Explorin
FRANCE

OTHER BOOKS IN THE *EXPLORING RURAL* SERIES

Series Editor: Andrew Sanger

Exploring Rural Italy
Michael Leech

Exploring Rural Spain
Jan S. McGirk

Forthcoming:

Exploring Rural Greece
Exploring Rural Portugal
Exploring Rural Germany
Exploring Rural Austria
Exploring Rural Britain
Exploring Rural Ireland

Exploring Rural FRANCE

ANDREW SANGER

CHRISTOPHER HELM
London

Line illustrations by Lorna Turpin
Maps by David Henderson
Christopher Helm (Publishers) Ltd, Imperial House,
21-25 North Street, Bromley, Kent BR1 1SD

British Library Cataloguing in Publication Data

Sanger, Andrew
Exploring rural France.
1. France — Description and travel — 1975-
— Guide-books
I. Title
914.4'04838 DC16

ISBN 0-7470-3001-4

Typeset by Leaper and Gard, Bristol
Printed and bound in Great Britain by
Billing and Sons Ltd, Worcester

CONTENTS

For Joe and Hilda Sanger

ACKNOWLEDGEMENTS

With many thanks . . .
to Peter Mills of French Railways, Pauline Hallam of the French Government Tourist Office, and many friends for their ready help and knowledge; above all to Gerry Dunham for her suggestions, ideas and companionship.

France — the regions and the routes:

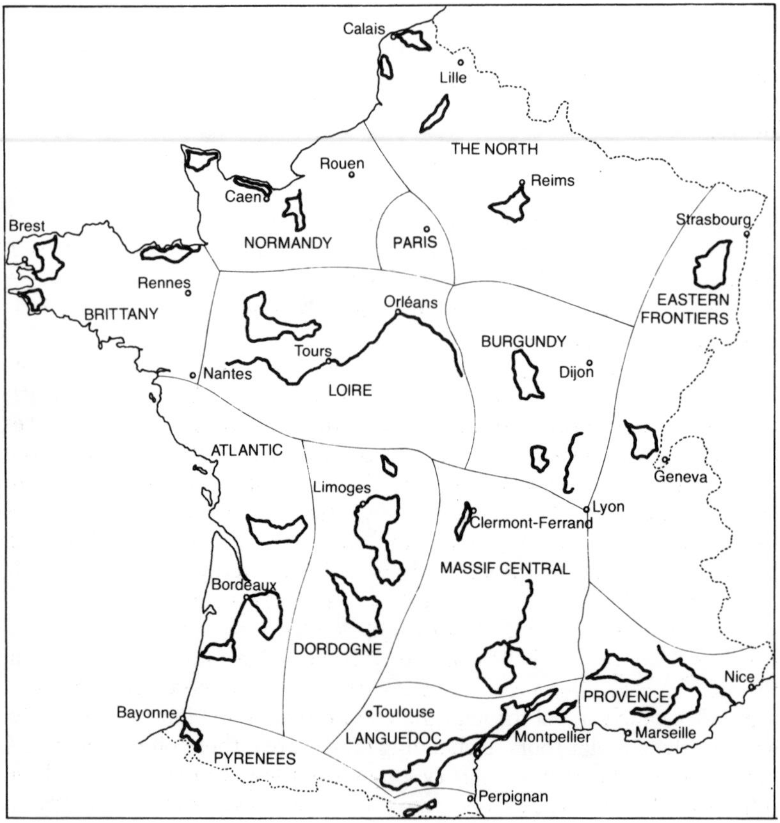

INTRODUCTION

Europe's largest country, the only one bridging the divide between the continent's northern and southern nations, France occupies a central place in European history and culture. In all the arts, and in philosophy, politics — and not forgetting that great indefinable, *savoir vivre*, the French have made a uniquely important contribution to our common civilisation.

The nation's vivacious capital, Paris, and of course its beaches on two oceans, attract millions of visitors annually. Yet France remains essentially undiscovered, unknown to most of the people who visit the country. For this is a predominantly rural nation, with vast areas of countryside undisturbed by industry, with few large towns, and a deeply conservative population of small farmers who are largely content to do things exactly as their fathers did before them.

Above all, France is a country of regions, each staunchly aware of its historic identity. Though it's not easy to define their boundaries, which have expanded and contracted over the centuries, the differences between these ancient provinces are plain to see and add much to the pleasure of travelling in France. Food and traditions vary from one to another, and in some, notably Brittany and Languedoc, local languages remain alive. Old village festivals continue to thrive, and it is a delight to arrive somewhere unexpectedly amidst all the energy and colour of its market day, when the region's produce is abundantly displayed.

This book is designed for the independent traveller who wants to become more intimately acquainted with one or several of France's rural regions. In each of them, I have described two or more recommended itineraries which travel through the countryside on exploratory, leisurely, and mostly, circular tours. Depending on the area, these offer from 1 to 4 days touring. Estimated journey times on these routes are based on unhurried driving, pauses to see anything of interest, occasional coffee or cake stops, and certainly a lunch break, whether on a grass verge or at a restaurant table. Every day's travelling is assumed to end in good time for dinner. Total touring in each province averages about one week.

There are no prizes for completing a route; all can be cut short, or extended, or simply treated as ideas to help in planning other off-the-beaten-track itineraries.

Indeed, the biggest problem in compiling this book has not been choosing the routes, but deciding which to leave out. Every region of

France offers a multitude of other equally excellent journeys — there is no limit, it seems, to the number of pleasant French rural rides to be discovered.

From Britain to France

The cost of crossing the Channel from Britain to France will vary according to the month, day of the week, time of day, number of passengers, age of child passengers and size of vehicle. It is also important to take into account the driving, meals and overnight expenses needed to get to and from each port.

Ramsgate-Dunkerque (2½hr) is the cheapest route, while Dover-Calais (ferry 1¼hr; hovercraft 35min) is the quickest (fastest loading and unloading too).

Other points: hovercraft are subject to frequent cancellation or delay in rough weather; Brittany Ferries charge the same for a car of any length.

However, final destination must be the deciding factor in choosing which Channel crossing to take. For all regions, consider Calais, Boulogne, or Dunkerque as possible crossings, but . . .

for the North: also consider Dieppe.

for the East, Burgundy and Provence: also consider Le Havre and Caen.

for Massif Central, Atlantic, Loire and Dordogne regions: consider Caen, Le Havre, Cherbourg, St. Malo.

for Languedoc and Pyrenees: consider St. Malo, Caen.

for Normandy: choose Caen, Le Havre or Cherbourg.

and for Brittany: choose St. Malo, Roscoff, possibly Caen.

I have included circular routes which start from Channel ports Calais, Boulogne , Caen, Cherbourg, St. Malo and Roscoff.

Motorail

French Railways' *Train-Auto-Couchette* services are a great resource. They're an excellent way to see the country and save time. The 800 km drive from Boulogne to the Dordogne, for example, becomes an easy overnight journey by rail, your car travelling on the same train with you. This can effectively add a day — or more — to each end of a holiday, allowing extra time to be spent in your chosen region rather than on the road to or from it. Current Motorail services from Channel ports include:

from **Boulogne** direct to Avignon, Biarritz, Bordeaux, Brive (Dordogne), the Côte d'Azur, Toulouse and Narbonne (Languedoc).

from **Dieppe** to Avignon and the Côte d'Azur.

from **Calais** to Narbonne and Nice.

For more information contact French Railways (in North America, French National Railroads): in Britain, 179 Piccadilly, London W1; in the United States, 610 Fifth Avenue, New York, NY 10020; 11 E Adams St., Chicago, IL 60603; 2121 Ponce De Leon Blvd., Coral Gables, FL 33134; 360 Post St., San Francisco, CA 94108; and 9465 Wilshire Blvd., Beverly Hills, CA 90212; and in Canada, 1 Dundas Street, Toronto, Ontario; and

1981 Avenue McGill College, Montreal, Quebec. (Include adequate return postage when requesting brochures or information.)
Routes have been included which start from Motorail arrival points Avignon (PROVENCE), Bordeaux (ATLANTIC), Bayonne (adjacent to Biarritz — PYRENEES), Brive (DORDOGNE) and Narbonne (LANGUEDOC).

Roads and Maps

Most of the touring routes in this book stay wherever possible on minor roads classified as *routes départmentales*, or 'D' roads. The name means that they are the responsibility of the départment. Most major roads are *routes nationales*, or 'N' roads. Some country lanes are only locally classified, as 'C' for *communale*, or 'CV', 'CVO' or 'V' for *chemin vicinale ordinaire*. But note that the status and numbering of roads alters frequently. There is, too, an excellent system of fast and modern *autoroutes* (motorways) which are ideal for covering a long distance from one part of the country to another. On most autoroutes tolls are charged, as they are privately run for profit on behalf of the Government.

Michelin road maps of France are the standard work on the subject. No.989 (red) covers the whole country, while the local (yellow) series shows almost all villages and minor roads and contour shading. There are 37 local maps altogether, or 16 in the larger format. All Michelin maps are readily available throughout France. For extensive travelling throughout the whole country, Michelin's Motoring Atlas of France is invaluable. Walkers are better off with the even more detailed Ordnance Survey style IGN maps (1:100,000 or 1:50,000). Car drivers making a long journey in July or August should get hold of the free Bison Futé map (literally, Canny Buffalo, supposedly a clever Indian brave who can find his way about) from garages and roadside traffic information booths (or, occasionally, from French Government Tourist Offices abroad). This shows when and where bottlenecks most often occur, and how to avoid them by using fast alternative roads signposted as Itinéraire Bis.
With each route, I have given the number of the Michelin yellow map which covers that area.

Driving and Parking

French Government Tourist Offices abroad give out a leaflet, 'Motoring in France', detailing rules of the road. The most important difference for visitors is the principle of *Priorité à Droite*, Give Way to the Right. Under this system all vehicles must give way to any other approaching from their right-hand side, unless there are indications to the contrary. Similarly, you have the right of way, or priority, over anyone on your left. However, in practice, except in town centres, there nearly always are 'indications to the contrary'. In particular, the **yellow diamond** roadsign tells drivers that their road has the priority. More important, the **yellow diamond crossed out** means 'you no longer have priority', and usually appears just before a meeting of two main roads or upon entering a town. Equally, **Stop** and

Cédez le Passage signs also mean Give Way. *Priorité à Droite* is being phased out at roundabouts; but remember to check by looking for a give way sign.

Other legal points: there are hefty on-the-spot fines for speeding and drunkenness. In the latter case you will be required to stop travelling until considered sober. The rules for parking can be idiosyncratic: often it's permitted on one side of the road only, on alternate odd (*impair*) and even (*pair*) days of the month. Zone Bleue parking is allowed only on display of a *disque bleu* permit, for which you have to pay.

Where to Stay

One of the things which makes France especially enjoyable and easy for leisurely touring is the great number of small, friendly and moderately priced hotels. Every little town, and many a tiny village, has at least one clean, adequately comfortable, unpretentious hotel or *restaurant avec chambres* (restaurant with rooms). Standards range from the extremely basic to the height of elegance and luxury. A star system is in force, but many hotels exist which fall well short of even a single star, while others far exceed the requirements for the maximum 4 stars.

There's no lack of campsites either, and these too are graded with stars: anything above 2 stars will have hot showers and good facilities. *Camping à la Ferme*, campsites on farms, tend to be more basic. Other possibilities: holiday villages, either for all the family or for children only, are popular with the French; Café-Couette is an organised system of pre-booked bed-and-breakfast accommodations in private homes (also known as French Bed and Breakfast); Gîtes de Vacances are simple cottages rented as inexpensive self-catering vacation accommodation.

Outside high season (July-August), booking hotels far ahead is rarely essential; except in popular holiday areas, it is usually sufficient to phone a few days before to reserve a room. Remember to specify if you would prefer *un grand lit* (a double bed) or *deux lits* (twin beds). Hotel accommodation is almost always rented by the room, not per person. Room prices must be displayed at reception and in the room itself (usually on the back of the door). Hotels expect reserved rooms to be claimed by about 7pm — if you are likely to arrive after that time, telephone to let them know.

Other curiosities: instead of pillows the bed will have a bolster. The pillows, if any, and spare blankets are in the wardrobe. And NB: don't bother to look for a room in the Hôtel des Impots (tax office), Hôtel de Ville (town hall), Hôtel de Poste (PTT office; though Hôtel de *la* Poste is OK), Hôtel des Ventes (auction rooms), or Hôtel de Police (police HQ)! Grand town houses are also called hôtels.

Most hotels have a dining room which is in fact a restaurant, since it is open to non-residents and offers a choice of set meals. Guests are not obliged to eat either the hotel's dinner or its breakfast, although some establishments try to give the impression that they can make that demand. In practice, it does give great pleasure at the end of the day to book into a comfortable hotel with a good dining room, enjoy a satisfying meal, and have nowhere farther to go afterwards than upstairs to bed. Hotel breakfast normally consists of *tartine* (French bread and butter) and perhaps a croissant, served with steaming jugs of coffee and hot milk. Hot chocolate or tea can be taken instead of coffee. Most hotels willingly serve breakfast in the rooms at no extra charge. Remember that when you are asked what you want for breakfast — 'Qu'est-ce que vous prenez?' — the question refers only to the hot drink you would like.

France has an exceptionally large number of hotel chains and federations. Most, whether luxurious or simple, concentrate on large urban areas, while some organisations specialise more in smaller towns and country locations. The most interesting are:

Relais & Châteaux — independently owned, top of the market, old-fashioned luxury and (especially those designated as 'Relais Gourmand') with excellent food.
Château Accueil — real, privately owned châteaux which take paying guests.
Chambres d'Hôte — bed-and-breakfast accommodation (often with evening meal too) in ordinary homes in country areas; no cheaper than hotels of similar standard.
Relais Routiers — truckdrivers' stops; cheap and cheerful roadside restaurants generally with a few basic rooms above; recognisable by blue and red circular sign outside.
Relais du Silence — top-quality hotels in especially quiet locations.
Logis et Auberges de France — the most valuable resource for travellers in rural France; a federation of almost 5,000 small, unpretentious, family-run independent hotels, nearly all with a good inexpensive restaurant (half of them specialise in regional dishes); rooms are adequate, reasonably priced; typically with 1 or 2 stars, rarely more; outside, a distinctive sign is displayed representing an old brick hearth.

Along most of the routes I have pinpointed a few good, reliable hotels and hotel-restaurants, most of which I have visited personally. Members of the Logis de France federation have been referred to simply as Logis.

Eating

Most French eating places offer a choice of about 3 *menus*, that is, fixed-price set meals, as well as *la carte*, a list of dishes individually priced. The price difference between one *menu* and another reflects not differences in quality but in quantity (i.e., number of courses) and difficulty of preparation.

In general, to get the best out of a French restaurant, order one of the *menus*. Prices will usually be higher and quality lower if you pick and choose from the *carte*.

The day's *menus* are always displayed outside the restaurant. Note what is included in the price. Service normally will be: 'TTC' (Tout Taxes Compris) means VAT included; *vin compris* means wine included (usually about a quarter or third of a litre of house wine per person); *boisson compris* suggests that you may have some drink other than wine. Coffee is not usually included in the *menu* price. Never ask for tea, coffee or milk with the food (not even with dessert): irate waiters and fellow diners will be appalled by such philistinism! Coffee after the meal is the thing. Decaffeinated (*café decafeiné*, or 'un deca') is universally available. Another alternative is *tisane*, herb tea.

It can be difficult to find something to eat outside normal mealtimes. The lunch break starts at 12 and goes on until 2-ish. The whole population sits down to eat at the same time and this is the main meal of the day. If you don't mind having a later or earlier lunch, between 12 and 2 is a good time for motorists to cover some ground — the roads are empty. Sunday lunch, often taken *en famille* at a local restaurant, lasts until 3pm. A little more flexibility comes into evening dinner hours, which range from 7 till 10, though 8pm is still regarded as the *correct* time to start dinner in most of the country. Be careful not to put off dinner too late, since restaurants frequently stop serving at about 9.30, especially in country areas. For cooked food outside these times, try a Brasserie — a bar which serves hot snacks and light meals.

Each region has its food specialities, its dishes based on local produce and tradition. While there is often a broad overlap of neighbouring regions, these dishes do capture much of the distinctive character of each part of France.
Regional specialities have been briefly described at the end of each chapter.

Excellent restaurants can be found everywhere, in towns, villages and in the open country, all over France. So can mediocre ones — avoid places which cater mainly to foreign tourists, or which offer an especially wide choice of dishes, or which are empty at mealtimes. In general the dining

rooms of Logis de France hotels reach a good standard.
Along the routes in each region certain eating places have been recommended.

Hotel and Restaurant Guides

All **Logis de France** hotels are listed in their handbook, free from French Government Tourist Offices (but enclose 50p in stamps to cover post and packing).
The inexpensive drivers' restaurants **Relais Routiers** are listed in their handbook; English edition from Relais Routiers Ltd, 354 Fulham Rd, London SW10.
The Red **Michelin** Guide details all hotels and restaurants in France which reach a reasonable standard, listed alphabetically by locality; restaurants which are far better than average are awarded a rosette, even better places get 2 rosettes, and the maximum score is 3 rosettes.
The **Guide Gault Millau** now edited only by Christian Millau, is witty, idiosyncratic, subjective, and sometimes so scathing that French restaurateurs are terrified of it. It awards toques (chefs' hats) to the best restaurants, with a maximum of 4 toques for the most outstanding.
If restaurants recommended on the routes have been awarded Michelin rosettes or Gault Millau toques, these have been mentioned.

Shops

The ever-present Tabac (or Bureau de Tabac), with its curious identifying pole outside, is more than just a tobacconist; it sells confectionery, stationery, newspapers, local bus season tickets and postage stamps. A more complete selection of stationery is found at a Papeterie. A Librarie is a bookshop (ask for the Bibliothèque if it's a library you're after). 'La Presse' could indicate a newsagents/tabac, but Pressing is a dry-cleaners. A laundry, Blanchisserie, or even a laundrette (dozens of names, properly called a Blanchisserie Automatique), are both astonishingly rare — most small towns don't have either.

For medicines, do not go to the Droguerie, which is what we would call a hardware shop or ironmonger's. Quincaillerie is hardware too, while a Mercerie, haberdasher's, is the place for a needle and thread. Medicines are bought at a Pharmacie, which is owned and run by a fully qualified pharmacist, who must also administer first aid, give medical advice and identify poisonous mushrooms.

There are almost no off-licences (liquor stores): buy food, wine and all other drinks at an Alimentation, general grocer's, often arranged as a 'mini-supermarket' with Libre-service, self-service. Despite what French teachers at school may have said, the name Épicerie is rarely used; but the occasional Épicerie Fine sells *vins fins*, high quality wines, and luxury or imported groceries.

Except in emergencies, buy bread only at a Boulangerie, where it is freshly baked on the premises twice a day. They have a selection of white breads and rolls, *pain complet* (wholemeal) and *pain de siègle* (rye). Most have morning croissants and *pain au chocolat*. Note that a Dépôt de Pain sells bread but does not bake it; theirs is usually factory-made. A Pâtisserie, literally a pastry-cook's, has better croissants, a selection of delicious little cakes and ice cream, everything being made on the premises by a master pâtissier. The Chocolatier or Confiseur sells chocolates and other confectionery, again made on the premises.

Boucherie means butcher's, or Boucherie Chevaline if it sells horse meat. A boon for picnics, a Charcuterie (properly a pork butcher's) sells a wide variety of cooked meats and other prepared foods, including salads. A Traiteur is like a delicatessen, again with plenty of prepared meats. Supermarché usually means nothing more than a big Alimentation, but the huge out-of-town Hypermarché, open long hours and sometimes 7 days a week, sells just about everything, at good prices, and often has a cheap and popular self-service cafeteria as well.

The ordinary town or village Marché, market, consists mainly of stalls selling fresh fruit and vegetables; traders' vans with dozens of cheeses, big rounds of butter, cold meats and charcuterie; other stalls with goats' cheese, cakes, honey, perhaps chickens alive or dead. Larger markets have traders selling natty blue workclothes, fabrics, households goods, excellent kitchenware, freshly gathered herbs, dried fruit and nuts, and much more. You'll rarely see a fishmonger, Poissonier, except in markets. Very common in rural areas is the travelling general stores van which turns up at the village once or twice a week.

Opening Times

The usual working day for **offices and banks** is 8 ot 9-12am, and 2-5pm, Mon-Fri/Sat am. Around these limits there are endless variations, of which the most common is to close on Mondays.

Shops also keep these hours in the north, with food stores perhaps opening a little earlier and closing later; but in the south, shops open from 8-12am, and 3 or 4-8pm. Though shops may legally trade on a Sunday, few are open other than the pâtisserie and butcher, for the morning only.

Museums, galleries, etc. tend to keep approximately to office hours, but are usually closed on Tuesdays. They may also be closed during the winter months.

Most **hotels and restaurants** close one day a week. They also close for an annual holiday of 2 to 4 weeks, or they may close for the whole winter in certain areas.

A lot of tourist amenities are open only from Pâques (Easter) or Pentecôte (Whitsun) to Toussaint (All Saints — 1 November).

Public Holidays

Banks, shops, museums and many restaurants close on public holidays (*jours fériés*). NB: if a public holiday falls on Thursday or Tuesday, many firms 'faire le pont' (bridge it), in other words they close on the Friday or

Monday as well to make a long weekend. Keep in mind too that banks and shops close early on the day before a holiday.
1 Jan. — Jour de l'An (important family holiday, gifts, etc.)
Easter Sunday and Monday — Pâques (March/April)
Whit Sunday and Monday — Pentecôte (May)
Ascension Day (in May, 5 weeks after Easter)
1 May — Fête du Travail (socialist and trade union celebrations)
8 May — VE Day 1945
14 July — Fête Nationale ('Bastille Day', spectacular events, fireworks)
15 Aug. — Assomption
1 Nov. — Toussaint (All Saints)
11 Nov. — Armistice Day
25 Dec. — Noël

Touring Information

French Government Tourist Offices abroad have masses of free information, maps, vacation ideas. FGTO in Britain is at 178 Piccadilly, London W1V 0AL; in the United States at 610 Fifth Avenue, New York, NY 10020; 645 North Michigan Avenue, Chicago, IL 60611; 9501 Wilshire Boulevard, Beverly Hills, CA 90212; 1 Hallidie Plaza, San Francisco, CA 94102; and World Trade Center, 2030 Stemmons Freeway, Dallas, TX 75258; and in Canada at 1 Dundas Street, Toronto, Ontario; and 1981 Avenue McGill College, Montreal, Quebec. (Include adequate return postage when requesting brochures or information.)
In France, almost every town has its **Syndicat d'Initiative**, a local information centre for both residents and visitors. There may also be a Maison du Tourisme, or Office du Tourisme, or some combination like Office du Tourisme-Syndicat d'Initiative.

Some French Words Used in the Text

appellation, appellation contrôlée (regional wine classification)
artisanat(s) (craft shops, etc.)
autoroute (motorway)
bastide (Medieval walled 'new town' built on grid pattern)
circuit touristique (marked route for tourists)
boulangerie (baker's)
charcuterie (sausages, black pudding, prepared meats, etc. — or shop which sells them)
département (administrative area similar to county)
fête (holiday, festival, celebration)
forêt (wild country, not necessarily tree-covered)
garrigue (or *maquis*: rough Mediterranean heathland)
Logis (Logis de France hotel)
Logis de France (hotel organisation)
Mairie (town hall, especially in village or smaller town)
méthode champenoise (method in Champagne for making sparkling wine)

nouvelle cuisine (the new, lighter style of haute cuisine)
Office du Tourisme (Tourist Office)
pâtisserie (cake shop — or the cakes themselves)
le patron, la patronne (the boss)
platanes (plane trees)
préfecture (administrative centre of départment)
Relais du Silence (hotel organisation)
Relais et Châteaux (hotel organisation)
restaurant avec chambres (a restaurant with rooms)
salon de thé (tea room)
sommelier (person responsible for serving wines)
Syndicat d'Initiative (local information office)
rosette (refers to rosette awarded to restaurants by Michelin inspectors)
route nationale (main highway)
toque (refers to toque, i.e. chef's hat, awarded to restaurants by Gault Millau inspectors)
Vieille Ville (Old Town — the old quarter of a town)

Abbreviations

av	*avenue*
bd	*boulevard*
D	with road number, e.g. D34, = route départmentale
m	metres
N	with road number, e.g. N1, = route nationale
pl	*place*, i.e. square
SI	Syndicat d'Initiative

Metric Conversion Tables

All measurements are given in metric units. For readers more familiar with the imperial system, the accompanying tables are designed to facilitate quick conversion to imperial units. Bold figures in the central columns can be read as either metric or imperial: e.g. 1 kg = 2.20 lb or 1 lb = 0.45 kg.

mm		in	cm		in	m		yds
25.4	**1**	.039	2.54	**1**	0.39	0.91	**1**	1.09
50.8	**2**	.079	5.08	**2**	0.79	1.83	**2**	2.19
76.2	**3**	.118	7.62	**3**	1.18	2.74	**3**	3.28
101.6	**4**	.157	10.16	**4**	1.57	3.66	**4**	4.37
127.0	**5**	.197	12.70	**5**	1.97	4.57	**5**	5.47
152.4	**6**	.236	15.24	**6**	2.36	5.49	**6**	6.56
177.8	**7**	.276	17.78	**7**	2.76	6.40	**7**	7.66
203.2	**8**	.315	20.32	**8**	3.15	7.32	**8**	8.75
228.6	**9**	.354	22.86	**9**	3.54	8.23	**9**	9.84

p		oz	kg		lb	km		miles
28.35	**1**	.04	0.45	**1**	2.20	1.61	**1**	0.62
56.70	**2**	.07	0.91	**2**	4.41	3.22	**2**	1.24
85.05	**3**	.11	1.36	**3**	6.61	4.83	**3**	1.86
113.40	**4**	.14	1.81	**4**	8.82	6.44	**4**	2.48
141.75	**5**	.18	2.27	**5**	11.02	8.05	**5**	3.11
170.10	**6**	.21	2.72	**6**	13.23	9.65	**6**	3.73
198.45	**7**	.25	3.18	**7**	15.43	11.26	**7**	4.35
226.80	**8**	.28	3.63	**8**	17.64	12.87	**8**	4.97
255.15	**9**	.32	4.08	**9**	19.84	14.48	**9**	5.59

ha		acres
0.40	**1**	2.47
0.81	**2**	4.94
1.21	**3**	7.41
1.62	**4**	9.88
2.02	**5**	12.36
2.43	**6**	14.83
2.83	**7**	17.30
3.24	**8**	19.77
3.64	**9**	22.24

Metric to imperial conversion formulae

	multiply by
cm to inches	0.3937
m to feet	3.281
m to yards	1.094
km to miles	0.6214
km^2 to square miles	0.3861
ha to acres	2.471
g to ounces	0.03527
kg to pounds	2.205

1 THE NORTH

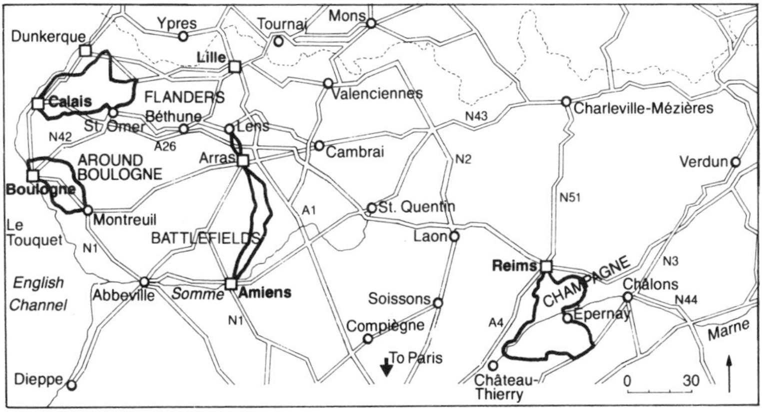

Away from the fast through-roads which cling to the high ground, this quiet landscape rises and falls in pleasant wooded valleys, villages retain an unexpected sense of remoteness, Gothic spires soar elegantly above city rooftops. Picardy and Flanders have their own patois and traditions and their own food and drink (beer, not wine), while further east, Champagne is thoroughly French. There are of course vast industrial areas too, of mining and manufacturing, which are best avoided perhaps, though these also contribute to the atmosphere and character of this tormented part of Europe. For going back to the Hundred Years' War and further, these Northern fields have changed hands again and again and have seen seemingly endless fighting, none worse than during this century, as neatly tended military cemeteries everywhere provide sombre reminder. Farms have been marched over, churches half knocked down — yet the people have survived together with their traditions and beliefs: churches and cathedrals have been patched up, streets rebuilt, farmland ploughed again.

Champagne

1–2 days/185km/from Reims

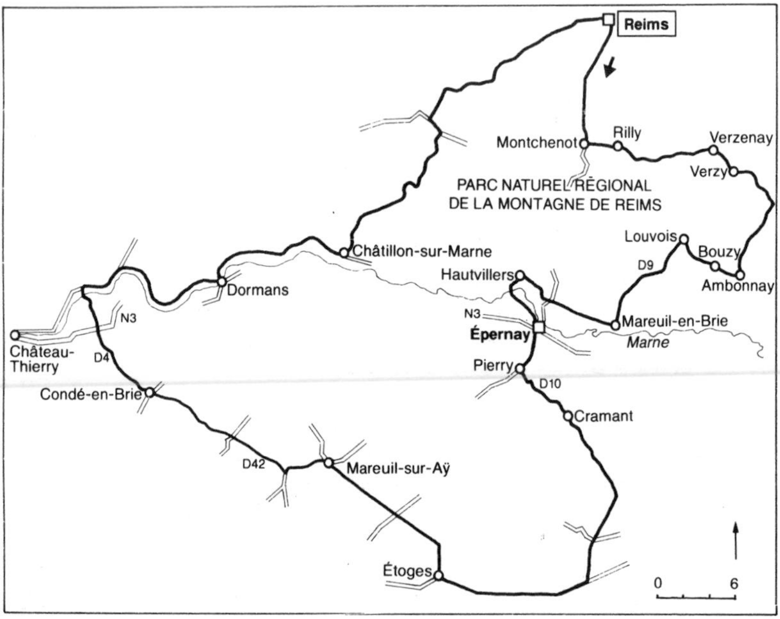

Beneath a thin cover of greenery, the Champagne countryside is pure chalk, a dusty and, one might think, unfertile terrain; yet it is this soil which, locals claim (the Government agrees), is the absolute essential if grape-growers are to make champagne. In recent years, thanks to the heavy use of chemicals, the region has begun to grow much else besides — grains, beet, corn, vegetables — and in vast quantities. But it is for one product alone that the area is world-famous, its very name a symbol of celebration and delight.

Champagne has 3 principal vineyard areas, Côte des Blancs, la Vallée de la Marne and la Montagne de Reims, which together account for most of the region's 24,000 or so hectares of grapes. Gauls, then Romans, cultivated the vine on these pleasant hills. Light, foaming champagne, made by the wine undergoing a second fermentation under pressure inside the bottle, was 'invented' in the 17C by the monk Dom Pérignon at Hautvillers, near Épernay. For centuries before that though, Champagne's fruity, often naturally *pétillant* (sparkling) wine (now called *champagne naturel* and still available) had been praised by emperors, kings and popes. The process of making champagne as we know it today is complex and precise. Only the best grapes are harvested, and different varieties mixed in exact proportions. Following the second fermentation, the sediment is literally frozen out and the bottles recorked. Nearly 200 million bottles are made annually, one-third produced by grape-growers themselves, the rest by the principal champagne houses whose careful blending ensures a reliable and unchanged product from year to year.

This is agreeable country for touring, and there is far more to this part of France than its famous wine. Reims, the principal town, holds a vital place in the nation's identity, for it was in its great cathedral that French monarchs would receive their crown. In the surrounding countryside, marked itineraries travel not just among grape-covered slopes but also, for example, along the Valley of the Ardre through villages with Romanesque churches. But our route, meandering and pretty, concentrates on the region's greatest fascination: the champagne vineyards. (The whole route can be found on Michelin map 56.)

REIMS (pronounced as if the M were a nasal *N*) pop: 182,000 Commercial centre, with nearby Épernay, of the champagne trade; many of the major champagne houses are based here and have their cellars in extensive subterranean corridors cut into the chalk beneath the streets. These labyrinths (used for shelter in periods of war) can be visited; the guided tours are instructive on the making of champagne. Veuve Cliquot-Ponsardin, Taittinger, Piper-Heidsieck, Pommery, Ruinart, Mumm, Heidsieck & Monopole, Charles Heidsieck and Lanson are all based here. Town almost entirely destroyed during World War I, and badly damaged again in World War II, but remarkably the cathedral survived both. German surrender signed here in 1945. Recommended: **Hôtel-Restaurant Boyer** (expensive and excellent Relais-et-Châteaux hotel, 3 Michelin rosettes, 3 Gault Millau toques: 26.82.80.80); restaurants **Le Florence** and **Le Chardonnay**, both with rosette and toque; and more down to earth with low-priced menu, **Restaurant Colbert**. Syndicat d'Initiative at 1 rue Jadart. See: Musée St. Denis, art museum; Roman triumphal arch and remains; above all visit the magnificient 13C Gothic Cathédrale Nôtre-Dame (note especially: portals, statuary, tapestries). In this building almost all the Kings of France were crowned.

Travel south (direction Épernay) out of Reims on N51. After 10km just as the road abruptly reaches the slopes of the **Montagne de Reims**, turn left at **MONTCHENOT** (good restaurant: **Auberge du Grand Cerf** — not cheap) onto D26 and follow this road through a succession of hillside villages encircling the Montagne. The Montagne de Reims is a gentle *massif* of chalk hills of which the slopes are cultivated with Pinot Noir grapes and the summits covered with woods of oak, beech and chestnut. Many of the villages make good starting points for worthwhile walks and drives into the higher ground: the Montagne is a *Parc naturel régional*, a protected area, and quite wild in places — you may even come across *sanglier*, wild boar, among the trees.

It is at **RILLY** that the great vineyards commence, and in the village church the sculptures feature vinegrowers; there are fine views and good walks. Continue along this picturesque road, by **CHIGNY**, **LUDES** and

MAILLY-CHAMPAGNE, to **VERZENAY**, one of the region's finest vineyard areas, and producing a good local wine. From here again there are magnificient views across the fields of vines stretching towards Reims. The hillside windmill which survives here was a World War I lookout post: the whole Montagne was British-held and proved unassailable. Neighbouring **VERZY** is an ancient vinegrowing community, home of another good local wine. Above the village (access on D34) are the 'Faux de Verzy', woods of low and curiously misshapen beech trees of astonishing age — many over 1,000 years old. The name comes not from the modern word *faux* but from local dialect Latin *faou*, beech. Adjacent to the woods, Mont Sinai observatory is the highest point on the Montagne de Reims (surprisingly only 283m). Verzy church has a statue of the Virgin Mary dating from 11C.

Through Villers-Marmery and Trépail carry on into **AMBONNAY**, a village pretty with flowers, host to various champagne events throughout the year, and producing a local wine classified as a Grand Cru de la Montagne de Reims. Hardly more than 2km further (on D19), aptly named **BOUZY** is particularly noted for a good local red wine, something unusual in the region; it is light and palatable, not *pétillant*, and classified as a Premier Cru de Champagne.

Take the road into **LOUVOIS** with its château and gardens once belonging to Louis XV's daughters and its humble 12C church. Head down (D9) through **AVENAY VAL D'OR** where the church has beautiful flamboyant façade and 16C organ, to the **Valley of the Marne**.

Here the *Vins de la Montagne* give way to *Vins de la Rivière*. **MAREUIL-SUR-AŸ**, where the road meets the Marne river near an 18C château, is one of the great Champagne vineyards. The firm Bollinger is based here. Turn right (towards Épernay) and, a little farther along the Marne, **AŸ** is another of the region's most eminent villages, whose wine was sent for by kings of France and England; still important today, its vineyards climb the hillside in attractive terraces — and the champagne to which they contribute is no less popular with kings than it used to be. A half-timbered house in the village is known, whether or not for good reason, as the winepress of Henri IV.

Instead of going straight into Épernay, continue through Dizy, taking D386 to hilltop **HAUTVILLERS**. This lovely village, with fine views, apart from being one of the prettiest locations in the region, is also distinguished as the place where Dom Pérignon, cellarmaster-monk at the Benedictine abbey here, devised a way to make the local wine effervescent — and so created champagne and the much-copied *méthode champenoise*. Dom Pérignon was buried in 1715 in the abbey church, which has since become the village parish church. Take one of the roads down the hill into Épernay.

ÉPERNAY pop: 29,000 Principal centre of Champagne trade. In some ways a dull town with little to see, apart from the grand premises of the world-famous champagne houses along the straight main street; more interesting are their miles of underground passages cut into the chalk on which the town stands. These are used as wine cellars (where humidity and temperature, incidentally, are constant), and can be visitied. Moët & Chandon (their subterranean network extends over 28km and contain around 50 *million* bottles), Mercier (their visit is by electric train, and includes a look at the world's largest barrel — holding 200,000 litres . . . that's 44,000 gallons), Pol Roger, Perrier-Jouët are all based here. Office de Tourisme: 1 pl Mendés-France. Recommended hotel-restaurant 5km north at Champillon: **Royal Champagne** (26.51.11.51) on N51; it's pricey but comfortable and imaginative, with accommodation in peaceful bungalows away from the road, and beautiful countryside views; choice of good if expensive menus with champagne included.

Leave town on the main road south, D51 (direction Sézanne), which straightaway reaches **PIERRY**. This is the start of **La Côte des Blancs**, a steep slope entirely covered, but for the wooded summits, with the finest white grape variety, Chardonnay. Surprisingly, most champagnes are made with 75 per cent black grapes and 25 per cent white. Since Chardonnay is a most essential ingredient, all the big champagne houses own vineyards along this Côte. However, the black grapes are not so essential: champagne made of white grapes only is called Blanc de Blancs. On the lower slopes of the Côte are the vinegrowers' villages with their narrow irregular streets, Romanesque churches and delightful views. At Pierry turn left onto D10. Stay on this road as it winds along the edge of the Côte, passing near **CUIS** (Romanesque church on terrace above village), and through a string of the most eminent champagne vineyards, **CRAMANT**, **AVIZE**, **OGER** and **LE MESNIL-SUR-OGER** (first class **restaurant Le Mesnil** has reasonable prices and wine-list including 120 champagnes), which all make renowned local wines as well. Follow the tortuous little road down the hillside to **VERTUS**, in medieval times an important commercial centre (natural fountains and springs; 11/12C church).

Go via D9 to Bergères-les-Vertus, where join the main D33. Just south of Bergères, **Mont Aimé**, though only 237m high, gives a clear view over the fields and terraces of the Côte des Blancs and, to the east across the plain, as far as Châlons-sur-Marne some 30km away. Understandably, such a good vantage point was first inhabited and fortified in prehistory, and in succeeding ages by Gauls, Romans and, finally, by the Counts of Champagne whose castle ruins remain with the evocative name Château de la Reine Blanche, Castle of the White Queen; from Bergères take D33 as far as **ÉTOGES** (moated château, still privately owned), where turn right onto D18 into **MONTMORT**. (Alternatively, from Vertus climb to Montmort directly across the forêt on D38, missing out Mont Aimé.) This quiet village with its sturdy red brick château, by the pretty little river Surmelin, makes a good base for excursions into the surrounding woodlands.

Follow the Surmelin valley first by taking D18 to **MAREUIL-EN-BRIE** (17C château) and on D11 to **ORBAIS** (fine 12/13C church remains of Benedictine Abbey founded in 7C). Agreeable D42 runs through riverside villages to **CONDÉ-EN-BRIE** (16C château; interesting covered market) where the Surmelin meets the Dhuys. Keep to the valley by taking D4 through St. Eugène and Crézancy all the way to Mézy on the river Marne. Cross the Marne and turn right onto D3 (changes to D320), travelling along the valley of the Marne towards Dormans.

DORMANS on the Marne is something of a '*Station Verte*' (countryside resort), with campsite and tourist office and watersports on the river. There's also a 17C (partly older) château and, in great contrast, a modern Chapelle de la Reconnaissance, with views across the valley, built to commemorate the 1914 and 1918 victories of the Marne. 1-star Logis **Hostellerie Demoncy** (26.58.20.86) is a modest *restaurant avec chambres.* Upriver from Dormans back to Épernay and Aÿ is the most important part of the Vallée de la Marne vineyard area. Leaving Dormans, return across the Marne, on the other side taking picturesque D1 (on the right) through Vincelles, Verneuil and Vandières to **CHÂTILLON-SUR-MARNE** (note the statue of 11C Pope Urban II, whose rhetoric created much of the Crusading fever of his era — he was born here). At Châtillon turn away from the Marne on the equally attractive D24 which winds up the valley of the aptly named Belval through Baslieux and Cuchery joining D386 at Chaumuzy. Turn left here, and after 1½km right onto main road D380, which skirts over the fringe of the Montagne de Reims (few vineyards on this part). Return on this road into Reims.

A Day in Flanders

1 day/160km/from Calais

Rather a long day, perhaps; this peaceful, rural journey through one of the most heavily industrialised regions of France could instead be extended over two (or more) days, or could alternatively be trimmed to make an easier day's ride. But it is too common a misconception that the broad, melancholy fields of Flanders deserve no more than the briefest glance. The very name evokes long centuries of history, of lost greatness, of decisive battles. Today's Flanders is no longer a country at all, merely an unloved countryside, scarred by its manufacturing areas (now in decline) and cut across by the Belgian border. Yet Flanders and the Flemish keep a character all their own, with a distinctive cuisine, a marked preference for beer instead of wine, a stolid robust capacity for endurance and work. While on the Belgian side the language survives intact, in French Flanders a curious patois evolved, neither French nor Flemish, which has contributed to the sense of a separate identity. Cobbled streets, big paved main squares, spacious meeting-hall churches, elaborate belfries (usually on the town hall, not the church) and tall gabled houses — where they have survived two world wars — capture the flavour of old Flanders. There are local customs and traditions too: many towns and villages celebrate their annual *Fête des Géants*, strange Giant Festivals with obscure origins, in which huge models of men and women

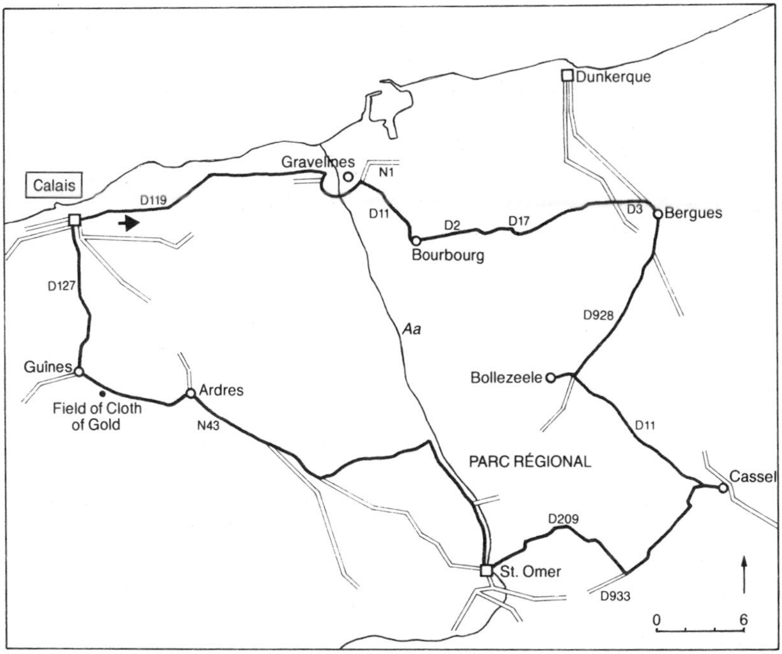

in medieval dress are wheeled through the streets at the head of lively processions. Each giant has a name and is regarded as a symbol, literally a figurehead, of the whole community. (Michelin map 51.)

CALAIS pop: 77,000 France's main passenger port, charmless, modern. From 1346 (Edward III) to 1558 (Mary Tudor: 'When I am dead and opened you shall find "Calais" lying in my heart.') ruled by the English Crown. Has the only church in France in English perpendicular style. Even the machine-made lace for which the town was once noted was introduced in 19C by manufacturers from Nottingham. Indeed, almost nothing predates the 19C: the town was almost destroyed by the Germans in World War I and again, more completely, by the English in World War II. 'Sights' include (none unmissable, frankly): Flemish-style town hall (early 20C) and, in front of it, Rodin's 'Six Burghers of Calais' (they offered their lives if Edward III would spare the rest of the town's population; he did — and spared them as well); unprepossessing 13C watchtower Tour de Guet in bleak pl d'Armes; Musée de Calais, more Rodin, 15C Flemish paintings, exhibitions of lace and of the town's history; more interesting Musée de la Guerre contains posters, leaflets, documents recalling the Nazi occupation. Office de Tourisme: 12 bd Clémenceau, opposite railway station. **Hôtel George V** (21.97.68.00) is a reliable 2-star Logis with good reasonably priced restaurant.

On N1 (or avoiding it by taking parallel D119) travel towards Gravelines between the coastal sand-dunes on one side and, on the other, one of Flanders' characteristic areas of *watergangs*, cultivated fields claimed from marshland and now separated by a grid of waterways. **GRAVELINES**, important port and site of a nuclear power station, comes as a pleasant surprise with its magnificent 16/17C fortifications. Standing at the mouth of the river Aa, a key access into the heart of Flanders, the town suffered frequent attack and even in World War II was a bastion in the defence of Dunkerque. For this route I have chosen to by-pass the refineries and factories of Dunkerque, but in its favour let it be said that at the heart of the encircling industry there is a likeable provincial town centre.

Instead take D11 from Gravelines to Bourbourg, where find D2 (changes to D17 and D3) to **BERGUES**, another small town staunchly defended by a ring of fortifications, here having the added protection of a system of canal-moats called the Couronne d'Hondschoote. Within the walls, entered by handsome gateways, the traditional houses, a fine belfry, the town hall and a local museum, all rebuilt after the war in their original 16/17C style, give the town much Flemish character. Take D916 (direction Cassel), turning right after 10km to **ESQUELBECQ**, which, though on a smaller scale, preserves just as much original Flemish appearance — as well as a sturdy old fortified château beside the river Yser.

If you do plan to spend the night somewhere *en route*, it would be well worth going (via D17 to Zegerscappel, left onto D928 to l'Erkelsbrugge, then right onto D226) to **BOLLEZEELE** (pronounced Boyezel). This tranquil village, as well as a superb ornate little town hall at its centre and farmyards on its edges where housewives walk to buy their half-litres of fresh milk, also has a comfortable 2-star Logis and Relais du Silence, the **Hostellerie St. Louis** (book ahead: 28.68.81.83), set back from the road in private gardens. The restaurant is good, though pricey, and *Monsieur le patron* is a master *sommelier* with a formidable cellar. From here return to the l'Erkelsbrugge crossroads and take D11, through slightly hillier, more attractive and more rustic country, to **CASSEL**, just before which the road begins to climb unexpectedly by pretty twists and turns to enter the surprisingly high hilltop town.

At its centre is the cobbled main square, Grand' Place, enclosed by the old steep-roofed houses with their dormer windows: most striking is the stone façade of 16C Hôtel de la Noble Cour, now housing a local museum. Excellent restaurant **Le Sauvage**, encompassing regional, classic and nouvelle cuisine in generous menus, can be found behind the pretty brick façade at no. 38. A few doors away, Hôtel d'Halluin is another impressive building, and outside the *place*, the collegiate church of Notre-Dame, in Flemish Gothic style, is typically vast and triple-naved. Steep, narrow, twisting backstreets, some in steps, rise up to public gardens, in which there's an 18C wooden windmill, at the summit of the hill (175m). From this spot, according to an old saying, 'one can see five kingdoms: France, Belgium, Holland, England, and above the clouds, the Kingdom of God'. Stretching a point perhaps, but a fine view none the less. Marshal Foch, commander of the French in the World War I, made his

Giant Festival at Cassel

HQ in Cassel during 1914 and 1915 and from these gardens was able to survey the positions of the armies. Cassel's Giants, Reuze-Papa and Reuze-Maman, lead a festival carnival procession through the streets on Easter Monday. Reuze-Papa comes out on his own on the first Sunday in March, and the June *ducasse*, Saint's Day festival, is the ancient Summer Solstice Fair almost unchanged.

D933 runs directly to St. Omer, but better to take, for part of the way at least, one of the backroutes (e.g. turn right onto D209 at le Nieppe) that pass through the **Forêt de Rihoult-Clairmarais**, a pleasant area with paths and picnic tables beneath the oak trees. **ST. OMER**, once great, has become a rather characterless town with cleaned-up and 'pedestriani-sed' old quarter, racetrack boulevards and a main square full of parked cars. True, rue Gambetta is still attractive with 17/18C mansions, and the 19C town hall (Syndicat d'Initiative inside) in pl Foch has a certain ineradicable magnificence. The more elegant Ancien Bailliage (now the national savings bank Caisse d'Epargne) too, and the Hôtel Sandelin (housing good collection of medieval Flemish art and crafts) are distinctive. A thick coat of grime obscures most external beauties of 13C Basilique Notre-Dame, tucked away in a quiet square. Huge inside, it does contain many notable items, particularly the 13C sculptures and astronomical clock dated 1558. Spacious and wooded public gardens cover the site of the old city ramparts, with a lofty view across the flat surrounding country.

To the left of D928 (becomes D213), along the river Aa as it flows away northeast of the town, is extensive 'reclaimed' marshland, formed into fields surrounded by water channels and canals. The inhabitants of this watery marketgarden area — *watergangs*, or in this district known as the Romelaere — get around by flat-bottomed boats on the quiet green-backed waterways under a big tranquil sky. Turn left at Watten onto D205 (becomes D221), and right towards Ardres on reaching busy N43.

Certainly **ARDRES** can claim some modest appeal of its own — a cobbled triangular main 'square', for example — but the greatest attraction for me has always been that this is such an incomparably better place to stay than Calais (17km away on N43). Charming and reasonably priced **Grand Hôtel Clément** (book well ahead: 21.82.25.25) is a family-run Relais du Silence and has an excellent restaurant (Michelin rosette, Gault Millau toque) with 3 no-choice set menus, a little pricier than average but well worth it. Or try smaller and cheaper 2-star Logis **Le Relais** (21.35.42.00). Close to Ardres was the site of the misconceived Anglo-French 'peace talks' between Henry VIII and François I which turned into nothing more than an undeclared war of ostentation, each side trying to outdo the other in the grandeur of its encampment. A simple stone block just beside the D231 on the way to **GUÎNES**, where Henry VIII based the English camp, records in gold letters 'Camp du Drap d'Or 1520 Field of Cloth of Gold'. Today, it's just another field of winter wheat. Just south of Guînes, footpaths wander through the tranquil young oak and beech woods of the Forêt de Guînes. Take D127 north for the 10km from Guînes back into Calais.

Battlefields

1 day/175km/from Amiens

> 'He's a cheery old card,' grunted Harry to Jack,
> As they slogged up to Arras with rifle and pack.
> But he did for them both by his plan of attack.
>
> (from 'The General', Siegfried Sassoon, 1917)

In both 1914–1918 and 1939–1945, northern France was subject to a relentless onslaught. While Germany's second world war resulted in greater and more deliberately planned suffering and more widespread destruction, their first exercises a particular fascination and had a peculiar

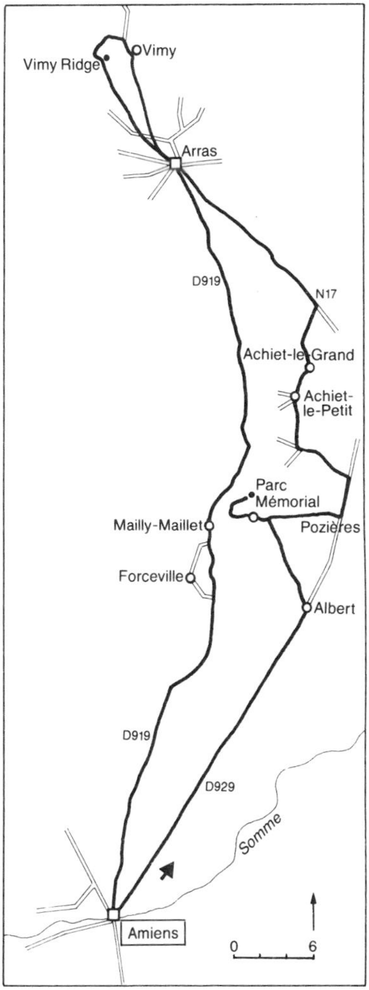

horror because of the calculated and laborious way in which tens of thousands of men, on both sides, with no better explanation than mere patriotism were so incompetently ordered to their deaths. Nowhere does the slaughter seem more meaningless and terrible than in the ponderous movement of the Front, slow lingering efforts to capture and then to recapture that strip of mud a few hundred yards wide, which was drawn through the valley of the Somme. This is a melancholy tour, yet compelling. It takes in one of the worst-hit areas and two of the most moving of the memorials which recall that era — Vimy Ridge and Beaumont-Hamel. (Michelin maps 51 & 52.)

AMIENS pop: 136,500 Capital of Picardy (now Somme département); hectic, busy, unattractive industrial town, much damaged in both world wars. Main Syndicat d'Initiative is in the Maison de la Culture, 1 rue Jean Catelas. See: Quartier St. Leu, a medieval district; the *hortillonages*, large out-of-town area of small reclaimed fields separated by canals on which farmers travel in flat-bottomed boats; don't miss the huge and majestic Cathédrale Notre-Dame, 13C Classic Gothic style. Note, inside cathedral, pillars bearing memorials to soldiers of various armies who died in the surrounding countryside.

Leave the town on D929, long straight road under a big cloudy sky, reaching **ALBERT** after 28km. There is a Syndicat d'Initiative at 4 rue Gambetta (summer only), which offers an explanatory leaflet ('Down Memory Lane') about a marked *Circuit de Souvenir*, a look at several nearby villages where fighting occurred and which have military cemeteries or memorials. Today an unappealing red brick town, Albert was all but destroyed by 1918. It is dominated by the appalling statue of the Virgin and Child on top of the brick church; the original church was bombed in 1915, and the original statue leaned precariously on the ruins for the rest of the war. For the moment, continue through Albert on

D929 just as far as the edge of **LA BOISSELLE**. Here the Front was formed in 1914. The Battle of the Somme started here on 1 July 1916, the Tyneside Scottish and Tyneside Irish Brigades launching the attack. A small monument beside the road marks the spot. Return into Albert and follow a sign for the *Circuit de Souvenir* (D50) which, after passing between council estate and campsite, leads out of town.

Stay on this marked *circuit* through Aveluy to **HAMEL**. Just outside the village is the **Beaumont-Hamel Newfoundland Memorial**, a part of the original battlefield on land which has been given in perpetuity to the Canadian Government. It has not been altered since 1919: cut with tortuous trenches and cramped dugouts, the ground distorted by the piled residue of these hasty earthworks, pockmarked by mortar craters, this was the site of fierce fighting on 1 July 1916, the Royal Newfoundland Regiment taking the brunt. From neighbouring village **BEAUMONT** Scottish soldiers of the 8th Battalion and 51st Highland Division joined the battle marching to the music of their bagpipes. By the end of that day 90 per cent of these men were dead. The battleground is being allowed to weather away, as memories do, though as yet remains little changed. A statue of a caribou, emblem of Newfoundland, with an inappropriate poem and incomprehensible biblical passage, are the only later additions to the site, where now all is silent but for birds singing. There are few visitors, and the visitors' book has been defaced by French school-children.

Unless you wish to continue following the signposted *Circuit de Souvenir*, from Hamel take D73 to **THIEPVAL**. This German-held village was taken after long bombardment by the 18th British Division, in whose honour and memory there is now a memorial. Close by, dominating the Ancre valley and visible for miles, is the chilling memorial listing the names of the Somme villages totally destroyed (one-third of the département) and all the 73,367 British soldiers killed in the area whose bodies were not recovered. Continue on D73 into **POZIÈRES** (important memorials), turning left onto D929 and going 2km on this road to **COURCELETTE** (Canadian monument) where turn left into the village. Take D107 to **MIRAUMONT**, D50 to **ACHIET-LE-PETIT** (German cemetery). At almost every village, and along the lanes between them, small military cemeteries parade their dead in neat rows of gravestones on clean, trimmed lawns. Take D9 through Achiet-le-Grand and Gomiécourt to Ervillers. Turn left here onto the main road, N17, and drive 16km into Arras.

ARRAS pop: 45,500 Traditional capital of Artois (now Pas-de-Calais département). Much rebuilt (in its original style) after extensive damage in both world wars, successfully preserving Flemish character and charm. Recommended: **Hôtel-Restaurant Le Chanzy** (excellent 2-star Logis, modest prices: 21.71.02.02). SI: 7 pl du Maréchal Foch. Arras was Robespierre's native town, which did not prevent him from having a guillotine erected here, in pl du Théâtre. See also: Grande Place and Place des Héros, two main squares at centre of town (lively morning markets Wed and Sat); with magnificient *hôtel de ville* rebuilt in former 16C style; and

Les Souterrains or *Les Boves*, underground network of vaulted rooms and passageways used for over 1,000 years to provide shelter for the citizens in time of war (entrance in *hôtel de ville*); Arras Memorial to the Missing, which records the names of almost 36,000 men whose bodies were not found after World War I battles in this area; *Mur des Fusillées*, the spot where 200 French Resistance members were executed by German firing squad in World War II. Yet after all it's been through, Arras is still a military town. Soldiers wander about and their barracks are soberingly close to the war memorials.

VIMY RIDGE 8km north of Arras (use D49e, D937 or N17), was the scene of tremendous fighting for 3 years up to 1917 until captured by the Canadians with crucial effect upon the subsequent development of the war. Vimy Ridge — the battlefield — was given to the Canadian Government, by whom it is maintained as a memorial. Part is kept intact, exactly as it was in 1919, complete with trenches, craters and tunnels, while another part is being allowed to erode in the wind and rain. Improbably, Vimy is a popular place for weekend family outings, and at the entrance, in an office, two bright and breezy Québecoise students hand out information, talk knowledgeably about the battle, and cheerfully announce that there are still 11,280 unrecovered bodies on the site.

Vimy Ridge

There is also at Vimy, on top of the ridge itself (Hill 145, as it was known during the war), an immensely tall memorial monument, distinctive and sombre, looking down onto a hellish industrial landscape of slag-heaps, mineworkings and smoking chimneys. It looks as devastated as the battlefield itself, and not so much a memory of war as a premonition.

About 3km away, just off N37, is Notre-Dame de Lorette, the French National Memorial and Cemetery, Apart from 20,000 individual graves on the site, another 20,000 unidentified men are buried in the Ossuary.

Return to Arras, and take D919 back to Amiens, 63km. Along the way are many quaint, tragic little military cemeteries, most of them British. Just beyond **SERRE**, which is again close to the Newfoundland memorial battlefield at Beaumont-Hamel, 2 British burial grounds and 1 French lie within a few metres of each other. I turned off the road by chance to visit the village of **FORCEVILLE** (about 2km from D919 near Hédauville); it is unremarkable, typical with British and parish cemeteries beside each other opposite a little farm with potatoes and chickens. This British cemetery is, like all of them, maintained with tremendous care by the Commonwealth War Graves Commission. The visitors' notebook shows that people call in about every 3 days. Comments are often trite — '*Trés bien*', 'Pretty', 'Very nice' —, some angry, and among them also 'Granddaughter' and 'Son'. Most are by local children, who have defaced the book. At Forceville there are '304 graves of soldiers and sailors' including 1 unknown British soldier, and 7 German graves too, as well kept as any of the others.

Around Boulogne

1 day/100km/from Boulogne

This is the most completely agreeable of the areas accessible by a short Channel crossing. Resolutely ignored by tourists, the gentle country behind Boulogne stays remarkably rustic and unspoiled, Luckily for any slightly more intrepid visitor, just a short ride inland offers some of the region's prettiest and most interesting places; this is one corner of Picardy and Flanders not quite so tortured by either industry or war — at least in the modern era. It also has some of the best restaurants in the North. (Michelin map 51.)

BOULOGNE pop: 48,000 Largest French fishing port. The port and lower part of the town, destroyed in World War II, are modern but not unattractive. The walled upper town — Haute Ville — escaped war damage and preserves several medieval and Renaissance buildings; it is dominated, however, by the curious domed Basilique Notre-Dame, built in 19C. Beneath the Basilica an interesting crypt contains remnants of a much older church (note frescoes) and of a Roman temple. An enjoyable walk on the park-like top of the broad ramparts takes about ½hr. Boulogne was an important harbour in Roman times: Caesar set out from

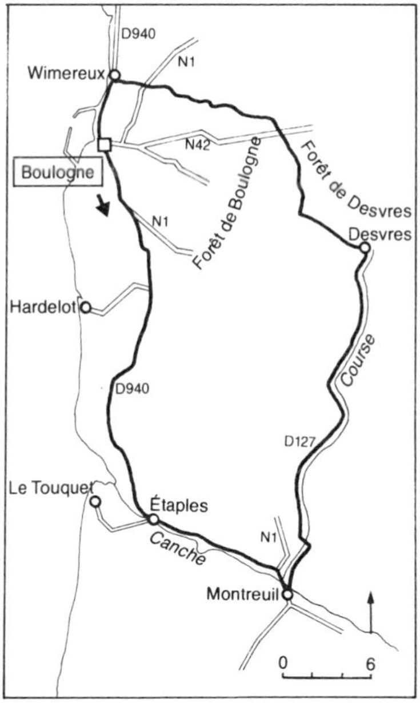

here on his conquest of Britannia in AD53. The Colonne de la Grande Armée, 3km north, recalls that Napoleon planned something similar in 1803. Syndicat d'Initiative located on ground floor of the covered walkway from the ferry terminal (gives address as Pont Marguet). Freshly caught fish and shellfish feature on the *menus* of almost every restaurant in town. Early risers can see the new catch being sold from quayside stalls each morning. Recommended: Restaurants **La Matelote** and, cheaper, **La Liegeoise**. (For a hotel, see Wimereux, 7km north, or Pont de Briques, 5km south, both on this tour).

Following signs to Paris, take busy N1 just as far as **PONT DE BRIQUES**. In the 18C château here Napoleon lodged frequently between 1803 and until after the Battle of Trafalgar in 1805, at which time he pragmatically gave up his dream of invading England. He marched off and conquered Austria instead. Unpretentious **Hostellerie de la Rivière** (21.32.22.81; Michelin rosette, Gault Millau toque; low-price menu on weekdays) offers 'the best and most *sérieux* meal in Boulogne', as Christian Millau describes it, and also has some simple places to stay. Continue south on D940 through the Fôret de Hardelot, pinewoods and dunes, and windy sandy seaward-looking villages all the way to Etaples. On the way, a detour into **HARDELOT**, old-fashioned beach resort with delusions of great elegance, makes an interesting comparison with **LE TOUQUET**, living on a past grandeur and now something of a weekend resort for wealthy visitors. If you do decide to take a look at Le Touquet, to which the only access from the north is via Étaples, remember that **Flavio's** cheerful and excellent (and expensive) restaurant can be found there (Michelin rosette, 2 Gault Millau toques). **ÉTAPLES** itself is a fishing harbour once fashionable with artists and still very pretty.

At Étaples turn inland on N39 along the valley of the Canche until the road, after reaching N1 and suddenly climbing away from the river, enters the gateway of **MONTREUIL-SUR-MER**. 'Sur mer' because, incredibly, in Roman times this town stood on the seashore and was a major port. Now 14km from the Channel, it stands aloof, protected by massive grass-covered fortifications (footpath on top), with a commanding view over the undulating countryside.

Almost everything in Montreuil has been built since the destruction of the earlier city by Charles V in 1537, at which time it is thought to have had as many as 40,000 inhabitants. The huge ramparts date mostly from 16/17C. There are some older sections, and parts of the imposing Citadelle — a separate fortress within the city walls — though, like the rest of the town, largely reconstructed by Vauban in the 17C, date from the 11C and 13C. The Citadelle, protected by a (now empty) moat and an entrance gate flanked by 2 powerful towers, is overgrown and unrestored, strangely spooky with subterranean chambers and 'Queen Berthe's Tower' in which are recorded the coats of arms of thousands of noblemen slaughtered at nearby Agincourt (present-day Azincourt, not far off to the east) by King Henry in 1415. Remarkably, Sir Douglas Haig, commander of the British forces in World War I, established his HQ in the Citadelle. Other things to see in the town include the Flamboyant chapel of the Hôtel-Dieu hospital (tremendously ornate exterior, tiny inside, good stained glass, fine carved wooden panelling) and in the same *place*, the Church of St. Saulve, originally 11C, but now a fascinating patchwork of repairs and reconstructions carried out following war damage in 13C, 16C and in the present century.

Even Montreuil's 'new' town, outside the walls and going down towards the river, has numerous picturesque corners and cobbled streets. Victor Hugo, struck by its atmosphere, used the town as the setting for Les Misérables, in which the main character becomes mayor of the town. Opposite the Syndicat d'Initiative in pl Darnetal (summer only; at other times apply to the Mairie), **Hôtel-Restaurant le Darnetal** (21.06.04.87) is friendly and unpretentious, with modestly priced *menus*. Close by, the beautiful old **Château de Montreuil**, standing in its private gardens, is now a magnificent, luxurious Relais et Châteaux hotel and a first-class restaurant specialising in light, fresh cuisine yet with an eye firmly on Northern specialities (rosette, 2 toques: 21.81.53.04).

From Montreuil our route is along the **Vallée de la Course**, but this can be hard to find. Leave the town by returning along N1, taking a right almost at once towards Neuville, where turn left and right to find D150 to rustic **ESTRÉE**. Turn left into the village, cross the river and follow the road round to the right. Continue up this picturesque road (D127) as it follows the twists and turns of the little valley. Carry on into lively **DESVRES**, a small town long noted for fine porcelain and pottery. Its Tuesday morning market is enjoyable. Like other towns and villages in the area, Desvres has its various fêtes throughout the year; not many others, though, have a Custard Pie Festival (November). However, I must reveal that these are not for throwing at people, but for eating — a far more French thing to do with a custard pie. Retrieve D127 by following signs to Calais and Marquise. The road remains attractive; just north of the town, it runs through the Fôret de Desvres, covering about 1,200 hectares, a popular area for picnics and walks.

Eventually meet busy N42, where turn left (direction Calais) and soon right onto D233 which travels along the lovely little valley, deep and narrow, of the Wimereux. Stay on this picturesque road all the way into the small seaside resort of **WIMEREUX**. From here a fine view looks both ways along the bright airy coast known as the Côte d'Opale. It was from the beach at Wimereux that Marconi made the first radio link across the Channel. In the parish cemetery is the grave of the poet Colonel John McCrae, killed in World War I. It was he who wrote 'In Flanders fields the poppies blow/Between the crosses, row on row'.

On the Wimereux waterfront there is a very good hotel-restaurant, **L'Atlantic** (21.32.41.01). D940 runs beside the shore back into Boulogne.

*

The people of Flanders, and to some extent the same is true of Picardy and Champagne, favour a style of cuisine heavier and more robust than in most regions of France. They like sausages (especially andouilles and andouillettes), tripe, pâtés, charcuterie, strong cheeses (milder in Champagne) and substantial stews. Fresh river and sea fish, especially herring, as well as eels and oysters, are popular too. The usual cooking fat is lard; and beer, the regional drink, works its way into many dishes. Most favoured vegetables are no-nonsense fillers like potatoes (in Picardy, it's chips with everything), cabbage, leeks and pumpkins. Northern specialities include carbonnade flamande (beef stew with beer), waterzoi (fish stew), flamiche (vegetable-and-cream tart), hotje potje or hochepot (i.e. hot pot, a stew of several kinds of meat with vegetables), ficelle picarde (rolled pancake filled with ham and mushrooms, and topped with creamy sauce). Finish with a generous slice of fresh fruit tart.

2 NORMANDY

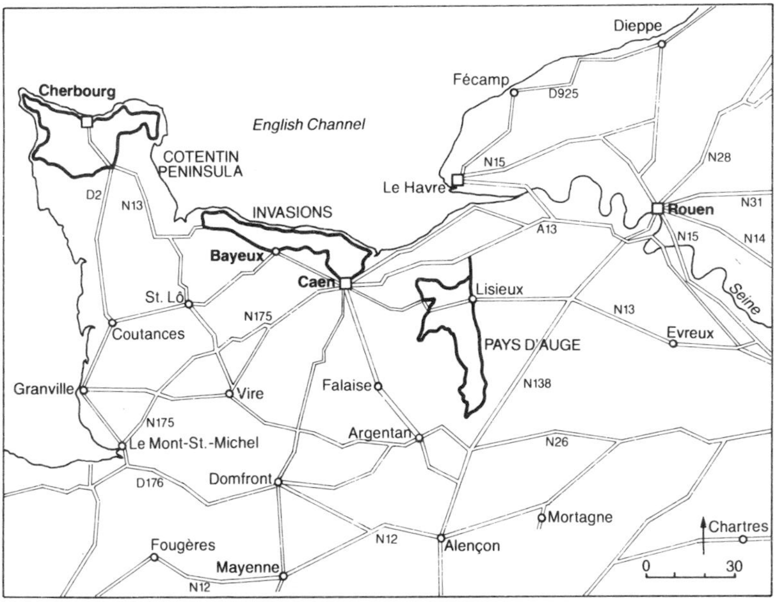

So peaceful now, Normandy saw more than its share of wartime devastation when the Allies landed along its coast in the 1944 liberation of France. Many great medieval towns, long famous for their beauty, were destroyed. Yet in the agricultural areas, in the rustic villages and farms, the traditional appearance survives. This conservative, profoundly rural region is noted above all for its fine cheeses, cider, delicious *crème fraîche* and — taking the name of one of Normandy's départements — Calvados, that elegant and fiery apple brandy. The coast provides much of Normandy's history and character, but inland the country lanes pass scores of superb old timbered houses, often thatched (and often with lilies growing in the thatch). The story of Normandy is, of course, the story of Britain: Vikings settled this French province in the 10C, and by the 11C were ready, under their charismatic leader William the Bastard, to take on the Anglo-Saxons across the Channel. William became The Conqueror, as is eloquently illustrated on the famous Tapestry at Bayeux, and the Normans became the English aristocracy, their culture eventually penetrating every area of British life.

Le Pays d'Auge

2 days/184km/from Pont l'Évêque (50km east of Caen on N175)

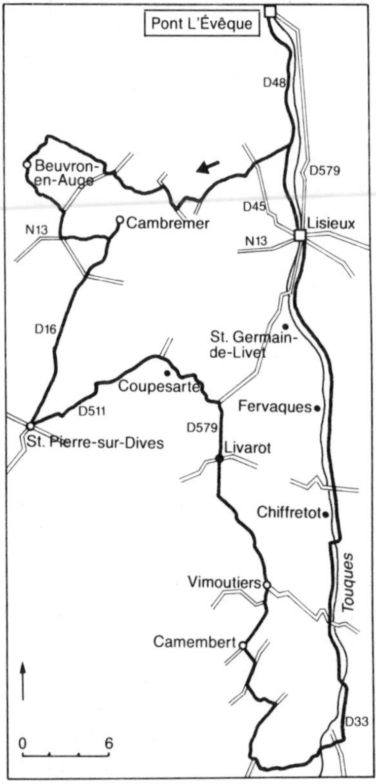

This is the Normandy of cheese and cider, of timbered cottages and tangled country lanes. The Pays d'Auge is the province's most picturesque, rustic region, green and rolling, with orchards and dairy farms everywhere. It is beautiful in late spring, apple-blossom time. While few Normandy cheeses are still made in the traditional way (they lend themselves particularly well to factory manufacture), all along the route signboards invite passers-by to try the farm-made *cidre bouché* (sparkling cider) and Calvados. The local wisdom is that every farm makes a different cider, and all deserve to be tried, but this route will take a lot longer than 2 days if you follow that advice! With or without the effects of *cidre bouché*, careful attention to the map is needed in this area (use Michelin nos. 54 or 55, & 60).

Like many towns in Normandy, **PONT L'ÉVÊQUE** suffered badly in World War II and little survives of its former medieval appearance. There are a few marvellous old houses remaining in rues St-Michel and de Vaucelles, there's a fine Flamboyant Gothic church, and the tourist office and town hall are in 18C Hôtel de Brilly. The atmosphere of this little country town is very pleasing and, of course, it has given its name to one of the best of the region's cheeses. Two roads head south from the town along the Touques valley: D579 on the right bank, and D48 on the left. Take D48, which is quieter, smaller and prettier.

Before reaching Lisieux, turn right at Coquainvilliers onto D270. Pass through Manerbe, taking D270^{A}. Turn right on meeting D59, just by the château-like former abbey Val Richer. Turn left at **LA ROQUE-**

Beuvron-en-Auge

BAIGNARD (17C château) to Montreuil-en-Auge, continuing to Léaupartie. There turn left onto D16 and immediately right onto D275: this leads through Rusmesnil where take the left turning to Forges de Clermont. This part of the drive gives some good views, as here the hilly Auge country meets the flat reclaimed *marais*, marshland, which stretches as far as Caen. At Forges, walk (10min) to the church of **Clermont-en-Auge** for a particularly fine panorama.

From Forges take D146 to **BEUVRON-EN-AUGE**. Beuvron itself is a remarkable place, a village which has managed to preserve its old appearance unchanged. It dares to claim that it is 'one of the most beautiful villages in France'; certainly it has the most extraordinary number of traditional, heavily timbered houses, one or two of them really magnificent with huge beams, and a fine manor house presiding over all. There's an excellent, reasonably priced restaurant too, **Le Pavé d'Auge** (31.79.26.71).

Take D49 past the hamlet of **VICTOT**; the impressive collection of buildings off the road here is a stables and stud farm, one of many in the area. On meeting D16, turn right, then left at the crossroads called *carrefour de St-Jean*. Go through Notre-Dame d'Éstrée and up a steep hill to St. Laurent-du-Mont. At St. Laurent turn down D101 to have a look at the plain, neat and down-to-earth village of **CAMBREMER** — the leading name in Normandy cider.

Returning to St. Laurent, carry on to **CRÈVECOEUR-EN-AUGE** (restored old manor house, now a municipal museum). Join D16, a rather dull straight road which goes into **ST. PIERRE-SUR-DIVES**. This likeable country town makes most of those characteristic wooden boxes, square or round, in which Normandy cheese are usually sold. It has more than that to recommend it though, and deserves a leisurely stroll. See the interesting Gothic church and chapter house, and the covered market rebuilt after World War II not only in its original style, but using all the original materials and tools — the effect is impressive (weekly market: Monday till about 1pm).

Leave St. Pierre on D511 (direction Lisieux). An interesting feature of this part of Normandy is its large number of wealthy fortified manor houses, mostly dating from 15/16C. Two can be compared just along this part of the route: at tiny village **ST. JULIEN-LE-FAUCON**, with its new and old timbered houses, take D269 on left for a few hundred metres to neighbouring **GRANDCHAMP-LE-CHÂTEAU**. Go past the tiny Mairie and village church to the 'château', which in fact is a splendid large country house, of which the older part is very much in the traditional Normandy style, with heavy timbers and patterned brick, and all surrounded by a very daunting broad moat with ducks swimming in it. This remains a private house, and certainly a fine one. But now return to St. Julien and take D47 (direction Livarot) a short distance to see, to the right of road, the smaller, more unaltered traditional 16C manor house of **Coupesarte**. This too is moated, far more picturesque though less grand, and is today a farmhouse, the surrounding land being a muddy, down-to-earth working farm. (For a small fee, you may approach the house to look at it more closely, but not go inside.)

Continue on D47 to D579, where turn right and go into **LIVAROT**, a pleasant and modest enough small town but a great name on the cheeseboard. Carry on along D579 to **VIMOUTIERS**, a slightly bigger town, not so attractive (much damaged in 1944), but another 'big cheese' of the region. It has a little Museum of Camembert adjoining the Syndicat d'Initiative, while in the main square there's a statue of farmer's wife Marie Harel (1781-1855), who was, according to the plaque, 'the possessor of the secret of making Camembert'. Another plaque says, unexpectedly, that the statue was 'offered by 400 men and women making cheese in Van Wert, Ohio, USA, with the cooperation of the committee on Aid to Vimoutiers'.

The obvious place to go from here is up the road to the village where Marie Harel lived, and where she created the most famous of all Normandy cheeses, **CAMEMBERT**. (Leave Vimoutiers on the Argentan road, soon turning left onto D16 and D246, following signs to Camembert.) The village, when you reach it, turns out to be marvellously obscure: tiny, quiet and simple, with a lovely view.

Go back down the hill on which the village rests so peacefully, across D246 onto an unnumbered road which climbs steeply to meet D16. Here turn right, and at La Bruyère-Fresnay take a left onto another unnumbered road (it has an old-fashioned blue roadsign pointing the way to 'Route de Survie' — i.e. D26). At D26 turn right, and enjoy this road through the tranquil fields and farms of the Auge. Take D299 on the left and follow it through Ménil-Hubert-en-Exmes to **MARDILLY**, tiny village in the Touques valley. (Alternatively reach Mardilly from the nearby town of Gacé by taking D979.)

The whole length of the Touques valley makes pleasant travelling. Follow it back towards the coast on narrow D33. On meeting D16 turn right and left onto D64. On the way the road passes close to several of the most interesting of the old manor houses and châteaux — **Chiffretot**, near les Moutiers-Hubert; handsome **Bellou**, with its village; **Fervaques**, right on the banks of the the Touques; and, best of them all, the unusual and impressive moated château **St. Germaine-de-Livet**, which is open (not Tuesdays) for guided visits. All these house are marked on the Michelin map.

Continue into **LISIEUX**, (pop: 27,000) which in truth is not a very charming town, being rather too big and busy for comfort. However, it is good for shopping, and does have some lingering signs of its former beauty (though it was largely destroyed in 1944), as well as a fine Gothic cathedral and a forceful and unusual Basilica high on a hill overlooking the town. Good 2-star Logis: **Hôtel de la Coupe d'Or** (31.31.16.84). Syndicat d'Initiative in rue d'Alençon.

Return from Lisieux to Pont l'Évêque on D48, on the left bank of the Touques.

Invasions

1-2 days/150km/from Caen

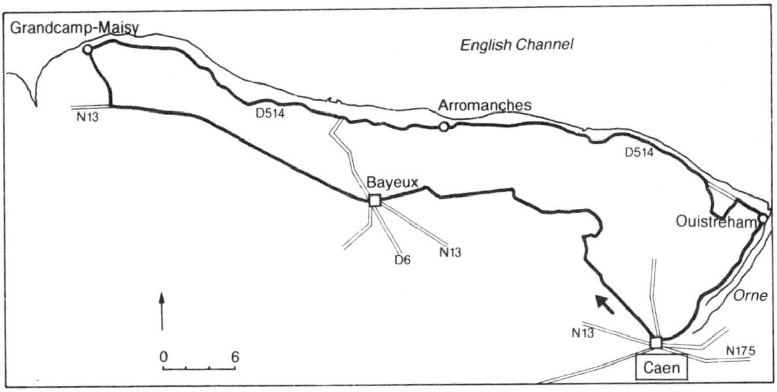

Not a very rural ride, this, and one which attracts, along parts of the route at least, tens of thousands of visitors each year. Yet this is one of Normandy's most fascinating and worthwhile journeys. Most people who come to see the invasion beaches along this coast have, in one way or another, been directly affected by events that took place here in 1944. But no less have they been affected by the events, recorded on the Bayeux Tapestry, which took place nine centuries before. This route takes in much else of interest, too, like the simple sea-facing villages along the shore, where local families, putting the wartime past far behind them, now calmly search the 'Landing Beaches' for shellfish. (Use Michelin map 54.)

CAEN pop: 117,000 Originally a Celtic town called Catumagus, meaning battlefield, the city has seen frequent fighting throughout its history and was almost entirely destroyed during World War II. It was rebuilt with great success from the attractive local Caen stone and is now a major industrial city, though with considerable character. This was a favourite town of William the Conqueror, who built a huge castle here, its impressive remains still dominating the central area. William and his reluctant wife Matilda each founded a fine abbey here, the Abbaye aux Dames, and the more unaltered Abbaye aux Hommes, in which William was buried, although his grave has in fact been empty since it was desecrated during the Religious Wars. See also: beautiful Gothic church of St. Pierre; Museum of Normandy; Museum of Fine Art. SI: pl St. Pierre.

Leave the city on D22 (direction Arromanches), turning right onto D170 after some 20km. Pass through **THAON** (attractive 11C church) to beautiful Renaissance **Château de Fontaine-Henry**. Take D141 (rejoins D22) to **CREULLY**, with its lofty fortified castle, and turn left onto D12 to continue straight into **BAYEUX**.

Bayeux is a largish country town (pop: 15,000) of immense charm with many old timbered houses and a fine 13C Gothic cathedral. The weekly Saturday market in pl St. Patrice is very pleasing. Fine lace-making, embroidery, tapestry and weaving are traditional local activities, and outside the School of Lace-making, Tapestry and Weaving in pl aux Pommes groups of women sometimes sit practising their craft. Of course the town possesses one of the world's most famous pieces of such work. Indeed most visitors do not explore the town at all, but come only to see, in the Centre Culturel Guillaume le Conquerant, the magnificent 70m-long Bayeux Tapestry (in fact an embroidery). This portrays colourfully in words and pictures, cartoon-style, the story of the Battle of Hastings, the reasons for it, and the consequences. It is well worth taking advantage of the tape-recorded commentary in English which you can listen to while walking round. There's also a Museum of the 1944 Battle of Normandy, and a British war memorial and cemetery. An excellent and moderately priced hotel-restaurant here is the 3-star Logis **Le Lion d'Or** (Michelin rosette, Gault Millau toque: 31.92.06.90).

Travel west along N13, pausing at **FORMIGNY** where, in 1450, the French defeated the English in what was to prove one of the final battles of the Hundred Years' War, so banishing the English crown altogether from France. Just after la Cambe, turn right onto D113 which leads to the little holiday resort of **GRANDCAMP-MAISY** on the coast. Turn right onto D514 to follow the coast road along the seafront which has become known as the Normandy Landing beaches.

Their story is dramatic enough; at dawn on 6 June 1944, British,

Commonwealth and American troops began a massive invasion of France through the Normandy coast. The key to the operation — masterminded and controlled by Generals Eisenhower and Montgomery, and codenamed Overlord — was artificial ports, which were floated across the Channel in darkness to be positioned against this coastline bristling with German defences (not so bristling, however, as the Calais coast, where the Germans expected the invasion). Airborne troops led the way, while the majority arrived in boats after an exceptionally rough night crossing. On arrival the men had to wade onto the beach, braving mines, barbed wire and gunfire, and attempt to head inland. Thousands were killed in the first few moments, but ultimately the Germans were driven back first from one position and then another, and on 12 August began their eastward retreat — only to be cut off by Canadian and American troops.

Just off D514 on left (15 min walk) is the headland **Pointe du Hoc**, a German stronghold and lookout point which has been left exactly as it was after the fighting. Press on to **COLLEVILLE-SUR-MER**, where, if you take the road down towards the beach, you'll find a monument and American cemetery recalling that this section of the coast — codenamed 'Omaha Beach' — saw some of the worst fighting. D514 skirts the attractive fishing village **PORT-EN-BESSIN** (or simply 'Port'), with its lively fish market each Sunday. From neighbouring Longues-sur-mer a track goes down to the rock formation of Le Chaos, looking out onto 'Gold Beach'.

Continue into **ARROMANCHES-LES-BAINS**, fishing harbour and small coastal resort, where one of the crucial artificial ports — here known by locals as Port Winston in honour of Churchill — was established for reinforcing the invasion. More than 2 million men landed here. The full story of the Allied invasion is graphically told in the local Musée du Débarquement (Landings Museum). Beyond Arromanches the coast road carries on past **GRAYE-SUR-MER** (in the Canadian-held 'Juno Beach' sector), where King George V and Winston Churchill made a brief inspection landing on 16 June 1944. At **LION-SUR-MER** turn just inland on D60 through **HERMANVILLE-SUR-MER** (British cemetery) and (on D35) the village of **COLLEVILLE-MONTGOMERY**, which adopted the name of the British commander of the 1944 landings, and erected a statue in his honour. Fittingly, Montgomery was himself descended from the Norman conquerors who crossed the Channel in 1066.

Take the road back to the seashore (Colleville-Montgomery Plage), which forms part of the beach resort of **RIVA-BELLA** (German blockhouse) and its neighbour (the two form a single *commune*) on the estuary of the river Orne, the old harbour town and modern cross-Channel ferry port **OUISTREHAM-RIVA-BELLA**. During the Hundred Years' War, Ouistreham was a frequent landing point for English troops.

D514 runs inland beside the Orne river and the Caen canal. At **BÉNOUVILLE**, the bridge over the canal was renamed Pegasus Bridge in commemoration of the insignia of British paratroops who, on the night of 5–6 June 1944, made the initial landing here in advance of the sea landings. Their first act, it is said, was to 'liberate' the café-bar which stands beside the bridge, before taking the bridge itself. A small museum records these first moments of the Battle of Normandy. There's an excellent hotel-restaurant here, too, suitably named **Le Manoir d'Hastings**; the cheaper menu is a particular bargain (rosette, 2 toques: 31.44.62.43).

D515 returns to Caen.

Cotentin Peninsula

1-2 days/200km/from Cherbourg

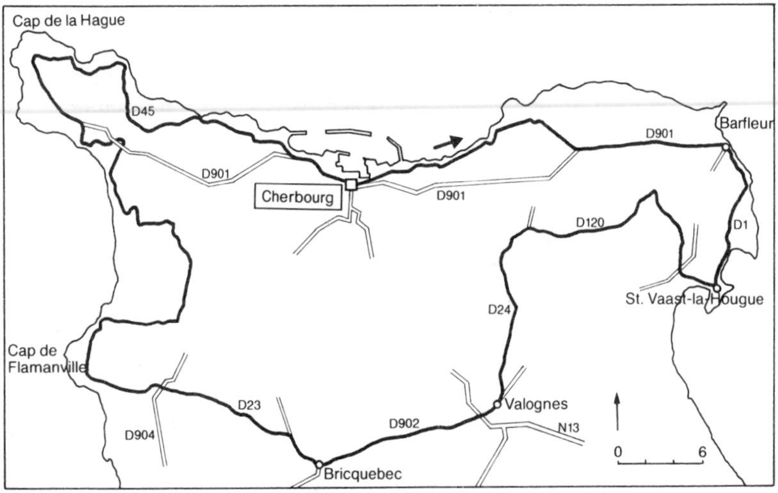

This unvisited corner of Normandy has a character and atmosphere all its own, alternating the starkest, wildest coastal hills with the gentlest, most rustic inland villages and valleys. The secret of this area is the narrow country lanes which thread the interior. The Cotentin Peninsula was the region most extensively settled by the Viking invaders who, after the treaty of 911 which 'allowed' them to remain (there was little that could be done to stop them) as an independent Dukedom within the Kingdom of France, became the great conquering Normans whose own kingdoms ranged from England to Jerusalem by the end of the 11th century. Place names on the Peninsula reveal these Norse origins: often seen are the Viking suffixes *bec* (stream); *ham* (settlement, hamlet); *hague*, *hougue* or *hogue* (hill); and *tot* (house, homestead). The Norman kings of England, especially Henry II upon his marriage to Eleanor of Aquitaine, acquired almost the whole of western France. Called upon to defend their title to these possessions, the former Viking warriors returned across the Channel in 1346, landing at St. Vaast-la-Hougue on the Cotentin Peninsula to fight the first battle of the Hundred Years' War. Six centuries later, their descendants returned once more ('Utah Beach' was just south of St. Vaast), to fight the Battle of Normandy and liberate France. (Michelin map 54.)

CHERBOURG (pop: 30,100) is certainly one of the pleasanter Channel ports, if only for its attractive location: the town, enclosing its harbour, is backed by green-topped slopes which give a distinctly rural air to this otherwise industrial and military centre. Lofty Fort du Roule, containing a museum devoted to the 1944 liberation, gives a good view across the town. There's a Fine Arts Museum in the town centre (Musée Thomas Henry), and the Syndicat d'Initiative is at 2 quai Alexandre-III.

Drive east out of town on bd Maritime, which becomes D116, the coast road (good views in places). At Fermanville a little access road leads down to Cap Lévy, a promontory with a fine panorama. From Fermanville take D210 to **ST. PIERRE-EGLISE** (18C château; 12C doorway of church), there picking up D901 to **BARFLEUR**. This attractive fishing and sailing harbour has a quiet waterfront, small stone houses and a curious church. The campsite on the opposite side of the harbour is a pity, but does not destroy the charm of the place! D1 from Barfleur to St. Vaast-la-Hougue is not the prettiest part of the route, though there are some fine manor-farmhouses in the Norman style on the way, as well as an 11C church at **RÉVILLE** and, close to that, a striking sea view from the Pointe de Saire.

ST. VAAST-LA-HOUGUE itself has plenty of charm: a busy fishing harbour, its quays are piled with the big lobster pots which are the key to the local economy. Hardworking, no-nonsense fishermen get on with their repairs and preparations at the waterside, their rough and ready boats moored to the quay. The harbour is large and interesting, providing some pleasant little walks; a long stone jetty projecting 400m into the sea, with a lighthouse at its tip, is the locals' favourite stroll. It was at St. Vaast that the English landed at the start of the Hundred Years' War, and they made many further attacks through this port in later centuries. Eventually, in the 17C, the village was fortified. There's an exellent 2-star Logis here, the **Hôtel de France et des Fuschias** (33.54.42.26); it has a pleasant, friendly atmosphere and good food at reasonable prices. Fuschias drape the front of the building like ivy: it's always a surprise to return to this hotel and find the fuschias still thriving.

Turning inland head first (on D1) to **QUETTEHOU**, where the church, standing high above the town, gives an excellent view back across to St. Vaast. Take D902 briefly out of town (direction Barfleur), soon turning left onto lovely D125 to Valcanville. Here take D25 (changes to D120), which follows the absolutely delightful valley of the Saire: the tiny river itself is not always within view, but this is exquisite countryside, with tiny villages, tiny lanes, muddy farmyards, and chickens scuttling off the road.

St. Vaast-la-Hougue

At inappropriately named **LE VAST**, the all-in-one Épicerie-Boulangerie-Café, which is also a restaurant at mealtimes, sells its own home-baked 'Brioches du Vast'. These are extra-large brioches, so eggy that they taste almost like soufflé or omelette, and are delicious with a jug of hot chocolate. Continue on D125, through the hamlet of Valognes, as far as the bigger and slightly busier D24, where turn left and drive to the busy market town of **VALOGNES**. Much damaged during World War II, Valognes has been successfully rebuilt, and has managed to preserve several of its exceptionally fine older houses, grimly elegant in grey stone. In one of them, the 15C Logis du Grand Quartier, there's now an interesting Cider Museum (summer only).

D902 goes on to ancient **BRICQUEBEC**, small country town dominated by what remains of an impressive 14/15C castle with a 10-sided keep. This was one of many French fortresses confiscated by the English after the Battle of Agincourt, but its new owner, the Earl of Suffolk, soon had to part with it again when he was captured by the French and forced to use the castle as a ransom. Amazingly, a comfortable and very reasonably priced 2-star Logis, **Le Vieux Château** (33.52.24.49), occupies part of the castle: the hotel dining room is spectacular, with massive stone pillars supporting a vaulted ceiling. From the upper platform of the castle keep there's a good view over the surrounding countryside and the nearby Trappist monastery, which stands a couple of km out of town (D121) in lush green farmland.

From the monastery, do not return into Bricquebec but take the steep road up to Quettetot, and from there follow D23 over pleasant country to les Pieux. Here D4 leads onto, and around, the headland of **Flamanville**, where there are several simple and traditional villages of unfaced stone, and an interesting 17C château. There's also one of France's numerous nuclear power stations, which is perhaps better seen from **DIÉLETTE**, a village built partly on the seafront (with a little harbour) and partly high up on a steep hill with commanding views. D4 (and several other little lanes) swings round to join main road D37, where turn left for a short distance.

Pass through another tiny 'Vastville' and turn off D37 again, taking the little road on the left which leads through Biville towards Vauville. The road forks to give a choice of routes to Vauville: make sure to take the magnificient D237, with its superb coastal views. **VAUVILLE** is a fascinating village of old stone houses and dry stone walls, with a Renaissance manor house. D318 runs up to Beaumont (on popular D901), and D403 goes back down again to the seashore before rising up an 18 per cent hill with marvellous coastal views.

It's unfortunate that the road re-emerges onto D901 just opposite the immensity and astonishing ugliness of yet another nuclear power station. Nothing daunted, turn left and follow D901 out to dramatic **Cap de la Hague**, the farthest tip of the Cotentin Peninsula. On the cape, take D45 (on right: signposted *Circuit de la Hague*) through a succession of picturesque villages. One of them, **PORT-RACINE**, a simple harbour sheltering a handful of small rowing boats, has a lovely 2-star Logis, **L'Erguillère** (33.52.75.31), a touch more expensive than the average but in a superb spot. Port-Racine claims to be 'the smallest port in France', but its neighbour **OLMONVILLE**, with 13C church and pretty little harbour, is no metropolis either. Stay on D45 all the way back into Cherbourg.

*

The result of all those orchards and dairy farms, of course, is meals with plenty of cheeses, butter, that delicious thick semi-sour cream called crème fraîche *and savoury cream sauces, apples and apple pastry, dry cider and fiery Calvados (brandy made from apples), and the sherry-like apple aperitif, pommeau. Many of the best-known French cheeses come from Normandy and carry the names of the towns and villages where they were first produced: Pont l'Évêque, Camembert, Livarot and others — all are flattish, strong cheeses with a thick natural rind. Normandy's butter too, processed and wrapped at Isigny, is widely exported. Other local favourites include charcuterie, especially andouillettes, and tripe, as well as fish and shellfish from along the coast. Most famous of the regional specialities is tripes à la mode de Caen (a stew of tripe, pigs' feet, vegetables, herbs and cider). Look out too for meat or vegetables cooked in cider or Calvados, and crêpes and galettes with fillings savoury or sweet. Meals in Normandy can be huge, and gave rise to the French gourmet habit of the* trou Normand, *literally the Norman hole (the French are so delicate when talking about food!), which is an interval between courses during which one has a glass of Calvados in order, so the theory runs, to relax the stomach muscles in preparation for the next course.*

3 BRITTANY

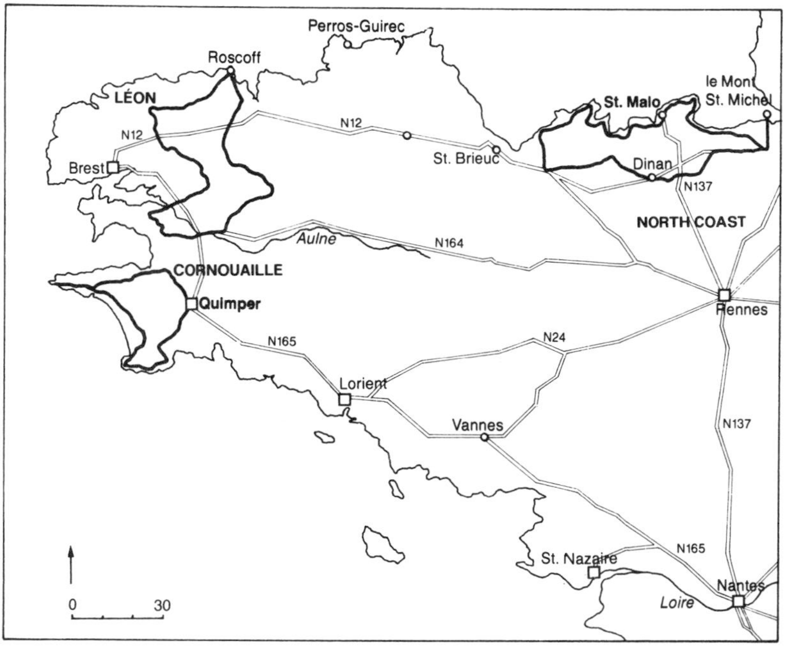

The great thing about Brittany is the sea: 1,500 kilometres of tortuously indented coastline — sometimes gentle sandy beaches, sometimes wild and furious rocky outcrops — reflect every variation of the ocean's mood. Great billows of cloud blowing across from the Atlantic create a magnificent, constantly changing sky. A low-lying peninsula pushing west from the Channel into the Atlantic Ocean, Brittany was seen by the Celts — who came here from Britain in the 5–7C and gave the province its name and its character — as two regions: the coast, which they called *armor*, the sea; and the interior, named *argoat*, the forest. The interior now is mistitled, for the woods have been cleared and the land farmed in rolling green arable fields separated by distinctive 'hedges' of trees growing from raised banks.

Whether officially ruled by French, English or native Breton kings, in reality the people of this windswept land remained for century after century almost ungoverned until World War I. Steeped in legend and superstition, struggling against direst poverty, each parish exercised a virtual independence over its affairs. No doubt this local communalism has contributed to Brittany's strong regionalist movement. Certainly, Bretons can justly claim that their province, with its Celtic identity, has stood apart from the rest of France.

Celts, with their mystical tradition and revered priesthood, always believed in the power of sacred sites, and death took an important role in their beliefs. The British Celtic invaders were nominally Christian, and had to conquer or convert the natives of the region who practised the old religion. An extraordinary number of the pre-Christian sites and monuments, dolmens and menhirs standing either lonely or in strange groupings, survive throughout the Breton countryside.

In a fusion of the two religions, each founder of a Christian village would be locally worshipped as a 'saint'. The church and its precincts were a walled sanctified area, generally constructed around a 'sacred' fountain or spring, and entered through a triumphal archway. This '*enclos paroissial*' (literally, parish close) received all the creative energy and as much of the wealth as a neighbourhood could muster. During the Gothic period, Brittany's farmers were not quite so poor and many *enclos* were grandly rebuilt. Locally designed and constructed (often copied from a nearby village), old Breton churches are traditionally lavishly ornate, with gaudy altarpieces, an elaborate baptismal font and organ loft, a large porch displaying statues of the apostles, and a distinctive bell tower. The church has the feeling of a large meeting hall, being often a square shape without transepts. Ceilings are usually wooden, barrel-shaped, and painted a 'heavenly' blue. Within the confines of the *enclos* should be, apart from the church itself, a graveyard (usually at the centre of the enclosure), an elaborate raised cross intended to represent Calvary (and sometimes flanked by the two thieves' crosses as well as statuary symbolic of the crucifixion) and an ossuary (in which were placed the bones from old tombs in the over-full graveyard). Scenes represented by the statuary in the *enclos* or inside the church reveal the naïve credulity of the Breton peasants.

Tourism, improved communications and escape from former poverty have brought many changes to Breton life and traditions. Inevitably, for example, each town and village is now surrounded by plain and inexpensive modern housing replacing the small and uncomfortable, if picturesque, stone cottages. French has almost entirely superseded the Breton language (Brezhoneg), even in the supposedly Breton-speaking area (west of a line from St. Brieuc to Vannes).

Yet Brittany does retain a strong regional identity and many local customs, as can be seen at the popular *Fest Noz*, night festivals, held whenever a community has something to celebrate. The most vital festival in the life of many villages is the *pardon*, when the whole population makes its way in procession to the *enclos* to beg the parish saint to cleanse them of their sins and cure their ills. Nowadays, *pardons* have lost something of their intensity and local importance. Visitors are welcome, and it is on these occasions that the curious lace headgear of the women and embroidered waistcoats of the men may again be seen, and the music of biniou (bagpipe) and bombarde (oboe-like flute) still heard.

Timing is important for a visit to Brittany. Many hotels and restaurants shut their doors from October to April. The province is a popular summer holiday destination and can be overcrowded in July and August. The best months are June and September. (Note that recent building of modern highways has led to renumbering of roads in places.)

Cornouaille

1–2 days/about 165km/from Quimper

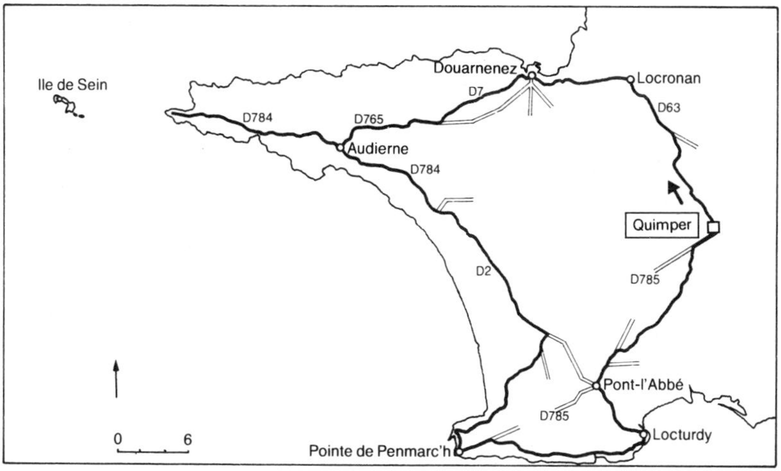

The Celtic invaders from Cornwall must have been struck by the similarity between this their adopted homeland and the country they had left behind. To the modern visitor too, this region seems startlingly like its namesake in southwest England. Quite apart from the placenames with such prefixes as Plo, Pol, Tre, Pen, there is the same tranquil countryside rolling down to broad inlets and estuaries, the small peaceful fishing communities built around a row of simple waterfront cottages. Cornouaille also happens to be the area where a visitor is most likely to see the old Breton style of dress and hear the Breton tongue spoken. (Michelin map 58.)

QUIMPER (pronounced Cam-pair) pop: 60,000 Capital of Cornouaille and préfecture of Finistère (= 'Land's End') département, and today something of a centre for Celtic/Breton consciousness. An exceptionally pleasant town built around the confluence (Breton *kemper* = meeting, coming together) of the murky Odet and Steir rivers. At the heart of an attractive old central area with numerous fine old houses (also many excellent pâtisseries and salons de thé) stands the Cathedral of St. Corentin (13–15C; spires 18C), high and impressive inside, with some beautiful stained glass, and built with a slight curve along its length. Fine Arts museum almost opposite the cathedral. Each summer the city hosts a fascinating week-long Festival de Cornouaille, a great chance to see Breton dress and dances and hear local folk music. Syndicat d'Initiative: rue du roi Gradlon.

Leave town on D765 (direction Douarnenez), soon turning right onto D63. Follow this wooded valley road, dotted with farms and hamlets, to **LOCRONAN**. Its cobbled square and side streets lined with the most extraordinarily well-preserved Renaissance stone mansions and cottages, the village of Locronan makes a picturesque sight. Its old buildings are all the more remarkable for their exceptional consistency of age and style. Of course the village attracts many visitors in summer, and devotes much energy to the selling of traditional Breton snacks, sweaters and souvenirs. In former days its wealth was made from the making of sailcloth, for which there was a huge demand in this seafaring province. Locronan's *pardon* is called the *troménie*; 'petit troménie' each year and 'grand troménie' — a longer procession — every six years (1989, 1995).

D7 leads to **DOUARNENEZ**, a large workaday fishing town set beside a beautiful bay. In this stretch of water, Breton legend has it, a city called Ys sank beneath the waves in punishment by the gods for the sinfulness of the king's daughter. Continue on D7, now a very minor road (this starts out from the town as rue du Commandant Fernand, off av de la Gare, by the main SNCF station), which passes by the interesting countryside church Notre-Dame de Kérinec (with open-air chapel). Join D765 and turn right for **PONT CROIX**, a village handsome with its whitewashed cottages overlooking the Goyen inlet, and on to picturesque fishing harbour **AUDIERNE**, at the mouth of the Goyen. An excellent, fairly pricey hotel-restaurant here is **Le Goyen** (Michelin rosette, 2 Gault Millau toques: 98.70.08.88).

D784 runs straight out west from here to the wave-lashed headland **Pointe du Raz**, from which can be seen the tiny bleak **Ile de Sein**, once a Druid burial ground. Reached by ferry from Audierne, the island has a quaint little harbour and village and supports a small fishing community. The Sein population were awarded the Cross of Liberation in 1946 for bravery during World War II, when every adult male islander (130 of them) sailed off to England to join the Free French brigade, taking with them 3,000 beleaguered French soldiers and sailors.

From Audierne, take D784 east (direction Quimper), at **PLOVEZET** (interesting church) joining D2, which heads south. At Plonéour-Lanvern, turn right onto D57 (direction Penmarc'h) and, soon after, turn right again (direction Mejou). This little road passes close to Notre-Dame de Tronoën church standing alone in open country (note the 15C Calvary), and goes round towards the fishing harbour **ST. GUÉNOLÉ**, where there is a good Museum of Prehistory. A great many prehistoric finds have been made in the immediate area, and all around St. Guénolé stand many dolmens and menhirs. A first-class seafood restaurant here — *avec chambres* — is **La Mer** (toque: 98.58.62.22).

Follow the road along this rocky weatherbeaten coast, past the massive lighthouse (Phare d'Eckmühl) to Pointe de Penmarc'h. Just inland (D785), **PENMARC'H** was once a major fishing port. Overtaken in importance by Nantes, it fell into such decline that now it has become no more than an obscure village. Note though its interesting 16C church, built by Breton 'privateers' (in other words, pirates). Return to the coast road, going through busy little fishing harbours **GUILVINEC** and prettier **LESCONIL**, to the popular resort village **LOCTUDY**. From here lovely views extend over a beautiful bay, while across the water at Ile-Tudy (accessible by ferry) there's an excellent beach. The 18C façade of Loctudy's village church conceals an intriguing Romanesque interior (note capitals).

Festival de Cornouaille

D2 runs north, passing 16C Château de Kérazan (housing Breton art and crafts), into **PONT-L'ABBÉ**. All this little corner of Cornouaille is called the Bigouden peninsula, after the ancient Breton tribe whose capital was at Pont-l'Abbé. Today, this is an area in which many old Breton customs have managed to survive remarkably well. In the streets of Pont-l'Abbé it's not unusual to see women wearing their tall lace coifes, or men in baggy trousers and embroidered waistcoats. The town has an attractive waterside setting, with many old houses and a Bigouden Museum (summer only; mainly local costumes) inside the round tower of a 13–17C castle. A couple of km southwest of town (D785), well-restored 16C **Château de Kernuz** has been turned into a comfortable and peaceful hotel-restaurant (98.87.01.59).

To return to Quimper, travel northeast from the town on D785, soon turning right onto D20, a more enjoyable minor road with views across the wide river Odet. D20 rejoins D785 just outside Quimper.

The Léon District

2 days/about 245km/from Roscoff

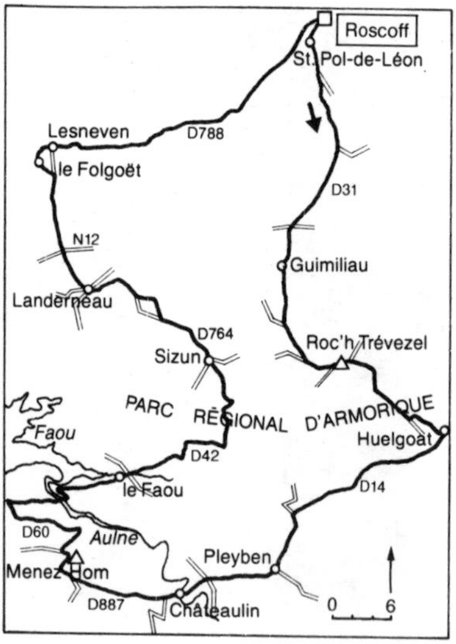

The Léon district, in the north of the département of Finistère, encompasses perhaps the best of Brittany's inland scenery and some of the finest traditional Breton architecture.

The small port of **ROSCOFF** is surprising with its backstreets of old stone houses and its sleepy Old Port used by fishing boats. **Hôtel Bellevue** (98.61.23.38) is a tranquil 2-star Logis with a sea view.

D769 leads south straight into adjacent **ST. POL-DE-LÉON**, a likeable country town dominated by its 3 splendid, ornate Breton-style spires. Two rise from the elegant and graceful former cathedral (12–16C: note stalls, reliquaries) and the other, the finest of them, is the belfy of the Kreisker Chapel (mainly 14–15C) where the town council used to meet. Climb the Kreisker tower for a good view over the Léon coast and interior.

Continue south on the same road, turning right at Penzé onto D31. Follow this road to tiny rustic **GUIMILIAU**; here, larger almost than the rest of the village, is a fine example of an *enclos paroissial*. In such a simple

Guimiliau — the enclos

setting one can readily understand the role that the *enclos* played in the life of the community. For a glimpse of ordinary daily life in these small Breton villages, stop in for a coffee at Guimiliau's Épicerie-Café-Bar.

Not so impressive as Guimiliau's in my view, but far better known, are the *enclos* at the larger neighbouring villages **ST. THÉGONNEC** to the east and **LAMPAUL-GUIMILIAU** to the west. (At St. Thégonnec, straightforward 1-star Logis **Auberge St. Thégonnec** has excellent inexpensive food: 98.79.61.18.)

Stay on D31 across flattish green arable land to **COMMANA** on the fringes of the Monts d'Arrée, and at the edge of the Parc Régional d'Armorique, a protected area within the Arrée hills. These 'mountains' do, by virtue of the contrast with the low-lying land on either side, manage to look like real mountains from a distance, but on climbing into them it turns out that they are modest wooded slopes, very attractive and with fine views, but having no arduous driving. The fine 16–17C church in Commana has an impressive porch. Continue through the village to meet D764 at a junction: facing you opposite is a lane to **MOUGAU-VIAN**, where there is a remarkable 'Allée Couverte' (covered alley) with pillars carved inside. Return to D764 and turn right, soon passing by the foot of imposing **Roc'h Trévezel**.

To climb to the top of this peak, turn down D785 for just 1km to reach the access path (about 15 min walk each way). From the summit (384m) there's a superb panorama; to the north lies the Léon countryside with its lofty spires; but to the south a sinister-looking nuclear power station rises from marshes, suitably known in Celtic as Yeun Elez, The Mouth of Hell. Even so, the middle of a regional park seems a typically unsuitable location for a nuclear power station.

Rejoin D764 and continue over the Arrée hills to **HUELGOAT** (Breton, 'high forest'). This little lakeside town, though perhaps too popular in season, is in the midst of an agreeable area of woodland in which are hidden a number of curious rock formations and prehistoric stone monuments reached by footpaths. Take D14 south, pausing at tiny **ST. HERBOT** on the road to admire the large Gothic church with its gloomy, crumbling and atmospheric interior (note oak screen). D14 eventually meets D785, where turn left and carry on to **PLEYBEN**. In the heart of this small town stands an unusually fine *enclos* with church, ossuary and, especially the Calvary, all richly ornate in Flamboyant Gothic style. Inside the church notice the rumbustious and sometimes quite bizarre carvings on the beams.

Here pick up N164 towards **CHÂTEAULIN**, an important river-fishing town on the Aulne. Salmon are caught by the thouands as they find their way along this winding river; one has even found its way onto the city's coat of arms. The main road (changed to D882) carries on west; as it approaches the 'mountain' of Menez-Hom, there are wide views down to the sea on the left, while on the right heath-covered **Menez-Hom** climbs to its summit. Though only 330m, it commands exceptionally wide views. To visit the top, take access road D83 on right. Every year on 15 August the summit is the setting for a lively festival of what the French call 'folklore' — traditional local dance, music and costume.

Immediately after the hill, take minor road C2 on right. This makes its way, over the crossroads with D60, to tiny **TRÉGARVAN**, poised prettily on the edge of the broadening Aulne as it reaches its estuary. The village has a walled churchyard-cemetery with a lovely little old church. Return to the junction with D60. Turn right and go through Argol, to bigger and busier D791. Here, turn right, and D791 soon crosses a spectacularly high suspension bridge over the Aulne, then runs along beside the beautiful Faou inlet: it's an enjoyable drive, with good views.

A turn on the left leads into **LE FAOU**, a former fishing village on the tidal Faou estuary. Interesting and attractive old stone houses, slate-fronted, line the single main street of the village, which unfortunately does become something of a resort in summer. D42 heads out of Le Faou, and into the Monts d'Arrée. The first village on this road, in a lovely setting, is **RUMENGOL**. Though hardly more than a hamlet, it has a substantial church surrounded by a walled grassy churchyard of buttercups and daisies. An open chapel at one side of the grounds is used on days of the popular local *pardon*, dedicated to Notre-Dame-de-Tout-Remède (literally, Our Lady of Curing All; Breton *rumen holl* = cures all). Beside the church a remnant of a Calvary stands rather incongruously, while the church itself has the distinctive Breton belfry and porch. The interior, without aisles or transepts, is typically ornate with gaudy retables and finely carved organ loft. Note, too, the bizarre 'reliquary' of '365 saints — one for each day of the year'.

Stay on D42 as it climbs again into the Parc Régional d'Armorique. Turn left onto D342, which passes by the mansion **Menez-Meur**, now the information centre for the Park, and makes its way (changes to D130 and D30) into **SIZUN**. Enter the *enclos* in this village through a striking 'triumphal arch'. Take busier D764 (direction Landerneau), perhaps making a detour off the road to see the exceptional church porches at tiny **LA MARTYRE** and its neighbour **PLOUDIRY**.

LANDERNEAU, former capital of the Léon district, though a large town (pop: 15,500), has a certain amount of charm. It has a number of picturesque old houses, and is well placed at the head of the long estuary of the river Elorn, spanned here by a handsome bridge dating from 1510. Cross the water and pick up D770 (direction Lesneven). Shortly before Lesneven, D32 on the left goes into **LE FOLGOËT**, a rather bleak small town with an impressive and ornate church which is the centre of a great *pardon* every September (the most popular month for Breton *pardons*).

LESNEVEN is a pleasant little town with several interesting buildings made of the local granite, some arcaded sidewalks and an attractive, if too busy, main square. In the square: Syndicat d'Initiative and a 1-star Logis **Hôtel de France** (98.83.00.06).

To return towards Roscoff follow signs on D788 to St. Pol-de-Léon (Roscoff itself is not signposted until much closer). The road is not as busy as one might expect, and follows a course between broad fields of cabbages. **BERVEN**, a small plain village on the road, has a very basic *enclos* but with an unusual triple archway and a Renaissance tower strangely more elaborate than the rest of the building. Just south of here, in open countryside, stands an impressive fortified 16C mansion, the Château de Kerjean (signposted).

Stay on D788 to return to Roscoff.

North Coast

1–2 days/275km/from St. Malo

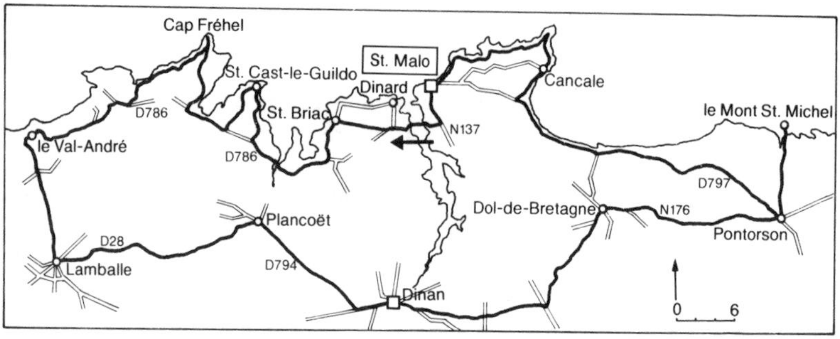

North-Eastern Brittany has a great cultural overlap with neighbouring Normandy and makes no claim to being Breton-speaking. Yet here, too, is Brittany's familiar landscape: great churches, simple villages and gentle green countryside, meeting the sea along a spectacular coast.

ST. MALO pop: 47,000 A thriving fishing and ferry port with a tremendously imposing walled old town ('Intra-Muros') best seen from the sea, which beats dramatically against the ramparts. In fact the 'old' town with its tall austere terrace was almost entirely rebuilt with perfect fidelity to its previous appearance, after being destroyed in World War II. A walkway encircles the top of the ramparts (mostly original 12C). Determinedly independent, the motto of the townspeople has been 'Not French, not Breton, from St. Malo I am'. However, the atmosphere today is very much that of a proudly Breton city. Many enjoyable little restaurants and hotels; a good traditional snackbar and crêperie with many Breton specialities is Ti Nevez, 12 rue Broussais. Syndicat d'Initiative at the marina.

Head south through St. Malo's holiday area **ST. SERVAN**, there taking the D168 (direction Dinard) across the top of a big dam which blocks the broad Rance estuary. After the bridge, ignore signs to the resort town Dinard and press on, taking D603, to **ST. BRIAC**. The village stands by a small pine-covered headland, with tiny islands offshore. Follow round (D786) through Lancieux and Poubalay, eventually turning right to go into **ST. CAST-LE-GUILDO** via Pen-Guen, keeping to the road which goes through town staying close to the seashore. On the way round it first passes Pointe de la Garde and then, after an attractive little harbour, Point de St. Cast. Both have good sea views. St. Cast is not so much a town as a group of villages (La Garde, Le Bourg, and L'Isle) which together have a pleasant atmosphere and some excellent sandy beaches.

Leaving St. Cast on D13 to little **MATIGNON** (lots of good boulangeries and charcuteries; big market every Wednesday), take D786 towards **Cap Fréhel**. At the village of St. Aide, turn right (signposted Cap Fréhel) onto a winding road through pleasant rustic countryside with glimpses of sea. At last it reaches the heather-and-gorse covered Cape, which is a nature reserve. Gulls screech and turn above the lichen-stained red granite rocks at the tip of the headland. Astonishingly, a precarious footpath winds its way round the head clinging to the cliff face. The view is impressive, showing a wide sweep of rocky coastline stretching away in each direction.

D34^{A}, with many good views along the way, runs above the shore from Cap Fréhel to well-named **SABLES-D'OR-LES-PINS** — a small modern resort with a long sandy beach backed by pines. Turn right onto the main road (combines D786 with D34) and follow signs to Le Val-André. First it is necessary to pass through horrible Pleneuf on the outskirts, but **LE VAL-ANDRÉ** itself is not so bad; it makes a good starting point for some excellent cliff walks.

Take D786/D791 inland, to **LAMBALLE**. This is a small town with a rocky escarpment in the middle of it: on the summit stands the drab Collegiate Church. Pl de Martrai, in the town centre, preserves a few handsome old buildings, many timbered in Norman style. The church, too, looks more Norman than Breton. Inside the most beautiful of the old timbered houses — called the Executioner's House — is the Syndicat d'Initiative and a local museum.

To leave town, at first take D786 (signposted St. Cast), but soon turn right onto D28 (signposted Plancoët). This unassuming country lane alternates farms and woods in a gentle, rather flat landscape. First village on the way is **LA POTERIE**, which has a good hotel-restaurant in a quiet waterside setting to the left of the main through-road: **Manoir des Portes** (Relais du Silence: 96.31.13.62). **PLEVEN**, soon after, is an old village of unfaced stone houses and a church, again in Norman rather than Breton style. Outside the village, the fine 16C Breton manor house **Le Vaumadeuc** has been turned into a quiet and comfortable but overpriced hotel. The road continues into **PLANCOËT**, a straightforward, agreeably bustling small country town of old stone houses. On D794 travel towards Dinan. The down-to-earth but not unattractive little town of **CORSEUL** on the way has Roman remains in its Jardin des Antiques.

DINAN is a large town (pop: 14,000), with quite a lot of traffic, but very attractive within its walled and fortified old centre. 'Vieux Dinan', with cobbled streets and superb old houses, is signposted and worth exploring. A vast basilica dominates the town, while a fine oval keep stands across the ramparts wall with tremendous views. 16C mansion Hôtel Kératry now accommodates the Syndicat d'Initiative. There's an excellent 3-star Logis in town, **Hôtel Avaugour** (2 toques: 96.39.07.49).

Leaving Dinan, at first follow signs to Rennes and Combourg (D794). These lead across a remarkably high viaduct over the river Rance. Turn left into the village of St. Solen. This turning, D68 (changes to D10), is misleadingly marked N794 on the old signpost. After St. Solen, take a left signposted to St. Pierre de Plesguen. This narrow road makes its way through the Forêt de Coëtquen, then across a tranquil country of woods, farms and hamlets. At surprisingly large St. Pierre, continue straight on, following signs to Lanhélin (D10). At Lanhélin, D10 crosses over D73 onto D75, which goes to **LE TRONCHET**.

The area around Le Tronchet is interesting, with the Mesnil forest close by (good walks), and dolmens, old *manoirs*, and the remnant of the lakeside 17C Benedictine abbey of Le Tronchet. Road numbering is confusing around here though. Follow the signs, along D75, D78 and D119, through villages sometimes Breton and sometimes Norman in style, to **DOL-DE-BRETAGNE**.

The most amazing thing about Dol is the number and age of its astonishingly well-preserved old houses. Stroll down Grand Rue des Stuarts, for example, in the centre of town, and see beautifully arcaded and timbered no. 27 (13C; now an antique shop), no. 25 next door has a remarkable wooden façade and doorway, no. 32 is part of the impressive 15C gateway into Cour des Charretiers, while no. 17 (now a florist) is a very beautiful 11C stone house with wide decorated arches. No. 18, the crêperie opposite, is a timbered 12C house. There are many more such buildings in the town — it seems impossible that so many houses in one place could survive for so many centuries. '*Dol*' is Breton for plateau, or high ground, and the town justifies the name, for it stands atop a high escarpment — an ocean-washed cliff-face when these houses were built — with a commanding perspective on the countryside to its north. Dol's massive St. Samson cathedral, a vast grey Gothic pile standing on the edge of the cliff, is visible from afar. Inside, it is impressively high, with lovely stained glass and an interesting statue of Christ-aux-Outrages. Note the cathedral's large, ornate porch. Promenade des Douves, behind the cathedral, makes an enjoyable stroll on the former sea-facing ramparts; from this vantage point there's a fine view of Mont Dol — formerly an island — rising from the marshy plain.

To continue on to **LE MONT ST. MICHEL**, take N176 from Dol to Pontorson, where signs lead to the Mont (on D976). Le Mont St. Michel, an enormous abbey rising pyramid-like from the sea-bound tip of a narrow causeway, receives more visitors than almost any other 'tourist sight' in France. Some absurd claims are made about it, such as (quoting a tourist office leaflet) that it is 'Man's finest achievement'! None the less, it is a magnificent construction and a quite fantastic location. In modern times the setting has lost some of the magic it must once have had, because the island is now easily reached by car, and because the surrounding waters are rapidly silting up and have even, in large measure, been 'reclaimed' and turned into fields where sheep now graze. For all that, the walk from the waterside, up the hundreds of steps to the awesome entrance of the abbey church, is rewarding. A hefty fee is payable to enter the church, which is of inspiring dimensions. Note especially the lovely Gothic Cloisters. Surrounding the abbey are powerful fortifications, with a ramparts walk. And there's a village of sorts in the shadow of the abbey buildings. Devoted, as it has been for centuries, to parting visitors and their money, the single street offers as gaudy and tasteless an array of souvenirs as can be found anywhere. A better bet would be to try the famous local speciality Omelette de la Mère Poulard (literally, Mother Hen's Omelette). Le Mont St. Michel, incidently, is officially in Normandy, not Brittany, the border between the two provinces traditionally being the river Couësnon.

Return to Pontorson, and find D797 (on the west edge of town) which runs across the reclaimed sea-marshes, through atmospheric fishing villages and, beside a long sea-wall, to **CANCALE**. At this popular little fishing harbour, seafood restaurants line the front and gaze out across the water. The most highly praised of Cancale's excellent eating places is **Restaurant de Bricourt** (rosette, 3 toques), which gives a rare opportunity to see inside a *Malouinière*, that is, one of the fine old mansions built in this district by the many rich *corsairs* (mere pirates — but loyal to the Crown) of St. Malo.

From here D210 runs back along the coast, with a succession of magificent sea views, into St. Malo.

*

Not a gastronomic region, in general Brittany favours plain food simply prepared. The sea rules the Breton table as much as everything else in the province: fresh fish and shellfish feature constantly on menus. Charcuterie, too, is much liked. Traditional Breton specialities include, above all, delicious caky tarts, eggy cakes, galettes and crêpes both sweet and savoury. Blé noir (buckwheat) and Froment (whole wheat flour) are both widely used, and every village and town has at least one crêperie. Galette fourrée is like a soft caky fruit pie; Far Breton is a popular caky tart with dried fruit; Kouign amann is another favourite, a round light buttery plain cake. For drinking, crisp dry white Muscadet wine — an ideal companion for the region's fish dishes — comes from around Nantes, where Brittany meets the Loire Valley. But cider or, surprisingly, buttermilk are often preferred with Breton cakes and pancakes.

4 LOIRE

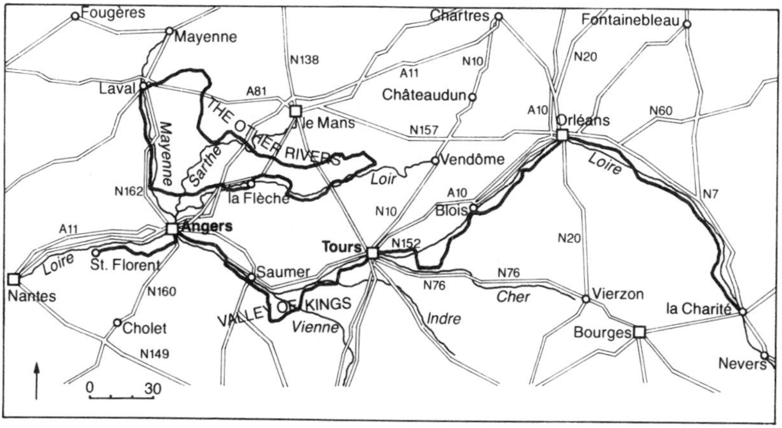

As it flows northwards from the hills of the Massif Central and along the edge of Burgundy, the river Loire grows constantly in majesty and dignity. At last it turns west in a stately sweep to face the Atlantic, and its valley broadens to become, in Victor Hugo's words, 'a plain drowned in verdure'; a rich, gentle, refined countryside which the French have called La Vallée des Rois, the Valley of Kings. With the river itself often hidden behind reeds, trees and floodbanks, it is the human life of the Loire, ornate Renaissance châteaux and noble castles, delicate wines, and old riverside towns and villages, not forgetting the strange cave-houses dug into the valley escarpments at many places, which give the region its special character. Remember, though, that the same civilised life and many of the finest châteaux and prettiest countryside are not only on the Loire but along its beautiful tributaries: the Cher, the Indre, the Vienne, Sarthe and Mayenne, and that other river Loir (without an 'e') which flows along about 40km north of its better-known namesake.

The Valley of Kings

4 days/about 455km/from La Charité-sur-Loire to St. Florent-le-Viel

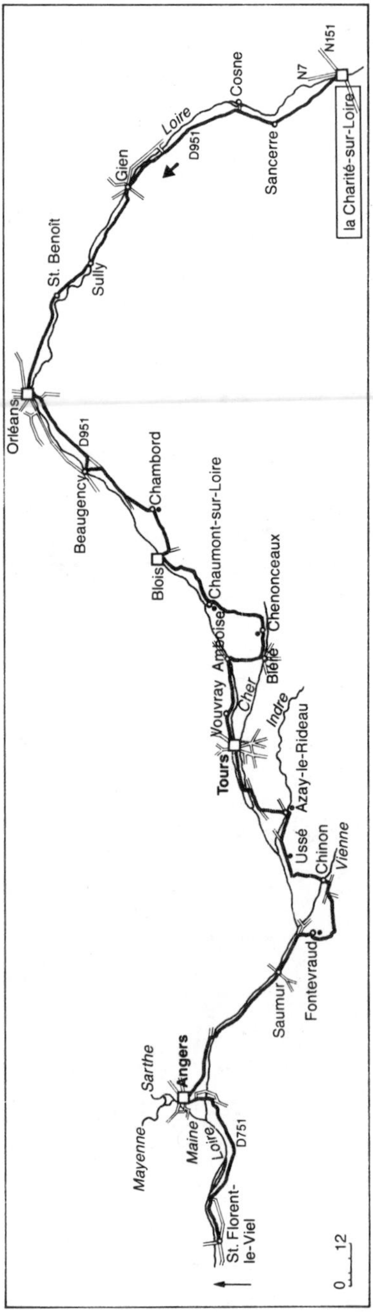

Wide, shallow, full of islands, concealed by greenery, the capricious waters themselves are veiled from view along much of the Val de Loire's length. Escarpments of tufa, that curious rock which gives beauty to Loire buildings whether château or cottage, rise unpredictably first from one bank, then from the other. Apart from these cliffs the valley is broad and flat, with its fields, farms and woods stretching away from the river under a vast, hazy brilliant sky. Prosperous and densely populated, the Loire valley seems somehow to have been deprived of a truly rural quality. Generally, the south or left bank is the prettier, but the Loire is not always especially picturesque: some sections have plenty of industry, and it has even been dubbed the *fleuve nucléaire* because of the number of nuclear power stations along its length. All the better-known stretches of the river are teeming with visitors in summer. Yet there are considerable compensations: many good hotels and restaurants, pleasant old towns and dozens of impressive châteaux.

Several French monarchs spent much of their time in the Loire valley, and many noble families also established themselves in securely fortified castles in the region. In later centuries, when concerns about security were allowed to give way to preoccupations with luxury and elegance, most of the fortresses were completely redesigned in the lavishly decorative Renaissance style. Despite one's instinct to avoid the crowds, many of these great stately homes, with their astonishing fairy-tale exteriors, are well worth seeing.

Most are built of the local tufa, a pale stone which has the fortunate quality of becoming ever whiter as time passes, and ever more striking under jet-black slate roofs. (To follow the whole route, use Michelin maps 65, 64 & 63.)

The first inkling of the Loire's grandeur can be felt at about **LA CHARITÉ-SUR-LOIRE**, a small and picturesque old former monastic town on the edge of Burgundy. Remnants of the abbey, entered through a splendid gateway, have become private dwellings. The existing church is just a part of the original larger building. The town (or rather, village) retains curious old overgrown ramparts, with a commanding walkway. Down by the riverside, set back in its own courtyard, there's a good hotel-restaurant, **Le Grand Monarque** (86.70.21.73). An impressive 18C stone bridge spans the river just here, giving a stirring view, full of promise.

Cross the bridge (N151), turning right onto D7 immediately on other side. Take this road to **SANCERRE**, well known for its excellent, fragrant dry white wine. It is also a good-looking town, poised on a round hill gazing across the neat vineyards and the river, its tangled old streets and lanes guarded by a 14C tower. As well as the local wine, try, too, some of the district's highly-praised goats' cheese called Crottins — perfectly delicious despite the name (it means 'goat droppings'!).

Continue north on D955, perhaps crossing the river to see **COSNE**, largish and busy but very likeable town. But staying on the left bank, take D751 (changes to D951) as it makes it way through **LÉRÉ** (village with remains of old ramparts) and Châtillon-sur-Loire, passing handsome **GIEN**, on the opposite side of the river (very striking 15C château with geometric pattern of red and black bricks).

Stay on D951 to **SULLY-SUR-LOIRE**, pretty little town with an awesome 14C feudal castle, cleverly 'moated' by the river Sange. (Note especially the splendid 600-year-old wooden roof inside the keep.) Voltaire spent long periods here as a guest of the Duke of Sully.

Take the bridge across to the right bank, turning left at once onto D60. This soon arrives at **ST. BENOÎT-SUR-LOIRE**. In this village stands one of the finest Romanesque buildings in all France, the Basilica of Saint Benoît, or as he is called in English, Saint Benedict. Founded in 7C on a site of great pre-Christian religious importance, the superb present buildings are mainly 11C. Note especially the richly decorative carvings on the capitals in the belfry-porch of the church. Down in the (older) crypt are the remains of Benedict himself, founder of the Benedictine Order whose influence was to spread so far and become so great during the Middle Ages. Close by, at **GERMINGNY-DES-PRES** on D60, there's a lovely little country church which, quite extraordinarily, dates from the year 806 — a rare survival from that distant era. It was originally built as a private chapel to adjoin the house of Theodulf, Abbot of St. Benoît at that time. Inside, on the roof of the east apse, there's a magnificient mosaic probably just as old as the rest of the building.

Stay on D60 into the pleasant market town **CHÂTEAUNEUF-SUR-LOIRE**, from there going directly into Orléans. (Or, to avoid Orléans and its city traffic, return to the left bank at St Denis l'Hôtel, taking D921 to La Ferté-St. Aubin, then D18/D103/D19 to Beaugency.)

ORLÉANS pop: 105,600 The town is best seen from the river itself. Not surprisingly, Orléans makes much of its patriotic and devout heroine Joan of Arc, who in May 1429 rode, armour-clad and triumphant, into the city from which she had driven the English troops. The town centre, with old streets and houses, cathedral and museum, extends along the north bank, but the prettiest parts of Orléans lie south of the river. SI: pl Albert-1er.

Take D951 or N152 (neither is very interesting) straight to **BEAUGENCY**. In former times, bridges across the Loire were few and had tremendous strategic importance. Joan of Arc's soldiers, unable to enter Orléans from the south, also found the bridge blocked at Beaugency, where English forces had massed. Today, the cobbled streets of Beaugency, rising gently from the river, retain a good deal of medieval atmosphere, and the splendid stone bridge with its 22 irregular arches spans the Loire as grandly as ever. A very enjoyable and reasonably priced hotel-restaurant is the creaky old 2-star Logis **L'Ecu de Bretagne** (38.44.67.60) in the main square. Slightly more upmarket is **L'Abbaye** (38.44.67.35).

Return across the bridge, taking D925 as far as main D951, where turn right. You will soon be treated to a spectacular view of a nuclear power station on the river banks. Press on to Nouan-sur-Loire, after which turn left onto D112B to enter the walled Parc of one of the most impressive of all the Loire Valley châteaux — **Chambord**, which comes suddenly and dramatically into view. In the midst of a large forest, and standing beside the little Cosson river, it was once no more than a fortified hunting lodge. King François I, who had a passion for hunting, transformed the building into the most regal of royal country retreats, crowned with a mass of spires, turrets, windows and ornamentation rising above the treetops. The interior, with over 400 rooms and a splendid Grand Staircase, is laden with gorgeous Renaissance decoration. The château's great hunting forest has become a preserve in which the animals — including wild boar — are protected.

D33 follows the Cosson to meet the Loire at **BLOIS**, ancient, handsome small town with basilica and cathedral. Its picturesque lanes are watched over by an immense château, a favourite of the French monarchy for generations. Interior decorations are lavish; the spiral staircase is a masterpiece of Renaissance art and craftsmanship. This château earned a notorious place in French history with the brazen, savage murder of the Duke de Guise actually inside the private apartment of King Henri III, who felt that the Duke posed a threat to him. 2-star Logis **Hostellerie de la Loire** (54.74.26.60) is an excellent little hotel-restaurant, reasonably priced.

Take the left bank road, D751, which passes below the lofty château of **Chaumont-sur-Loire** in its clifftop gardens. Catherine de Medici, that royal lady who at various times stayed as a guest in most of the region's best château, owned Chaumont until, by an unsavoury combination of flattery and trickery, she managed to swap it for its much grander neighbour, Chenonceau. To reach Chenonceau, leave Chaumont on D114, soon turning right onto D27, which continues, via Vallières-les-Grands, to Chissay-en-Touraine, on the banks of the river Cher. Here turn right and travel the short distance to pretty, flowery, but crowded **CHENONCEAUX** village. It is filled with hotels, for here is possibly the most popular of all the Loire châteaux, and deservedly so. Chenonceau (only the château is spelt without an 'x') is an exceptional flight of imagination, as well as an astonishing achievement in construction, the whole mansion standing in the waters of the Cher, with a long gallery going clear across the river. Elegant gardens and a sumptuous interior complete the effect.

From Chenonceaux village, travel on either side of the Cher downstream to **BLÉRÉ**, a pleasant small market town with a quietly civilised atmosphere. Looking onto pl de l'Eglise there's a nice 2-star Logis, **Hôtel du Cheval Blanc** (47.57.90.04), with comfortable rooms, beamed ceilings and excellent reasonably priced meals.

Cross the Cher on D31 and head into **AMBOISE**, the agreeable old town on the south bank of the Loire where Leonardo da Vinci lived as a guest of François I. Leonardo became fascinated by the soft brightness of the light over the wide Loire Valley and wrote that his great wish was to know 'how to render this light accurately' on canvas. The last three years of his life were spent living in the town at le Manoir du Clos Luce, now an intriguing museum of Leonardo's scientific designs and plans. A secret passageway gave him direct access to the château. The château of Amboise, remnant of a much larger complex of buildings poised on terraces high above the town and river, looks its best from across the water on the north bank. Very pleasing 2-star Logis **Le Lion d'Or** (47.57.00.23) has a river view and good food (including home-made croissant for breakfast).

Stay on the north bank (N152), skirting pretty village **NEGRON**, then passing through **VOUVRAY**, little town at the centre of the district producing one of the Loire's most prestigious white wines, ranging from dry to very sweet, and from slightly *pétillant* to sparkling. So respected are the wines of Vouvray that the SNCF, in building the TGV Atlantic line, decided to run their 270km/h trains through a tunnel beneath the vineyards to avoid any disturbance to the vines — despite an established policy, adhered to everywhere else, to run TGVs above ground only. Another underground phenomenon around Vouvray — and on the opposite side of the Loire — is the large number of curious cave-houses carved into the cliffs. N152 runs into Tours.

TOURS pop: 136,500 The city is built on an 'island' between the Cher and Loire rivers. This part of France, the heart of châteaux country, is known to the French as Touraine, with Tours as its capital. And to the French mind, the city of Tours is the very essence of what these aristocratic châteaux are about. It has a reputation for incomparable civilisation and refinement, and the Tours accent is considered the 'best' in France. Its château has been largely destroyed, and much of the old town was damaged in World War II. Nevertheless, what remains of the old quarters down by the Loire is attractive, with several splendid old houses. See: 13–16C cathedral; 13C church of St. Julien; Fine Arts Museum. SI: 1 du Marechal-Leclerc.

Leave Tours as near to the south bank of the Loire as possible, eventually coming out of the city on D88. After St. Genouph this becomes a picturesque riverside road. Follow it round to **SAVONNIÈRES** (note Romanesque church doors) and take D7 into the lovely, peaceful old village of **VILLANDRY**. The château at Villandry is one of the few which still has the sort of gardens or park that it would have had in the 16C (they have not survived since that period, but were re-established in the 19C). Formal, intricate, neatly laid out on three terraces, there's a water garden of fountains and cascades, an ornamental garden with flowerbeds and clean-cut hedges of yew and box, set out in patterns, and delightful kitchen garden. The courtyard has a fine view over the Cher and Loire.

After a short distance along D7, a left turn on D39 leads across

Château d'Azay-le-Rideau

country to tiny **AZAY-LE-RIDEAU** on the bank of the river Indre. Azay's château was the first of the old strongholds to be converted. This little castle, enclosed by woods and reflected in a calm lake, managed to establish a standard of elegance and beauty which few others were ever to match. The way its earlier grim fortifications have almost been parodied in the ornamental turrets and castellations is really delightful, while the river Indre provides a pretty moat. As a final touch, Azay village is also very endearing — though, of course, often crowded.

Cross the Indre and pick up D17, which follows the river and skirts the oak woods of the Chinon forest. Turn left onto D7, which runs along next to the Indre as it flows parallel with the Loire. Beside the road, overlooking both rivers, the brilliant but forbidding white château at **USSÉ**, with its towers and turrets and terraces, looks like something straight out of a fairy story — and indeed, it was supposed to have been the setting for Sleeping Beauty. (It's best from outside.)

To avoid yet another *centrale nucléaire*, take D16 on the left, through Huismes, to the atmospheric old town of **CHINON** on the river Vienne. Rabelais was born nearby and spent or mis-spent his youth here, began his writing, and perhaps the excellent local red wine can be blamed for his notorious appetite for drink. Chinon gives marvellous views over town and country, and 15–17C houses line its network of narrow medieval streets and lanes. It is clear to see that the ruined château of Chinon was three separate castles, each moated and fortified. Here, in 12–14C château de Milieu (i.e., the middle castle), Joan of Arc picked out the heir to the French throne, defeated and in disguise, and urged him to claim his crown. Thanks to her zeal and leadership, he was swept forward to fulfil her prophecy that he would be 'anointed and crowned in the city of Reims'. Also to see in Chinon: 6–12C chapel St. Radegonde inside a cave (note 12C fresco); 10–11C church of St. Mexme; 12C church of St. Maurice: 15C Flamboyant Gothic church of St. Etienne; Museum of Old Chinon.

Cross the Vienne on D749, turn right onto D751 and left onto D759, and take a right turn, D117, to see the 15C house of the Rabelais family at **LA DEVINIÈRE** (guided visits). Stay on D117 (changes to D48), passing pretty **LERNÉ** to reach D147/D947 where turn right for **FONTEVRAUD L'ABBAYE**, a village based around what is the largest group of monastic buildings anywhere in France, now the 'Centre Culturel de l'Ouest'. The original monastery — in fact 5 separate monasteries, founded in 1099 — prospered and found favour with the nobility. Most unusually, it was for both men and women, under the rule of an abbess. The French King and Queen of England, Henry II and Eleanor of Aquitaine, and their son Richard the Lionheart, are buried here in the crypt. Wholesale destruction by Huguenots and Revolutionaries, and also under Napoleon's rule (during which time the abbey became a prison, and so remained until 1963) took its toll, yet the 12C abbey church (note superb 13C sculpture), the 16C cloister and chapterhouse, the original refectory, and, especially, the fascinating Romanesque abbey kitchens, remain intriguing and beautiful. See also the attractive tufa parish church, with covered 'arcade' outside. A popular Logis here — impossible to understand why it has only 1 star — is the hotel-restaurant **La Croix Blanche** (41.51.71.11).

Turn right onto D751 for **CANDES**, a beautiful site at the confluence of the Vienne and Loire (see 12C church with 15C fortifications). Neighbouring **MONTSOREAU** has a fine view, a handsome château, and a delicious white wine. At this point Touraine ends; beyond it lies Anjou, the country of the Plantagenets, who became the English royal family. When Henry Plantagenet, King of England, married Eleanor of Aquitaine, almost the whole of western France came under the English crown. Hence the Hundred Years' War — which was one reason why so many stately homes in this area needed to be heavily fortified.

D947 stays close to the Loire's south bank to reach **SAUMUR** (pop: 34,000), important and historic town spanning the river and capital of an excellent white wine district. A powerful castle stands high above the town with a commanding view over rooftops and river. An attractive old quarter surrounds the château, and there's a delightful Romanesque chapel, Notre-Dame-de-Nantilly (decorated with 15/16C tapestries). SI: 5 rue Beaurepaire.

Leave Saumur on D751, on the outskirts of town passing through **ST. HILAIRE-ST. FLORENT**, where all the makers of Saumur's *méthode champenoise* sparkling wine are based. Continue through little **CHÊNE-HUTTE-LES-TUFFEAUX**, with its white tufa houses, its caves renowned for cultivated mushrooms and a lovely Romanesque church. Soon after, slight remains of a great castle at **TRÈVES-CUNAULT** have become the village church. But a little farther on, at **CUNAULT**, stands a much more impressive church (originally monastic), a magnificent Romanesque building (11–13C), severely elegant, beautifully white, surprisingly spacious. The finely carved capitals — 223 of them — are superb, though so high and so detailed that it is in fact hard to appreciate them with the naked eye.

Some half-dozen prehistoric dolmens form a line across the countryside behind neighbouring **GENNES**, where take the minor riverside road D132. Where this passes through tiny **LE THOUREIL**, a former river port, there's a fine view over the Loire. Just 2km farther on, the ruined abbey of **St. Maur-de-Glanfeuil**, now an ecumenical centre, was originally built (6C) on a Roman villa; in the abbey courtyard remnants of a Roman temple have been uncovered. On reaching a bridge over the river (D55), cross the Loire to enter St. Mathurin-sur-Loire; turn left onto busier D952 to reach Angers.

ANGERS pop: 141,200 Anjou's imposing old capital presents something of a contrast with the château country upriver, for, instead of pale tufa, here the buildings are made of dark schist. Angers' château commands respect with its 17 sturdy towers (inside: superb collection of 14–17C tapestries). A peaceful old quarter separates the château from the beautiful Gothic cathedral (12–13C). See also: several other 12C and 13C churches; a Fine Arts Museum; tapestry museum Musée Jean Lurçat in fine former hospital dating from 1180; and much more — for details call in at Syndicat d'Initiative, pl Kennedy or in main SNCF railway station.

Beyond Angers the Loire seems to lose some of its pomp and grandeur, and gains something of genuine rural character. Leave the city heading south on N160 through **LES PONTS DE CÉ** (15C castle; good views of river), soon after turning right onto D751. Along this stretch the Loire is much broken up by islands and tributaries, as can be seen to good effect as the road climbs onto slightly higher ground. D751 between little **ROCHEFORT-SUR-LOIRE** and **CHALONNES** winds and twists along the cliff-face, giving the best views right across the Loire river, and so is called the Corniche Angevin. South of the road spreads the Layon vineyard region. Even after Chalonnes the villages and road offer some excellent views, for example from **MONTJEAN-SUR-LOIRE**, where take the waterside road D210. The river narrows considerably along here and, seen from the south bank, **INGRANDES** on the opposite side of the river looks attractive. This once-busy river port was a centre for the smuggling of salt, on which hefty taxes used to be payable. The salt tax was called La Gabelle, and on reaching **ST. FLORENT-LE-VIEL** you'll find on the little quayside of this village a former salt-tax customs house which has become the pleasant 1-star Logis with good restaurant, **Hostellerie de la Gabelle** (41.78.50.19). At St. Florent, a quiet place nowadays, the execution of the king in 1793 sparked off the short-lived but bloody Royalist insurrection which, as it was mainly confined to the département of the Vendée, became known as the Vendéen War. The uprising finished where it had started, in St. Florent, where Republican citizens gathered fearfully inside the church, which stands on high ground above the rest of the village. However, the plan to massacre them all was abandoned by the Royalists; one of the people sheltering inside was the father of sculptor David d'Angers, who in gratitude carved a fine tomb for Royalist leader Bonchamp (buried here). The terrace in front of the church looks across the Loire.

D751 continues along the river's south bank to Nantes, passing through rolling country with quiet little towns and many fine viewpoints, as the Loire reaches the southern edges of Brittany and, at last, broadens to pour into the Atlantic.

The Other Rivers

3 days/about 380km/from Laval

Just north of the Loire, out of sight of that immense wide valley under its pearly sky, lies a far less well-known region. More rural and less grand, yet quietly civilised, adorned with elaborate châteaux and attractive old towns, with broad valleys and producing delicate white wines, this is the

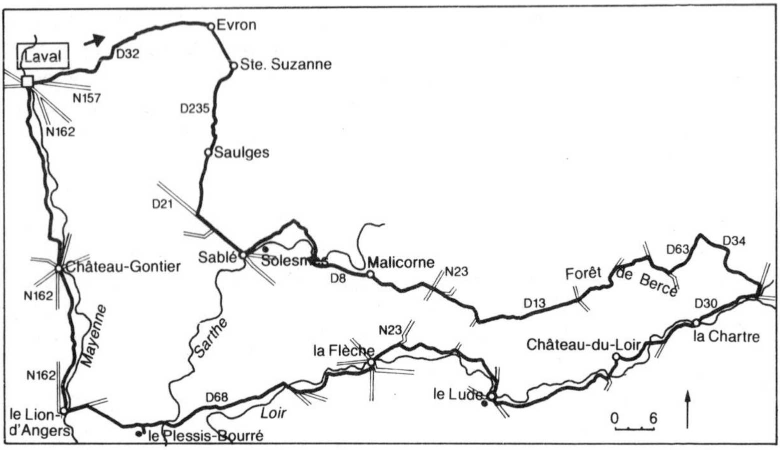

Loire's 'back country'. Our route covers it from the river Loir — remarkably similar to the Loire — across to the Mayenne, which is quite different. (Use Michelin maps 60, 63 & 64.)

LAVAL pop: 54,000 Préfecture of Mayenne département. Industrial but attractive town on river Mayenne. New area on one bank and, on the other, old quarter of 16–18C houses clustered around sombre 12C château (see: magnificent roofbeams in the keep; Romanesque chapel). Renaissance-style 16C Nouveau Château ('new palace') serves as today's Law Courts. Modern Pont Neuf and 13C Pont Vieux link the two halves of the town. Syndicat d'Initiative in the main square, pl du 11-novembre.

Leave the town on N157 (direction Le Mans), almost at once taking D32 (on left) to **EVRON**. This is quite a large town and, on the outskirts, industrial; the principal activity is slaughtering animals, and in honour of this grisly trade each September there's a Fête de la Viande (Meat Festival). Yet its centre is not unattractive and, rising over all stands the majestic Basilique Notre-Dame. The simple, strong Romanesque tower and nave date from the year 1100, while the rest of the building is elegant 13–14C Gothic.

D7 runs straight across the fields to **STE. SUZANNE**, which comes as something of a surprise: standing on a hill, this very picturesque fortified medieval village could all too easily have been by-passed without a glance. It deserves exploration. There are fascinating old cottages, remains of an 11C fortress and 17C château, and the old ramparts give marvellous views over the idyllic little river Erve and surrounding green countryside. Down below you can see a pretty riverbank farm with a working waterwheel. Close by are lovely woodland walks and drives.

Follow the river by leaving Ste. Suzanne on D125 to Chammes, shortly after which turn left onto D235. This agreeable country road winds its way through rustic dark-stone villages and rich fields. After St. Jean-sur-Erve and St. Pierre-sur-Erve (note narrow old pedestrian bridge across river), it arrives at **SAULGES**. This quiet village has an interesting parish church, but opposite is the far more remarkable church of St. Pierre, very simple and small, with obscure frescoes and, down steps, an atmospheric chapel dating from as long ago as 7C — a very rare survivor from the pre-Romanesque period. There's a good, inexpensive 2-star Logis next door, **L'Ermitage** (43.01.22.28). Stay on D235, which joins D24 at Ballée; D24 runs into D21, where turn left for Sablé.

The busy, largish country town of **SABLÉ-SUR-SARTHE** is well enough known (in France) for a type of biscuit — called sablés — small thin discs, sweet, crisp and very buttery. They can indeed be bought here from most local pâtissiers, though the ones sold elsewhere in France tend to be factory-made. Sablé has some grand Renaissance buildings dotted about, and the beautifully curved main shopping street, rue Carnot, is especially striking. There's a dominating, rather severe château, now used as a library. Sablé's watery location is pleasing — the river Sarthe and its tributaries, the Erve and the Vaige, seem to be all over town.

Stay close to the Sarthe river, leaving town on D22 to reach neighbouring **SOLESMES** village, approached by crossing a fine bridge at **PONT DE JUIGNÉ**. Solesmes consists of little other than its massive grey abbey, a huge ugly edifice, more imposing than pleasing, largely rebuilt in 1833 supposedly in 12C style. Most of the abbey, still serving its proper purpose as a Benedictine community, is closed to the public; however, enter the main gate and pass into the courtyard (a good deal better looking than the exterior), at the rear of which is the dark, incense-filled church into which visitors are allowed, and to which genuine worshippers are called by resounding bells. Here monks chant the service in Latin — this is one of the only places where outsiders can hear the Gregorian plainchant (other than on the famous recordings of it which were made here). Weekday services: 9.45am; 1pm and 1.50pm; 5pm; 8.30pm. Sundays and fêtes: 10am; 1–1.30 pm; 5pm; 8.30pm. If there is no service going on, take the opportunity to look at the skilful and elaborate 16C tableaux of statuary, called the Saints of Solesmes, in the transepts.

Cross back over the Pont to the Sarthe's north bank. Turning right, pass through Juigné-sur-Sarthe, and head into little **ASNIÈRES-SUR-VÈGRE**. Asnière's new bridge over the Vègre is nothing special, but the narrow older bridge, with the cattle ford and old cottages alongside, is a lovely spot. The older part of the village deserves a stroll; the small Romanesque village church of St. Hilaire has an interesting roof and remnants of intriguing 13C frescoes which obviously entirely covered the walls at one time.

D57 returns to the Sarthe via pretty **AVOISE**, with its riverside vegetable gardens. Follow D57 to **PARCÉ-SUR-SARTHE**, a small, charming old town climbing up from the banks of the river. It has a solid old belfry and an interesting church in two sections of different ages. A mill stands beside the water. Cross the river on D309, and pick up D8 to

MALICORNE-SUR-SARTHE. Just before going into the town, beside the road, you'll see its moated Renaissance château, entered across an ornate bridge. In the town centre several remarkable old houses survive, some with turrets. Hand-made pottery is still a great local speciality here, as can be seen from the local shops. Though not a big place, Malicorne has a confusing one-way system: leave on D8 heading east (initial direction, La Flèche).

Stay on D8 (do not be led off to La Flèche), eventually crossing busy N23 into la Fontaine-St. Martin. Shortly after this village take D189 on right, and follow this quiet route to Mansigné. Turn left onto D13, which runs across often wooded country, via Pontvallain and Mayet, eventually coming into the beautiful oak-covered hills of the marvellous **Forêt de Bercé**. Footpaths and *routes forestières* give excellent opportunities to explore this woodland at leisure.

Take any turn on the right to St. Vincent du Lorouër. Turn right in the village onto D304. Next village on the road is St. Pierre du Lorouër, where turn left onto D63. This soon joins the pretty valley road beside the Etangsort. On meeting D34, turn right for Vancé, on the river Tusson. Staying on D34 carry on down the densely populated little Tusson valley until the road meets larger D303.

Turn right onto D303 for **PONT DE BRAYE** in the valley of the Loir. D303 meets D305, where turn right to travel along the Loir valley. While Pont de Braye itself is not particularly interesting, the road soon begins to pass through a succession of more attractive villages of pale tufa houses, many quite grand. Just before **PONCÉ-SUR-LE-LOIR**, notice the château standing high on the wooded slope to the right of the road, while to the left stretches the wide valley (and narrow river) of le Loir. (This river is masculine, while its larger and more famous namesake, la Loire, is feminine — one of those grammatical niceties which are so mysterious to English-speakers.)

The road soon reaches **LA CHARTRE-SUR-LE-LOIR**, a nice little old town with an arm of the Loir running through it. Houses eat into the soft cliff-face in the backstreets, which climb the hill on the southern edge of the town. Some are right inside the cliff except for their front walls. On the summit of a high grassy knoll on this side of town, a medieval-looking watchtower turns out to be, in fact, a 1914-1918 war memorial (steep climb; approach from steps off rue de St. Vincent). From this height the view extends aross the neat black rooftops to the winding, tree-lined Loir and the river-plain beyond. A good hotel-restaurant stands in La Chartre's main square, a creaky old 2-star Logis with satisfying and inexpensive *menus*, the **Hôtel de France** (43.44.40.16).

Leave town on D305, but at **MARÇON** turn right, past the attractive old church, onto minor D61. Cross the river on a narrow bridge at **LE PORT-GAUTIER**, a former river port, and turn left onto D64. It's amusing somehow, on reaching the next village, to discover that the Loir has its very own **VOUVRAY**; and this too, like its incomparably more illustrious namesake on the Loire, is a wine-making village simple, old-fashioned, and without conceit. Try its appellation contrôlées called

Château of le Lude

Jasnières and Côteaux du Loir; there's a *dégustation*, a tasting, in the Mairie on weekend afternoons throughout July and August.

Follow signs into **CHÂTEAU-DU-LOIR**, an important local centre, pleasantly bustling, but with very little to see. The only 'sight' to which visitors are proudly referred by the tourist office is the much-altered ('the work of several generations of builders can be seen') church of St. Guingalois, with 13C east end, Romanesque crypt and some worthwhile statuary. Despite the town's grand name, not only is it completely by-passed by the river Loir — it stands at the confluence of two tributaries, the Yre and the Guerpenay or Profondevaux — but there is not even any sign of a château! The château which once dominated this site was wrecked during its period as a prison, and eventually a road was built right through the ruins. A remnant of the keep, with prison cells beneath, survives near the town's florid town hall. Leave on D10, following signs to 'Nogent — Château la Vallières — Route Touristique de la Vallée du Loir'.

Just after crossing the river bridge, turn right into Nogent and continue on C2 (i.e. left-hand fork) to La Bruère. This is all horse-breeding country, with many stables and stud farms. Turn right onto D11 (sign-posted Vaas, but don't go there), and where this meets D30, cross straight over onto V3. This backroad carries on to the little village of **CHAPELLE-AUX-CHOUX** (literally, Cabbage Chapel). There is a tiny church here, but apart from the rustic setting no obvious reason for the name. Turn right onto D141, and follow this minor road (it does not cross the river). It meets D306 just beside the impressive white back-entrance gateway into the extensive grounds of the château of Le Lude.

Turn right to enter **LE LUDE**. A fine Renaissance-looking town, pleasant to walk around, Le Lude's most splendid possession is the lovely château, ornate, four-square with a big tower at each corner, and surrounded by a broad dry moat with a footpath at the bottom. More approachable, less remote than many other such opulent dwellings, the château of Le Lude is well worth a visit (1 Apr–30 Sept only). Almost every Friday and Saturday evening from 12 June to 5 Sept a most extravagant riverside son et lumière is put on at Le Lude, overlooked by the château. Amid lights, fireworks and music some 350 local people in period dress put on a rather stylised performance supposedly telling the history of the castle and the town. Not very educational, but good fun.

Cross the Loir (at the foot of the château) and turn left onto D307. After 2½km take left-turn V4 (signposted Mansigné), a pleasant road mounting onto higher ground. Turn left onto D214 and head into **LUCH-PRINGÉ** village with an interesting 13C church (note exterior carvings; choir in Angevin style; 16C Pièta). Taking D13, carry on towards La Flèche, maybe pausing (just after Pringé village) to admire the château de Gallerande and its gardens with peacocks wandering about. Still a private home, the château cannot be visited, but is clearly visible from the road.

LA FLÈCHE, hectic, busy, large and industrial, has little to justify a long visit. The town's most famous building is the Prytanée, leading military training academy situated in the elaborately Baroque buildings of a former Jesuit college and chapel founded in 1604 by Henri IV. On the west side of town stands the appealing and interesting Romanesque chapel, Notre-Dame-des-Vertus, with unusual Renaissance wood carvings. The impressive riverside Hôtel de Ville, in the old Château des Carmes, can be seen without going into the town centre; the river, château and bridge at this point make an attractive ensemble.

Passing the Hôtel de Ville, turn right onto D37 (signposted Fougue). Cross the new main road and at a little junction take the right-turn V24 (changes to C3) to Cré-sur-le-Loir. At Cré turn right onto C1 (changes to D70) beside the river.

Approaching **BAZOUGES** there's an enticing little riverside château standing on the opposite bank. A narrow stone bridge — with a lovely view of the château and cottages beside the water — crosses into the village. Return to the south bank and travel on D70 beside the river to **DURTAL**, a larger village yet a very picturesque spot. Durtal's striking 15C château has been turned, rather wonderfully, into an old people's home. The château, windmills and old houses make an attractive view from the bridge over the Loir.

Follow signs (D68) on the north side of the river to **TIERCÉ**, located on what is almost an island of flat watery land cut off by the broad meanderings of the Loir and the Sarthe. Cross the Sarthe on D74 into Cheffes, soon after which a turning on the left, D508, leads over flat hazy country to the splendid **Château du Plessis Bourré** (signposted). The

15C château, white stone under a dark slate roof, designed with simple elegance yet with military considerations firmly in mind, rises dreamlike from its wide moat, crossed by a long low bridge of many arches. Four round towers and a sturdy gatehouse stand guard to protect this palatial country house where kings and queens have stayed. Guided tours inside reveal impressive halls and rooms with lavish decor and furnishings. Note especially the wooden ceiling of the guardroom, beautifully painted with bawdy allegorical scenes.

Go back to D74, turn left, and continue (turn left on meeting D770) to inspiringly named **LE LION-D'ANGERS**, picturesque small town on the Oudon, a tributary of the nearby Mayenne. Its Église St. Martin is largely Romanesque with 16C murals, and there's an 18C château. Continue on D101 (direction Château-Gontier), straight away turning right to the village of Montreuil-sur-Maine. From here quiet and agreeable D187 works its way up the deep, wide valley of the winding Mayenne. It climbs first to **CHAMBELLAY** village, from which a long driveway gives access to the 15–17C Château du Bois-Mauboucher, well-located among its lakeside woods. Climbing again, the road reaches **LA JAILLE-YVON**, attractive clifftop village giving a fine view over the river. Soon after, crossing into the Mayenne département, D187 becomes D267: follow this road, often very pretty and sometimes with good views, perhaps pausing at 17C Château de Magnannes (just before Ménil village), all the way into **CHÂTEAU-GONTIER**.

This busy, pleasant, sturdy old town rising above the Mayenne seems somewhat larger than its population total (8,400) would suggest. Climb up to its beautiful church of St. Jean, poised on an escarpment overlooking the river. The lovely Romanesque façade, well restored, opens into a harmonious, simple, solid interior (the modern stained glass seems completely in keeping somehow). Beside the church, tree-shaded gardens — called the Bout du Monde ('end of the world') — cover former priory grounds. Walk down the narrow streets to the riverside and town centre, passing the local museum (with good 15C wooden statue of Ste. Martha) and many fine old mansions and attractive houses. A little away from the centre, rooms at rather grand 3-star Logis **Parc Hôtel** (43.07.28.41) are a bargain.

To head out of town on our route, follow signs to 'Mirwault' or 'Hôtel Mirwault'; minor road VC2 travels to **Hôtel Mirwault** (43.07.13.17), a tranquil *restaurant avec chambres* standing right on the edge of the Mayenne. The road turns to get round the hotel and runs along perilously close to the waterside as far as La Roche. Follow it round to the left (signposted Loigné-sur-Mayenne) and turn right on meeting D112.

Stay on D112, which meanders over the gently undulating farmland on the Mayenne's left bank. It passes through occasional villages, each arranged in a circle with a church at the centre. On the approach to Laval, you'll notice D103 heading off to Entrammes on the right. A short way down this road is the Cistercian abbey, **La Trappe de Notre-Dame du Port du Salut**, which now has a proper factory next door to make the popular strong-tasting cheese, Port Salut, which it created. Continue north on D112 to get back into Laval.

*

The Loire region has absorbed the cooking of every other part of France, and equally has contributed its own style to every other province, so that it is no longer possible to say that there is a local cuisine in this area. However, an abundance of rivers has made freshwater fish a great feature of menus here. Charcuterie is very popular, too, as are tasty and filling caky fruit desserts. Of course, the Loire is far better known for exquisitely light, deliciously fruity white and rosé wines; there are some good red wines made as well, these too having that superb delicacy typical of the region.

5 BURGUNDY

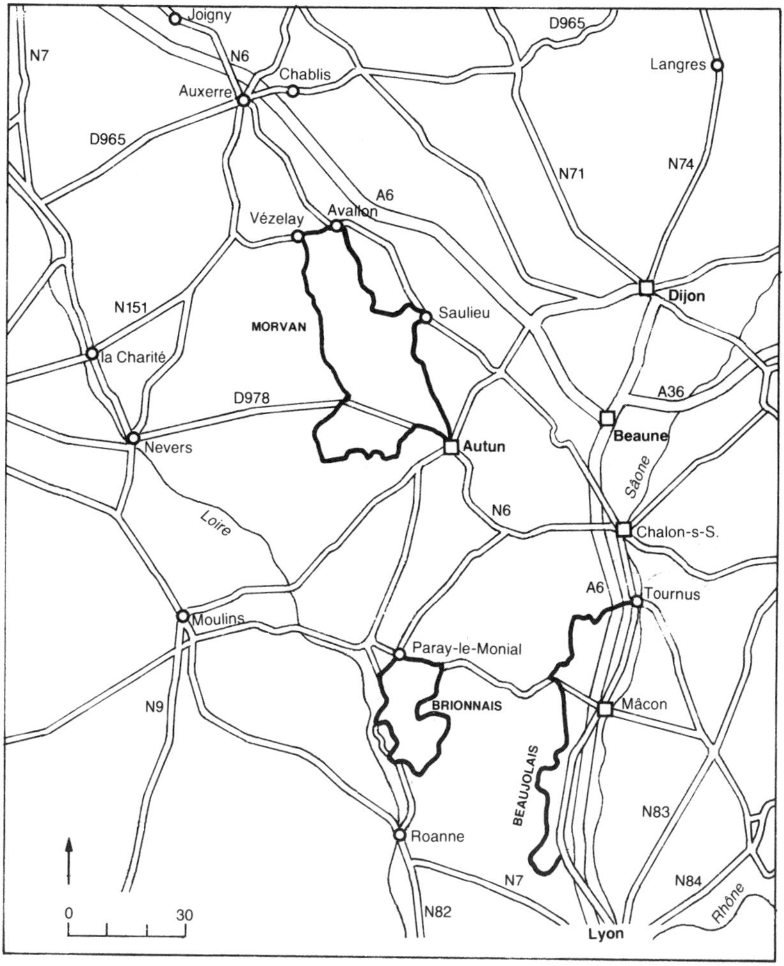

Green, prosperous Burgundy is today one of the most thoroughly civilised regions of France, renowned above all for good food and fine wine. For centuries the dynasty of Dukes who rules here stood quite apart from the French monarchy, and by the end of the Hundred Years' War (during which Burgundy joined with England against France) the Dukes had an empire of their own which extended throughout Franche-Comté, Alsace-Lorraine, Picardy, and all of Flanders into Holland. Burgundian patronage helped to establish Flemish artists and craftsmen as the leaders of their day, and it was from Flanders that the tradition came of decorated rooftiles, now regarded as typically Burgundian (and rarely seen any more in Flanders). In 1477 the marriage of the Duke's daughter divided the Burgundy possessions into two, and the French crown finally took control of the great Duchy. Impressive abbeys, churches and castles rising up from the medieval streets of tiny villages recall the past, and in many ways of Duchy's sturdy self-reliant character, its richness and love of the good life remain unchanged. In the little country towns peace and quiet reign, and there is an abundance of good pâtisseries, charcuteries and restaurants.

Across the Morvan

2–3 days/about 250km/from Avallon (on N6 100km west of Dijon)

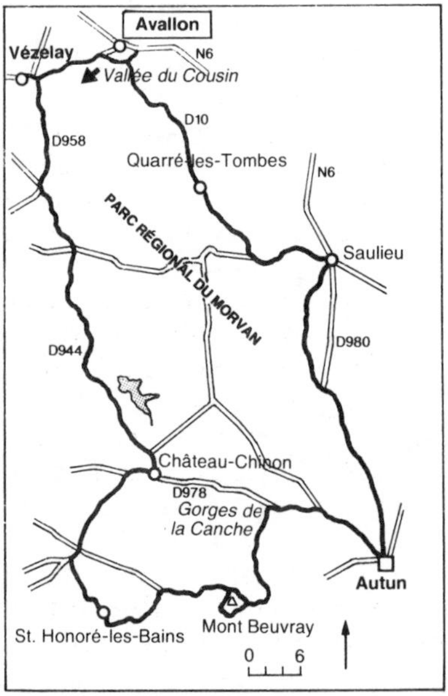

In France, any large area of countryside which has never been much use for farming tends now to acquire a 'leisure' aspect. Certainly this is true of *le Morvan*, the granite *massif* which lies at the heart of Burgundy. In former centuries its main resources were timber and, curiously, peasant women employed as wet nurses . . . neither today having its earlier economic importance! Much of the area, 1730sq km, was made a Regional Nature Park in 1970 — just one way in which the Government tries, by attracting tourism, to breathe some life into the economies of undeveloped rural regions. Here are clear clean rivers and tranquil lakes, small empty villages, rolling tracts of unspoiled oak, beech and pine woods, heathland and high pasture with broad airy views. Though steep in places, in general the hills are not too severe (never above 1,000m), and lovers of walking, riding, canoeing, or just gentle touring, are actively encouraged to come and enjoy the wild landscape and fresh air. Yet apart from a few especially popular spots like the Lac des Settons, it remains little known. On the fringes of the Nature Park area you'll discover historic towns Avallon and Autun, both good starting points for a visit. Villages and towns in the Morvan are proud of the fact, and try to keep alive — though it is all slowly becoming what the French call 'folklore' — their folkdances (in clogs), festivals and traditions. For details of village festivals ask at any Syndicat d'Initiative in the Park or in Avallon or Autun for the pamphlet *Morvan en Fête*. Viollet-le-Duc did a lot of work around here, and restored many of the handsome Romanesque churches of the region. The awe-inspiring abbey-church at Vézelay, Viollet-le-Duc's greatest work, stands on the northern edge of Morvan. And a further attraction; there are some superb restaurants on this route, including a couple reckoned among the best in France. (Use local Michelin maps 65 & 69.)

The small and ancient town of **AVALLON** is superbly situated high up in beautiful country. A particularly pretty part of the deep valley of the little river Cousin skirts the town walls. Avallon's 'new town', with several wide roads, tree-lined squares and 17/18C buildings, is quietly bustling, while the atmosphere of the older part of town, within the ramparts, is calm and peaceful. There are many unfaced stone houses and narrow cobbled streets; here hardly anything dates from later than the 1700s.

Grande Rue A. Briand is the main street through the old town, though it has practically no traffic. It passes beneath a handsome 15C bell tower and continues to the fascinating 12C church of St. Lazare, which stands, most unusually, slightly below street level and has to be entered by going down steps. The exterior is in terrible condition, with mouldy columns and badly damaged tympanum, but the portals are fine none the less, with much detailed carving. Looking into the gloom, the interior is hard to appreciate at first, but notice the interesting frescoes and domes. Almost opposite the church is the Syndicat d'Initiative in an attractive restored 15C house. At the far end, the road passes through the ramparts between Tour Gaujard and the Bastion de la Petite Porte to a delightful esplanade of lime trees. From this high, fresh vantage point there are precipitous views across the plunging wooded valley of the Cousin. From here a walk round the outside of the ramparts begins, going from one fortified tower to another.

Avallon and its neighbourhood are well-served with good places to stay or to eat, though bargain prices are few. Early 18C **Hostellerie de la Poste** (86.34.06.12) in the main square, pl Vauban, is rather grand and terribly expensive, with carefully tended gardens and much character; its restaurant has a Michelin rosette and a toque from Gault-Millau. Just as highly commended, but not so expensive, is restaurant **Le Morvan** (86.34.06.52), 7 rte de Paris. More modest, though still far from cheap, **Les Capucins** (86.34.06.52) is a 2-star Logis with an excellent restaurant.

Leave Avallon either from the Petite Porte esplanade or by going back through the new town to the Route de Lormes; either way runs steeply down to the **Vallée du Cousin**. The Cousin is exquisite, twisting and changing, sometimes rushing, sometimes calm, always shaded by mossy trees. A narrow winding road (D427) with hardly any traffic runs between a wooded rocky escarpment on one side and the river on the other. Along the way are several old watermills, a few now turned into enviable private homes and small luxury hotels. The most enticing of these, indeed verging on the idyllic, are **Moulin des Ruats** (86.34.07.14) and **Moulin des Templiers** (86.34.10.80) — and surprisingly, neither is particularly expensive. The river passes through hamlets, rustic, tranquil, with Romanesque churches. At larger **PONTAUBERT**, there's a 12C Templar church, and fountains in the street with fish swimming in them; many houses and farmyards have unusual elaborate wells, often with steps inside climbing down to the water level.

At Pontaubert, leave the Cousin. Take D957, a high, hilly road with expansive views across the farmland and woods of the northern Morvan.

Abbey Church of La Madeleine at Vézelay

The Eglise Abbatiale de la Madeleine, the great Abbey Church standing high above the rest of Vézeley, is clearly visible from several km away. The village of **VÉZELAY**, picturesque, old, its steep lanes of stone cottages perfectly restored, with lovely ramparts and medieval gates, was abandoned and collapsing just 100 years ago. Since then it has transformed itself into a chic, upmarket little *ville touristique*. There are top-quality restaurants, expensive hotels, art galleries and the usual *artisanats*. But the reason for it all, the Abbey Church, has remained unscathed by the commercialism.

From outside, the church appears deceptively plain, large certainly, with flying buttresses and square towers. But the interior is stunning: immense, light, overwhelming. From a vast vestibule, huge double doors standing open (note the tympanum over these doors and over the main doors outside) lead into the nave, the scale and proportions of which make the people inside look tiny. Apart from the stonework itself (especially the carved capitals) there is almost no decoration, no distraction. Around the choir, dim traces of old frescoes on some columns and parts of the ceiling show that it was not always so bare. Simple wooden crosses fixed to the walls were put there after the last world war, in 1946. A side chapel, slightly less plain, is used for ordinary services. In the dark crypt a little shrine contains relics once thought to be the bones of Mary Magdelene, brought here from St. Maximin in Provence.

How many Catholic churches claim to have pieces of the skeleton of one saint or another? One wonders if these saints were ever given a decent burial. In any event, the collection of bones at Vézelay — whomsoever's they may be — attracted many thousands of pilgrims each year for centuries. The 2nd and 3rd Crusades effectively started from here (1146 and 1190) because of them. The tyrannical and extortionate abbots, much hated by the local people who rose up against them periodically, became enormously rich. But it all came to an abrupt end in 1280 when it was discovered that the 'real' relics of Mary Magdelene were still in the church at St. Maximin. The Abbey went into a rapid decline, and subsequently was badly damaged by Protestants and then by Revolutionaries. By the time Viollet-le-Duc came here and decided to have it restored, the Abbey itself had completely disappeared and its church was almost in ruins. Supposedly using old texts and plans, Viollet-le-Duc rebuilt the church between 1840 and 1861. Whether it did originally look like this is debatable; what is undeniable is that the Abbey Church today is an exceptionally beautiful building. It's cool inside; take a sweater.

If you can, try to visit Vézelay sometime outside the crowded months of July and August and, if possible, come soon after breakfast to be here before the tour buses start to arrive.

From Vézelay return 2km down the hill to **ST. PÈRE**. Turn right (D958), just before the bridge over the river Cure, into the old village. For such a small place it can boast quite a number of attractions: an extraordinary 13C church which is a mass of ornament; the strange *Fontaines Salées* (salty fountains — to visit them, call at the house facing the church); and one of the most lauded restaurants in France,

L'Esperance (86.33.20.45), where chef-proprietor Marc Meneau merits his 3 Michelin rosettes and 4 Gault-Millau toques — the maximum score from both organisations. There are rooms as well, but note that meals and the impeccable, tranquil accommodation are both very expensive (though still an undoubted bargain). The road leaves St. Père and shortly passes tiny **PIERRE-PERTHUIS**, beautifully situated on the rushing Cure. Turn off the road for a moment, or walk down, to see the old bridges and the river in its narrow gorge; on the opposite bank you'll see the 'pierced rock' which gives the village its name. Between high fields of pasture continue on D958 through **BAZOCHES**, where Vauban, the military architect whose fortifications can be seen in so many French towns, was buried in the village church in 1707 (a century later, 'his heart' — though surely not much was left of it by then — was removed and buried in Paris). After 8km turn left (D42) to hillside **LORMES**, a good base for some manageable walks (Gorges de Narvau; Etang du Goulot; Mont de la Justice). Take D944 south towards Château-Chinon, perhaps pausing on the way at the dam and lake of Pannesière-Chaumard, one of the Morvan's largest.

CHÂTEAU-CHINON, though proclaimed the capital of Morvan, in truth is just a fairly charmless small town. However, it does offer some very good views from the summit of a rather morbidly got-up Calvary hill outside town. 2-star Logis **Au Vieux Morvan** (86.85.05.01) has a low-priced menu. The tiny Office de Tourisme (summer only), bursting with useful pamphlets about the region, can be found by going through the narrow door and up a creaky flight of steps actually inside the archway of the medieval town gate Porte Notre-Dame, in pl Notre-Dame. If you want to foreshorten the journey across Morvan, there's an attractive road (D378 — D977bis) directly from here to Saulieu through the heart of the Park, and allowing easy detours to beautiful Lac des Settons (watersports) and the resorty hill-village Montsauche. Otherwise take D978 west out of Château-Chinon, turning left (D37) to **MOULINS-ENGILBERT** with its old houses and market, 2km after the village taking D985 on left to **ST. HONORÉ-LES-BAINS**, a thriving and agreeable little spa in the midst of green and pleasant walking country just outside the Regional Park boundary. The Romans considered its naturally sulphurous waters of great benefit, and since the 19C it has been re-established as a centre for the treatment of asthma and respiratory illnesses. There's a 2-star Logis, simple but with charm, **Hôtel Henry Robert** (86.30.72.33): it's nicely located, has pretty gardens and offers good meals.

A narrow, winding and picturesque route runs over and around the hills from the spa town to **Mont Beuvray**. From St. Honoré take D299; at Sanglier turn left onto D227, then turn right at junction with D18. Mont Beuvray was the site of Bibracte, an important Celtic settlement and, under the fiercesome Vercingetorix, a centre of the Gauls' resistance against the Roman colonisation. Little survives of the Celtic period, but it is none the less a striking spot. Steep D3 struggles to the summit, 821m, which allows a tremendous sight of the wild woodlands and peaks of the southern Morvan. One-way D274 encircles the base of the mountain, about 8km round. In the nearby village of St-Léger-sous-Beuvray take the left turn (D179), another narrow, hilly and unfrequented road which leads eventually through the twisting gorges of the little river Canche and onto busier D978, where turn right towards Autun.

AUTUN pop: 122,200 Important country town with pleasant atmosphere. Large Gallic settlement before Roman colonisation of 15 BC. Augustodunum — 'Rome's sister', Caesar called it — grew to great stature, a centre of education, art and commerce, with a large population of Roman civilians. The medieval town walls, mainly still standing, follow the line of the Roman fortifications (modern Autun hardly extends outside them even today). There's a ramparts walk for part of the way round. Two of the four city gates survive: Porte St-André is large, designed for a considerable passage of people, with 2 big arches for traffic and 2 smaller arches for pedestrians. As well as being a fine, elegant piece of work in really remarkable condition, the very sight of it sets the imagination going on the everyday scenes of Roman life. Porte d'Arroux is smaller and more graceful, though not as well preserved. See also: the town's huge main square, the Champs de Mars; town hall with library of ancient manuscripts; superb 12C Cathedral of St. Lazare (note especially: impressive entrance, with tympanum which was saved from damage during the Revolution because, ironically, it had been plastered over when Voltaire declared that he did not like it; excellent stone carving throughout; spiral stairs inside interesting bell tower); outside the Cathedral, elaborate Fontaine St. Lazare (beside which market each Saturday). Office de Tourisme at 3 av Charles de Gaulle (main road off Champs de Mars) organises tours of the town. Some superb restaurants with astonishingly low-priced menus: **La Clé des Champs** (85.52.12.30) slightly out of town near the airfield on the Château-Chinon road has imaginative cuisine; somewhat cheaper, almost as good, with more classic dishes, **Hôtellerie du Chalet Bleu** (85.52.25.16) at 1 rue du Bourg St. Pantaleon. Hotels **Les Arcades** (85.52.30.03 — no restaurant) and **Moderne et Tête Noire** (85.52.25.39) are both reasonable 2-star Logis.

Leave Autun by passing through Porte d'Arroux on D980 and continue to Saulieu. For a more scenic route part of the way, after 24km turn left onto D149, following this country lane which becomes D20, D121 (right) and D26. **SAULIEU** on the N6 is another good Morvan base. It's a pleasing little town which, perhaps surprisingly, has been included inside the Park area; it has a long history as a halt for travellers (the N6 follows the course of a highway which existed even before it was made into the Via Agrippa), and still has a number of excellent restaurants and hotels. Most notable of them is the pricey 2-rosette, 4-toque 17C *restaurant avec chambres* **le Côte d'Or** (80.64.07.66) where the *patron-chef*, Bernard Loiseau, is now reckoned one of the best in France. For a much cheaper, but most adequate hotel-restaurant, try 2-star Logis **La Poste** (80.64.05.67). Take a look too at the fine Basilica of St. Andoche, where pilgrims have stopped on their journeys since the 12C.

Return to Avallon not on the N6 but on the attractive smaller road which starts out from Saulieu as the D977bis. After 10km take D6 (right), which soon skirts **ST. BRISSON**, the Regional Park's main information and exhibition centre. At a junction 10km further, take D211 which becomes D20, **QUARRÉ-LES-TOMBES** on the road, standing above and between the Cure and Cousin valleys, takes its strange name from the startlingly large number of tombstones — said to be over 2,000 — found here. The explanation, researchers eventually discovered, was simple enough: this happened to be the place where tombstones were made for sale to other communities. D10 continues from here into Avallon.

Brionnais and Charollais

1–2 days/about 130km/from Charolles (55km west of Macon on N79)

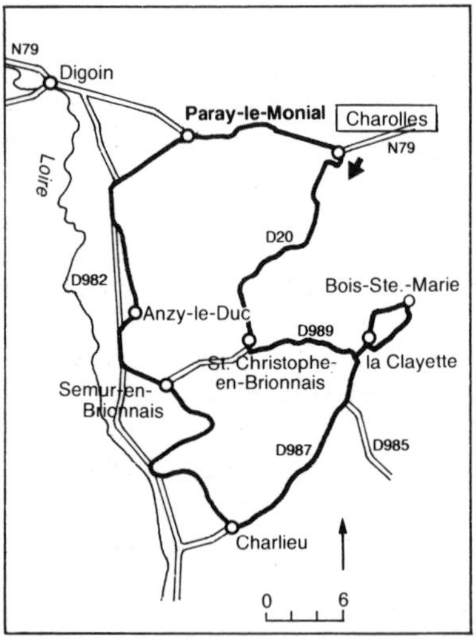

Across the whole of Burgundy, Romanesque churches imitating the once-great abbey at Cluny rise from tiny unknown villages. One of the most intriguing concentrations of all is in the Brionnais. This southernmost corner of Burgundy, one of the 19 '*baillages*' of the ancient Duchy, broadly overlaps with another area equally tranquil and rustic, yet with a name well-enough known to cattle farmers all over Europe — the Charollais. For here a breed of cattle (properly known as *Charolais* with a single *l*) was developed, completely white and exceptionally heavy with their lean meat. Today, they can be seen everywhere in France, and increasingly in other countries too. The nearer one approaches to the small market town of Charolles, the more numerous are these impressive white animals standing in their green fields.

Every day of the week, at one or another of the villages on this route, there is an open-air market. Marcigny, on market day, with its crowded alleys of covered stalls, looks as if it has not changed in centuries. The biggest is at Paray-le-Monial, on Fridays. This pretty old town, where the Catholic cult of the 'Sacred Heart' originated, is rather remarkably the second most popular place of pilgrimage in France (after Lourdes), and is the capital of the Brionnais.

Without a map it would be no easy matter to find one's way around these two small regions: together they constitute a veritable Kingdom of Little Roads, with lovely tangled lanes and, of course, plenty of junctions without signposts! (Michelin maps 69 & 73 will keep you on the right track.)

CHAROLLES is a small, sedate, charming old town in green and hilly countryside. The Arconce and Semence rivers and the Canal du Moulin twist and wind throughout the town, which has altogether 30 little bridges. It has few 'sights' other than the remnants of the castle of the counts of Charollais, which now houses the Town Hall. Through one of the former gateways, at the foot of a 14C tower, Le Tour de Charles le Téméraire, a pleasant public garden now covers part of the ramparts and gives agreeable views across the surrounding rolling country. The tourist office is in the 16C Ancien Couvent des Clarisses, where Marguerite-Marie Alacoque (see Paray-le-Monial, at the end of the tour) had her first communion, in 1656. Apart from cattle, the town is noted too, in a smaller way, for its *faïencerie*, fine earthenware. **Hôtel de France**, (85.24.06.66) and **Hôtel Moderne** (85.24.07.02) are just a few doors away from each other in av de la Gare. Both have 2 stars and similar prices, but the Moderne is rather more comfortable, and is a Logis de France. The **Hôtel de la Poste** (85.24.11.32) at 2 av de la Liberation could perhaps be classed more as a *restaurant avec chambres*: it has a few modest and inexpensive rooms, but a charming dining room with excellent food and wine.

Take the D985, south from Charolles (direction La Clayette), turning right after 8km onto D20. Continue through St-Julien-de-Civry and take a right turn (D108) to **VARENNE-L'ARCONCE**. This tiny village has a fine Cluniac church dating from the early 12C, robust, sturdy, and made of local sandstone with the simplest design and barest decoration, dominated by an elegant 4-sided belfry. Through pretty pastoral country D34 goes to another equally tiny place, **ST. CHRISTOPHE-EN-BRIONNAIS**, where until recently the weekly cattle market was the largest in France. Still the second largest, each Thursday morning it sees thousands of Charolais bought and sold for cash. The market begins at 4am, but is still going strong at 7, when the farmers settle down to big cooked breakfasts in the nearby cafés and bars. Along the short main street of the village, every bank in France has a branch, open only on Thursdays.

The road to La Clayette (D989) passes by **VAREILLES**, where there's another simple but graceful Romanesque church, this time smaller and more village-y, with an interesting bell tower. **LA CLAYETTE** (pronounced La Clett) is a bustling local centre, a small market town on the bank of the Genette, which broadens here to make a lake, attractive with *platanes*: a suitably impressive setting for a 14C moated castle with sturdy round towers (extensively restored in 19C). The 15C outbuildings rather incongruously house a good automobile museum. The Syndicat d'Initiative is at 6 pl Fosses (July/August only) and there are a couple of pleasant and reasonable small hotels: the 2-star Logis **de la Poste et du Dauphin** (85.28.02.45) and, slightly cheaper, 1-star **de la Gare** (85.28.01.65). Each has a good inexpensive restaurant.

It's worth making the short detour from here to the splendid 17C Château de Drée, 4km north, built in Classical style of golden stone and standing alone in a wood; and to the village of **BOIS-STE.-MARIE** where the church is most unusual, one of the oldest in the Brionnais, 11C and pre-dating Cluny. Head back to La Clayette and make your way (D987) to attractive **CHÂTEAUNEUF** on a peaceful wooded hillside overlooking the Sornin. Here stands a château together with one of the last Romanesque churches ever built, yet a fascinating example of the style, with sturdy grace and some intriguing sculpture. If you're looking for somewhere to stay at this point, the **Hostellerie du Château** (80.33.00.23) is quiet, comfortable, and has a good view.

Follow the Sornin (D987) down to **CHARLIEU**, a small market town with many medieval houses and, at its centre, remnants of a fine Benedictine Abbey founded as long ago as the 9C, though nothing survives from that period. The exceptional 12C vestibule and carved doorway — le Grand Portail — is particularly noteworthy. Much of the Abbey's original stonecarving is now in the adjoining museum. A short walk away along rue Rouillier is the curious 15C cloisters of the Couvent des Cordeliers, all that's left of a monastery which, foolishly and tragically, has been dismembered and taken away to the United States. Syndicat d'Initiative is in narrow rue André Farinet, off rue Charles de Gaulle (Easter-Sept only). The **Relais de l'Abbaye** (77.60.00.88), a 2-star Logis on the other side of the river, has a good restaurant with some Charollais specialities.

Setting out from Charlieu (D227), follow the signs of the marked *Circuit des Eglises Romanes du Brionnais* all the way up to Paray-le-Monial. Not only does this take in several more of the region's Romanesque churches, but it follows an attractive route along minor roads most of the way. There's something of interest at nearly every village church: **FLEURY-LA-MONTAGNE** (tympanum), **IGUERANDE** overlooking the river Loire (11C, good capitals), **ST. JULIEN-DE-JONZY** (much damaged, but still with excellent belfry, doorway and tympanum). Handsome **SEMUR-EN-BRIONNAIS**, in the midst of vines and orchards, has one of the more beautiful examples of the Brionnais churches, and one of the last to be built; the bell tower is octagonal, as at Cluny, and the doorway finely carved. **MARCIGNY**, with 15C dwellings, has a much less striking church, but the next village, **ANZY-LE-DUC**, has the best of them all, a lovely golden-hued building with unchristian-looking frescoes (and note especially: tympanum, capitals, bell tower), believed to have been the model for the huge abbey church at Vézelay (see p. 77). Finally via **MONTCEAUX-L-ÉTOILE** (unusual tympanum) join the slightly busier and faster D982, leading through uninteresting St-Yan onto D352bis and into **PARAY-LE-MONIAL**.

Paray, 'of the monks', a lovely country town on the banks of the poplar-lined river Bourbince, is the centre of one of the most peculiar of the Catholic cults. For it was here, in 1673, that Marguerite-Marie

Alacoque, young novice nun and daughter of a prominent local *notaire*, told her fellow nuns, her confessor and the Mother Superior that Christ had physically appeared before her with his chest ripped open and the heart visible inside. He had said to her 'Here is the heart which so loved Man'. The Mother Superior, for one, did not believe this story. So many others did though (the confessor proved a useful ally) that the Mother Superior declared that she had moved from incredulity to uncertainty. Thus began the cult of the Sacré-Coeur. Marguerite-Marie Alacoque had the vision again and again until her death in 1690. Strangely though, the devotion to the Sacred Heart only really took off in earnest over a century later, during an 18C religious backlash against the Revolution. Marguerite-Marie was beatified in 1864, and in 1873 it was decided 'to consecrate France to the Sacred Heart of Jesus', hence the building of the impressive Sacré-Coeur basilica in Paris. Marguerite-Marie was made a saint in 1920 — a coup for Paray's hotel trade.

The town's beautiful Basilique de Notre-Dame, now generally known as the Basilique du Sacré-Coeur, has nothing to do with the cult and predates it by many hundreds of years. Built in the early 1100s, it was intended as a smaller copy of the huge Abbey Church at Cluny, no longer standing, and reveals something of why Cluny was so much praised. True, it could do with a clean-up; but the building is dignified, strong, sturdy, massive yet elegant. The secret of its beauty is simplicity. The curve of the ambulatory is exquisite, the columns delightfully slender. In its spacious gardens on the edge of the peaceful Bourbince, from outside, Paray's Basilica looks superb. By night it is illuminated and, reflected in the river, looks yet more splendid.

Some of Paray's other popular sights have a good deal less to recommend them! Behind the Basilica is a small museum about Sainte Marguerite-Marie, called the Chambre des Reliques. It contains a jumble of items connected with her, such as an ordinary table fork said to have been hers, and several awful pictures, of which the silliest must be the 'photograph of an imagined portrait'. The room where it is alleged that she had her visions has become the Chapelle de la Visitation, object of much veneration. Musée Hieron, rue Pasteur, is a museum of religious art with little of interest apart from an impressive 12C tympanum in good condition which comes from Anzy-le-Duc. In contrast to the simple finesse of the Basilica, Paray's *hôtel de ville* is gorgeously tasteless. A 16C building, originally named Maison Jayet, it was at one time the private house of a wealthy cloth merchant. It has an absolutely extraordinary façade, heavily covered with sculpted ornamentation, including odd little figurines either naked, or clothed in improbable outfits. St. Nicholas' church opposite is now deconsecrated and has been turned into an interesting art gallery.

There are several places to stay, many with inexpensive restaurants. During our visit, unfortunately, the highly-spoken-of 2-star Logis **Aux Vendanges de Bourgogne** (85.81.13.43) was full. Instead we booked into cheaper **Hôtel Terminus** (85.81.08.80), and were very happy with the room, dinner and service. There's a helpful Syndicat d'Initiative in pl de la Poste. Paray has big open-air markets: the *marché fermier* on Saturday mornings is the smaller; the Friday market fills rue du Marché, Place du Champs Foire and Cours Jean Jaurès.

To complete the circle, **CHAROLLES** lies 12km east of Paray on the busy N79. Alternatively, 13km west on N79 is **DIGOIN**, small ceramics town standing remarkably at the meeting point of the Loire, the Arconce, the Arroux and the Bourbince rivers, as well as having the Canal du Centre crossing the Loire in a superb aqueduct to join another canal. Digoin is hardly a '*ville touristique*', but it does happen to have, apart from all these waterways, one very good restaurant — *avec chambres* — **La Diligence** (85.53.06.31), 14 rue Nationale, with a most reasonably priced *menu* of classic cuisine, Charollais specialities, and a Michelin rosette.

Mâconnais and Beaujolais

2–3 days/160km/from Tournus to Villefranche-sur-Saône

The journey from Tournus to Villefranche, both old towns on the river Saône, is a mere 70km on the autoroute and takes little more than half an hour to drive. Yet just to the west of that fast highway, and within sight of it, the hills of the Mâconnais and Beaujolais deserve a thorough exploration. Cluny, once so important in European religion and politics, today rests quietly among these green woods and rolling fields. Attractive, agricultural, rich in history, the two areas merge indistinguishably into one another. Both are eminent wine-making regions: the Mâconnais, producing first-rate whites and modest reds, extends from Tournus down to Mâcon; Beaujolais, noted for its fresh red wines, continues south almost into Lyon. (Michelin maps 69 & 73.)

The railway, route nationale and autoroute charge by the edge of walled **TOURNUS** (the *s* is silent), a very small, quiet and old-fashioned town which looks from its riverside *quais* over the broad and curving Saône. Arcaded sidewalks and shopfronts, and some imposing *hôtels*, make the town centre a most attractive place to shop in its delicious pâtisseries and épiceries. Close to Quai du Midi, modest little 12–15C Eglise Madeleine has a superbly simple interior, whitewashed, almost without decoration, with broad side aisles but a narrow centre aisle. At the other end of town (by the main road), the huge Abbey Church of St. Philibert is unusual: 3 churches built on top of each other in the course of a couple of centuries — 9–11C — finally constituting a single curious and original building in pure Romanesque style, though with castellations as if to repel attackers.

Enter through a lovely dark vestibule, a forest of pillars under a low ceiling, which opens out into the light, tall, magnificiently sturdy yet elegant church with thick unadorned brick columns. The central nave is barrel-vaulted, strangely, crosswise; but the side aisles are rib-vaulted, an odd combination. And the stained glass, though modern and out of keeping, is not unattractive either. Standing on top of the vestibule is

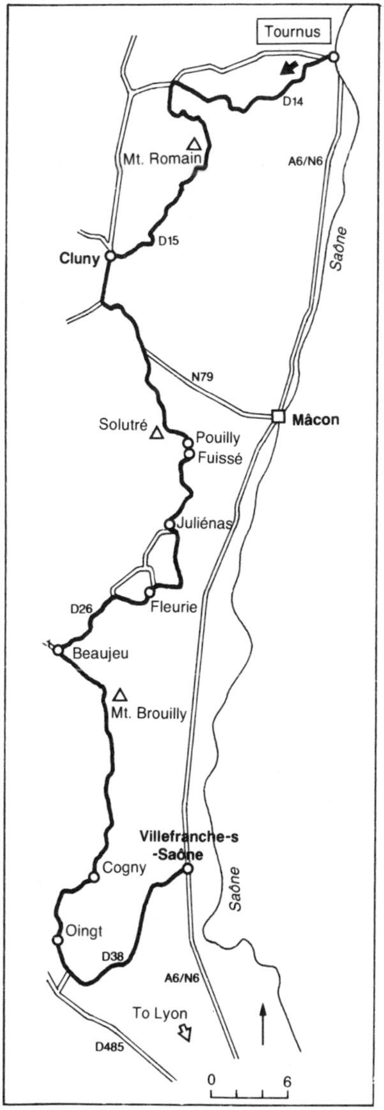

another church, St. Michel, reached by an outdoor staircase. Extraordinarily, this part of the Abbey was built before the nave of the main church. Yet it is neither antiquity nor architecture which makes the Abbey so interesting: it has an uplifting, spiritual quality. See too the cloisters and other Abbey buildings.

Tournus' Syndicat d'Initiative is in pl Carnot (summer only). A big street market fills the town centre every Saturday morning. Hotels: **de la Paix** (85.51.01.85) is a pleasant Logis with inexpensive menu; **Le Rempart** (85.51.10.56), close to the Abbey, is pricier, has a classier restaurant (with rosette and toque); **Le Sauvage** (85.51.14.45) is a little more modest, but comfortable and satisfying. **Restaurant Greuze** (2 rosettes; 2 toques) is expensive but has character and excellent food.

Take winding D14 13km west from Tournus to **BRANCION**, a picturesque walled village on a rocky ridge between two ravines, with medieval castle, 15C covered market, lovely old houses and 12C church clinging to the limit of the spur. It's a thriving local centre, and has been for centuries. 6km farther, at the end of a forest drive, **CHAPAIZE** is dominated by an even older (11C) church with a distinctive square bell tower. Turn south on D282 to **LYS**, a small and very traditional village, where take D187 on left. This road climbs up and down through handsome *forêt* around Mt. Romain. At Col de la Pistole, where the road forks, follow D446 on the right (soon after, on the right there's a steep access road to the summit of Mt. Romain — 579m — good views). Deep caves, *grottes*, underneath the mountain can be entered just by **FOUGNIÈRES** on the way to **BLANOT**, where among the narrow lanes, old cottages and stone walls of the tiny village are a 12C Romanesque church and remnants of a 14C abbey in the Cluny style. On reaching the D15 at **DONZY-LE-PERTHUIS** (very old houses and 11C church; ruined 12C Cluniac priory), turn right towards Cluny.

CLUNY, now hardly more than a village, agreeably situated beside the little river Grosne, was once the seat of the largest and most powerful abbey in Western Christendom, at a time when kings and emperors could hardly move without religious approval for their acts, when every act of naked personal ambition could be camouflaged by seeming to be condoned by God. The approbation of Cluny was such a moral victory that it could virtually ensure the triumph of one party over another. Only the Pope had greater influence — but he would not have risked a split with the Abbot of Cluny, who frequently undertook the role of the Pope's adviser. A number of Popes were themselves from Cluny. Of course, the vying for Cluny's intervention was all on the material level, often through generous gifts made to the Abbey. By the 13C, as well as everything else, it had thus become immensely wealthy, and the life of the Abbots was extremely comfortable.

The Abbey was founded in 910. Benedictine rule was introduced in 926. Cluny grew in influence, reaching its height during the 11/12C. Eventually excessive wealth jeopardised its moral superiority, and in the 15C the Abbey came completely under the control of the French monarchy, which 'appointed' the Abbots it wanted. The buildings were damaged during the Wars of Religion, and finally, during and after the Revolutionary period, were totally destroyed, being in fact mainly dismantled for their fine dressed stone.

Cluny Abbey was immense, its church the largest in the world (until St. Peter's in Rome was built — just a few metres longer). The choir alone had 250 seats. It perhaps says something about the significance of the Abbey at Cluny that the town today still basks in the sense of that importance, and several hotels thrive on it, even though the buildings have gone. All that's left is a handful of ruins and a small undamaged fragment which now serves as a school of arts and crafts. Yet the minute fraction which remains is not disappointing. Pillars, doorways, corridors, vaults of such celestial proportions speak volumes about the grandeur of the place as it was. Surviving towers mark the edges of the Abbey: the Tour de Fromage (entrance inside SI) offers a suitable vantage point from which to imagine how it once looked, in its green and rolling countryside setting.

Visits inside the Abbey are on ½-hr guided tours only. See also: Musée Ochier, displaying remnants of stonecarvings, reconstructions and an extensive collection of ancient books and manuscripts; several houses and superb Romanesque design and decoration (especially in rue Avril) dating from 12/13C. Syndicat d'Initiative (summer only), 6 rue Mercière, runs 1-hr tours of the town (in French). In av de la Gare there are some inexpensive places to stay or to eat — in particular, **Hôtel de l'Abbaye** (85.59.11.14), 1-star Logis, has character and is good value. Better but far dearer are the **Bourgogne** (85.59.00.58; rosette and toque) hotel-restaurant beside the Abbey, and slightly out of town the **Moderne** (85.59.05.65; toque), a favourite stopover of President Mitterrand.

D980 runs south 5km to N79, where turn left (direction Mâcon). In

Porte d'Honneur de l'Abbaye, Cluny

the space of the next 10km the road passes very close to several points which reward a quick stop: **BERZÉ-LE-CHÂTEL**, on left (feudal castle); **BERZÉ-LA-VILLE**, on left (chapel with remarkable 11C Byzantine-influenced frescoes); and **MILLY-LARMARTINE** on right (where the poet Lamartine — greatly admired in France — spent his childhood). Driving through Milly-Lamartine, continue through villages on narrow lanes to the massive and intriguing 500m-high **Solutré rock** around the base of which a phenomenal quantity of animal bones have been discovered — mammoth and bison, horse and reindeer — in a layer of 4,000sq m and up to 2m thick. The explanation remains a subject of academic debate, but the rock was clearly of importance to prehistoric Man and not a few modern visitors also seem to regard it with nearly mystical fascination.

This southern corner of the Mâconnais (large, industrial Mâcon itself is only 10km away) contains, in a compact area, the very finest of the region's vineyards: from Solutré rock, go through **POUILLY** village, join D172 into **FUISSÉ**, thence to little **CHASSELAS**, which has given its name not to a wine but to a variety of eating grape now found on dinner tables throughout the world.

Beyond to the south lies the Beaujolais, a long narow *massif* between the great valleys of the Saône and Loire, its hills and terraces pretty with woods and vineyards in which Gamay is almost the only grape variety grown. A signposted **Route du Beaujolais** makes its way among the villages, where local wines can be tasted at the *caves*. A tangled multitude of narrow meandering lanes provide any number of alternative routes; make a point of calling in at some of the *crus*, meaning in Beaujolais those villages which produce the best of the area's wines: from **ST. AMOUR** and **JULIÉNAS**, take the road to **CHENAS** (restaurant **Robin** recommended, first-class cooking, nice setting and service, not terribly expensive), to **ROMANÈCHE-THORINS** (lovely 3-star Logis with pretty garden and rosetted restaurant, **Les Maritonnes**, 85.35.51.70), and to **FLEURIE** (**Auberge du Cep** restaurant highly recommended, top-class cooking, fairly expensive, booking essential: 74.04.10.77). Up the valley, through the **CHIROUBLES** vineyards, reach the high and attractive D26, turning left to **BEAUJEU**, the old village from which the whole region takes its name — although it does not produce any wine. It has a 12C church and remains of the castle of the local Beaujolais nobility, one of whom has had a good, reliable *restaurant avec chambres* named after her: **Anne de Beaujeu** (1-star Logis; 74.04.87.58). She, incidentally, the daughter of Louis XI, was a 15C regent of France while her brother Charles VIII was too young to take the throne.

Either on D37 or one of the parallel lesser roads, follow the valley down towards the foot of **Mont Brouilly**: Côtes de Brouilly is another of the Beaujolais *crus*. Access to the summit of the 'mountain' (altitude 483m, with good views) is by a steep road off the D43. At the top there's a little chapel to which the local vinegrowers make a pilgrimage each year on 8 September.

Follow D43 south, turning right onto D19 at St-Etienne. Stay resolutely on this road through all its twists and turns, crossing D504 and continuing past Cogny, soon after which, at a meeting of minor roads on the picturesque pass of Saule-d'Oingt, take D120 into **OINGT**. The Beaujolais is a region of diverse character, and in this southern part, between Villefranche and the Azergues valley, it is called the country of *pierres dorées*, golden stone. Houses, châteaux and the rocks of the landscape itself are a warm, pleasing honey-yellow. This is perhaps, to the eye at least, the most pleasing part of Beaujolais country. The tiny village of Oingt, its narrow streets lined with beautiful old houses, climbing to the church which was once the chapel of the ruined castle, captures the essence of its charm. There are many unostentatious claims on your interest, castles and panoramas and Romanesque houses, in all the surrounding countryside and villages, which are a delight to explore. D120, driving south of Oingt, gives great views across the hills and vines; after Le Bois d'Oingt join D38 and follow the signs to Villefranche-sur-Saône (or to Lyon, if you're heading that way instead). Just off the road, as it turns to Villefranche, **BAGNOLS** village, hardly changed since 15C, with its castle (note flamboyant chimney), church and lovely porticoed houses, makes an enjoyable pause.

VILLEFRANCHE-SUR-SAÔNE pop: 29,000 Handsome walled town on N6 and autoroute A6, 30km north of Lyon. Became the regional capital of the Lords of Beaujeu after the 13C. Retains some charm and a good deal of local importance and is the commercial centre of the Beaujolais wine trade. See: old houses along the old main street rue Nationale. Office de Tourisme: 290 rte de Thizy. Recommended places to stay and to eat, both with modest prices: **Hôtel Plaisance** (74.65.33.52;

its restaurant is called **La Fontaine Bleue**) and, much cheaper, **Restaurant Potinière** (*avec chambres*; its hotel is called **La Bourgogne**: 74.65.06.42).

*

Few regions are so much associated with rich, refined cooking and excellent wines as Burgundy. A great abundance of animal and vegetable produce has encouraged the development of a generous cuisine. Meat cooked in a cream and/or wine sauce is the local tradition, giving rise to such well-known regional specialities as coq au vin (chicken cooked with onions and mushrooms in wine), boeuf bourguignon (beef — usually Charolais — cooked with onions and mushrooms in wine) and saupiquet (ham in cream and wine sauce). River fish are plentiful, and they too are cooked with wine, for example as fish-and-wine stew (pauchouse). Escargots (snails) done in various ways are tremendously popular as a starter. Just a few cheeses are made, notably the powerful Époisses and Pierre-Qui-Vire. Fruit-based tarts and puddings are typical local desserts. Burgundian wines, of course, are world-famous, especially from Chablis (dry and elegant whites), the Côte d'Or (rich, prestigious reds and whites), Côte Chalonnais and Mâconnais (superb whites, everyday reds) and Beaujolais (highly drinkable uncomplicated red). For an aperitif try a kir, properly made with the black currant liqueur Cassis de Dijon in a glass of sharp white Bourgogne Aligoté; and as a digestif, Burgundy's marc (brandy made by distilling the residue of grape pressing) is reckoned the best and smoothest in France.

6 EASTERN FRONTIERS

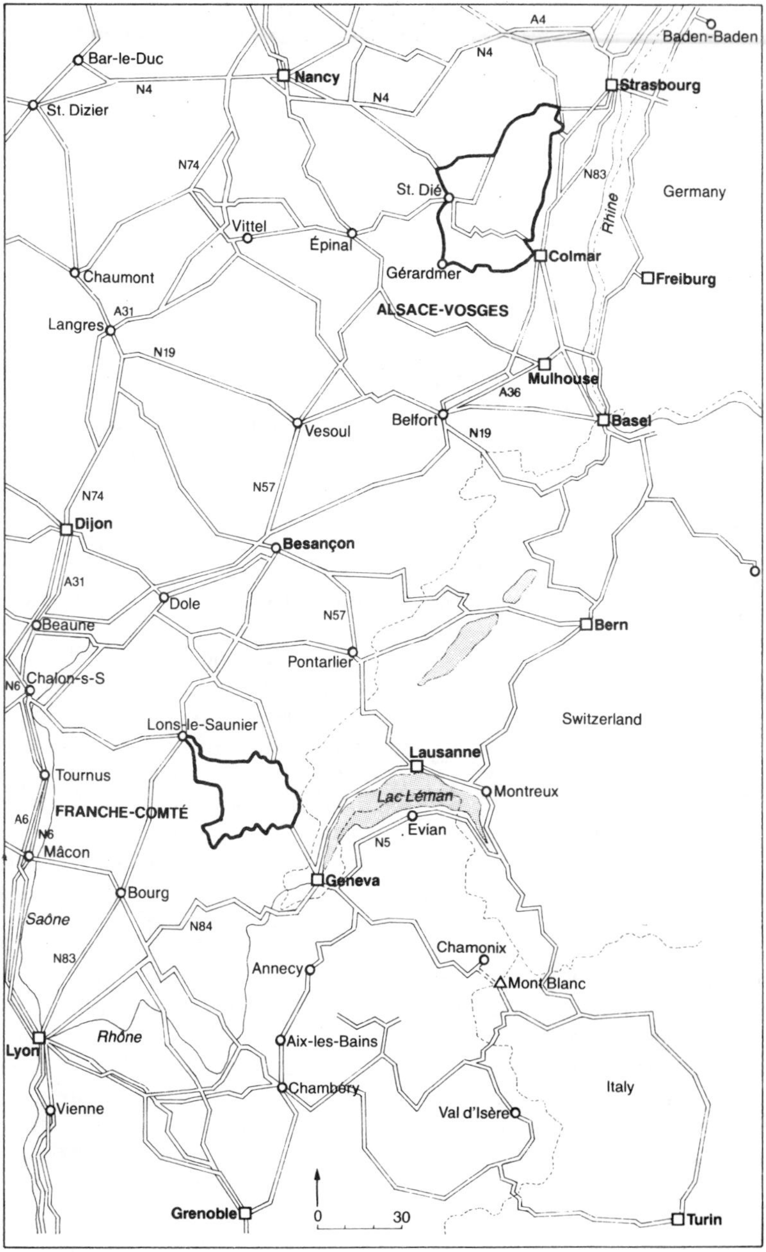

Along the whole length of France's mountainous eastern border are territories, much disputed over the centuries, with a not-quite-French flavour. From Alsace up in the north, with its unenviable story of constant invasion and annexation by Germany, all the way through the Jura and the High Alps with their close kinship to the Swiss, and right down to the Mediterranean Riviera, which, until a century ago belonged to Italy, this side of France has developed a fascinating overlap of culture and customs with its neighbours. This makes for interesting touring; the Alpine scenery is magnificent, too, and apart from the resort towns this remains a region thoroughly rustic in character, with simple, hardy villages, and dairy cattle clanking their cowbells in cool, peaceful pastures.

Alsace-Vosges

3–4 days/250km/from Colmar

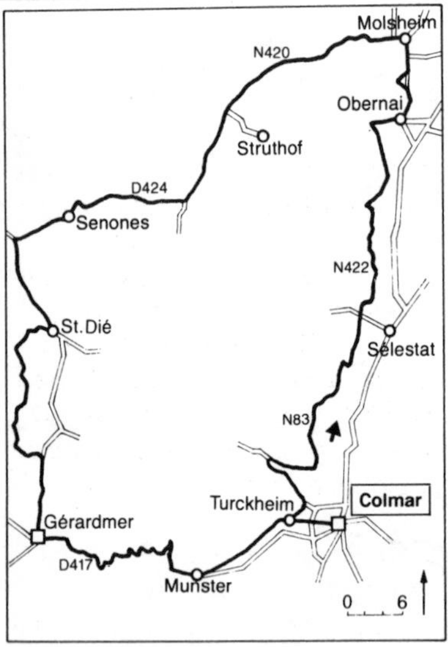

Of all the parts of France which can claim a separate regional identity, none is quite so completely different as Alsace. Yet far from demanding separation or independence, it is staunchly pro-French. During the Roman era, Alsace was part of Gaul, but since that period it has spent most of its time under German occupation. From 1681, when it was first retaken by France, to 1945, when the Germans were driven out yet again, this beleaguered region was constantly disputed between the two nations and frequently changed hands. Although speaking a German dialect, eating German food, and indeed looking like Germans, Alsatians have no love for true Germans from across the Rhine. This is hardly surprising, for the German way of bringing Alsace back into the fold was always to impose upon it the cruellest oppression. During the late 19C 'Germanisation', all French-sounding personal names had to be changed and the use of French words (with which Alsatian speech is heavily seasoned in some areas) was punishable by prison terms. That was nothing compared to the Nazi occupation, which saw mass deportations and executions, detentions in the concentration camp at Struthof, or for the lucky ones the option of being drafted into the German army.

Alsace is one of *the* great French gastronomic regions, though offering dishes rather unlike those served anywhere else in the country. Look out for *bretzels*, *kouglhopf*, and other delicious bakery; fruit pies and substantial vegetable tarts; of course real home-made sauerkraut, here known by its French name *choucroute* and heavily garnished with local *charcuterie*; as well as an abundance of terrines, pâtés, hams and sausages. And besides producing fragrant dry wines neither German nor French in character, Alsatians make (and drink) a lot of beer, and also have a taste for a multitude of powerful *apéritifs* and *digestifs* made from the wild mountain berries.

Alsace looks its best during the bright, delicate spring or mellow autumn. This route, to whet the appetite for further exploration, visits what is surely, with its flowery villages and craggy ruined castles, the prettiest vineyard region in France. It travels across the green crests of the Vosges mountains, and takes just a quick look at more industrial, more war-damaged Lorraine (not German in character, although the Germans seized it along with Alsace) on the other side. There are first-class restaurants every step of the way. (Michelin map 62.)

COLMAR pop: 64,000 Capital of the upper Rhine. Pleasing town on the Alsace plain at the foot of the Vosges mountains. At its centre are many picturesque streets and old half-timbered houses. See: ornate 16C dwellings; 15C Customs House; Musée d'Unterlinden, reputed art museum (note especially Grünewald's 16C Issenheim altarpiece) housed in old convent buildings around cloisters; 13/14C Basilica of St. Martin ('the Cathedral'); Church of St. Matthieu (good 14C stained glass and an early organ); Dominican church (more 14C stained glass and Schongauer's 'Virgin with Rose Bush' on display); the Krutenau quarter, with attractive waterways. For tourist information phone 89.41.02.29. Best restaurants: **Schillinger** (89.41.43.17), **Le Rendez-vous de Chasse** (part of quiet, comfortable, central **Hôtel Terminus-Bristol**; 89.41.49.14), **Au Fer Rouge** (89.41.37.24) — all with rosette and 2 toques, and none terribly expensive. For a good cheaper meal, **Restaurant Unterlinden** (89.41.18.73) is opposite the museum.

In a neat line along the foot of the Vosges range are the Alsace vineyards, their villages linked by country lanes which together are known as the Route du Vin. To get onto this **'Wine Road'**, drive 7km east out through the Colmar suburbs to **TURCKHEIM**. Beside the river Fecht, and noted for its white wine (Le Brand), this handsome walled town is triangular in shape, with main square and 3 gates, and preserves a thoroughly Renaissance appearance. In full traditional attire and 3-cornered hat, here the last town crier in Alsace does his round at dusk. His role has definitely changed though, from public address system to tourist attraction, for he can only be seen these days from May to September! One of the many attractive buildings is 17C **Hôtel des Deux Clefs**, an inexpensive 2-star Logis (89.27.06.01). Other good hotel-restaurants, both 2-star Logis: **Des Vosges** (89.27.02.37), and cheaper, **Auberge du Brand** (89.27.06.10).

Take D10 north through Ingersheim, and turn left onto N415 into **AMMERSCHWIHR**. Largely rebuilt after war damage, this village in the midst of vines, has achieved again a certain attractiveness and can at least offer one pleasant inexpensive hotel, **A l'Arbre Vert** (2-star Logis: 89.47.12.23) which has a restaurant and *winstub* (wine bar with local dishes) specialising in Alsatian dishes, and one superb *restaurant avec chambres*, a little dearer but still a bargain, **Aux Armes de France** (2 rosettes, 2 toques: 89.47.10.12) with light, imaginative food that on the whole is *not* especially Alsatian.

Continue to the junction with D28, where turn right into **KAYSERSBERG**, lovely small town on the river Weiss where Albert Schweitzer was born in 1875. There are 16/17C houses and town hall in German Renaissance style, an interesting church with gilded wooden altarpiece and, on the other side of the fortified bridge which crosses the river, a ruined castle with banners flying. **Hôtel-Restaurant Chambard** (rosette, 2 toques: 89.47.10.17) is a delight: rooms comfortable and rather pricey but restaurant remarkable value. D28 carries on down by **KIENTZHEIM** (vineyard museum in castle: summer only) and **SIGOLSHEIM** (early Gothic church; sobering war memorial) to junction with D1b, where turn left.

D1b continues through well-kept vineyards and weaves by a succession of villages hardly 2 or 3km from one to the next. **RIQUEWIHR** (on D3, left), the most visited of the Alsace wine villages and so often uncomfortably crowded, has an elaborately timbered 13C gate-tower (the Dolder), magnificent 16/17C houses, fortifications, fountains and flowers. There's a small Jewish ghetto in a corner of the village, an Alsatian Postal Museum in the old castle (1539), and much else besides. Riquewihr also manages to produce one of the region's, one of the world's, best Rieslings. **Auberge du Schoenenbourg** (89.47.92.28) is an expensive, luxurious

Riquewihr

restaurant with peaceful, inexpensive rooms. Carry on via **HUNAWIHR** (to left of road; fortified church and village) to larger **RIBEAUVILLÉ**, with flower-covered fountains and restored old houses beside the Strengbach valley, beneath the ruins of feudal St. Ulrich Castle. Ribeauvillé makes a good white wine: try it at **Hôtel-Restaurant Les Vosges** (bargain-priced Logis with rosette and toque: 89.73.61.39). Not quite as cheap, **Clos St-Vincent** (rosette: 89.73.67.65) is in tranquil vineyard country just outside the village (staying on D1b towards Bergheim).

Through medieval **BERGHEIM** and **ST-HIPPOLYTE** (producing a red wine; recommended hotel-restaurant **Aux Ducs de Lorraine**, a Relais du Silence and 3-star Logis, yet not terribly expensive; 89.73.00.09), with a possible detour up to **HAUT-KOENIGSBOURG** (impressive feudal castle, good views), stay on D1b (changes to D35) to **KINTZHEIM** (stork sanctuary — storks have special significance to the people of Alsace, who are concerned about the declining numbers of the species). Carry on to **CHÂTENOIS** (unusual Romanesque tower; note too the 15C gateway strangely called the Sorcerer's Tower) and **DAMBACH-LA-VILLE**, walled village (another one with 3 gates) beneath the slopes of a steep wooded hill and now the focus of an eminent wine district. The towers on the fortifications, the flower-decorated wooden houses with cast iron signs over the doorways, make it a delight. Just off the road to the left (on D235), tucked away in the valley of the Andlau, is old **ANDLAU** village, with its flowers, hilltop castle and — worth visiting — 11C abbey church (note porch, crypt, Romanesque frieze). Take D35 through hillside **MITTELBERGHEIM**, ancient wine-making village (Renaissance houses arranged around the main square) and **BARR**, important regional centre of commerce, to **OTTROTT**, with two (quite dissimilar) medieval castles and two good, inexpensive hotel-restaurants: **Hostellerie des Châteaux** (a Relais du Silence: 88.95.81.54) and, slightly better and slightly dearer, the very accurately named **Beau Site** (88.95.80.61). Ottrott makes a good red wine.

Turn onto D426 for **OBERNAI**, a larger town, but with a pleasing central area enclosed by the ruin of ramparts, a particularly beautiful old *place du Marché*, an interesting former corn market, and Renaissance houses, wells, fountains. There's no lack of hotels and restaurants: among its 7 (!) Logis are a couple with 3 stars. Lovely-looking and well placed in the main square, restaurant **La Halle aux Bles** has reasonably priced menus with typical Alsatian dishes.

D422 runs straight and quick from Obernai to Molsheim on the flatter ground, but take a detour back into the hills to **ROSHEIM** (on left) to see the oldest house in Alsace, 12C Maison des Païens ('Pagans' House'). North of Obernai the vineyards thin out, and at **MOLSHEIM** (fortifications and 15C gateway, old streets and houses, 16C Metzig or meeting hall) our route leaves the Route du Vin. Instead turn west (on N420) into what becomes, after very few km, the wooded and picturesque **valley of the Bruche**. The thick woodland climbing away to each side is really an extension of the Black Forest on the other side of the Rhine.

From time to time, worthwhile detours can be made. At **NIEDER-**

HASLACH, for example, 3km to right (on D218) of the valley road, there's a fine 13C abbey, originally founded by an Irishman in 7C, on the very edge of forest. More grimly, after **SCHIRMECK** (small lively local capital, industrial), D130 leads through the trees to the small concentration camp — the only one in France — at **STRUTHOF**. Barbed wire fortifications, watchtowers and gas chambers remain as a ghastly reminder of the German occupation. Inmates numbered 40,000 altogether, of whom 10,000 were killed.

Turn right onto D424 which, climbing over the Col du Hantz, leaves Alsace and enters Lorraine. The two neighbouring provinces, despite having become welded together during the 19C German occupation, have little in common. Culturally, Lorraine is truly a part of northern France – hardworking, industrious and industrial, perhaps long-suffering, and created by invaders of several lands — while Alsace, isolated from France by the Vosges hills, has a clearer Franco-German identity of its own. If cuisine reveals anything, and in France surely it does, Lorraine is much fonder of eggs, milk, cheese and cream. Egg and vegetable tarts (notably quiche lorraine, of course), meat pies, bacon-with-everything are the local taste, washed down with beer rather than wine. Lorraine also has a great tradition of desserts and sweets, many towns and villages offering their own speciality.

SENONES on D424, former capital of the tiny principality of Salm — 'around which,' according to Voltaire, who spent a month here in 1754 and, one suspects, covered the terrain pretty exhaustively, 'a snail could travel in a single day' — retains at its centre the princes' château, the abbey which was the origin of the town and an 18C *hôtel de ville*. Although the little town itself is now somewhat industrialised, the tree-covered hills rising like an amphitheatre around it provide a magnificent setting. Keep to the same road through **MOYENMOUTIER** (beautiful 18C church) to **ÉTIVAL-CLAIREFONTAINE** (12C abbey) where join busy N59 (direction St. Dié).

ST. DIÉ pop: 25,000 Unappealing town but the setting, in hills of red rock and pine, is attractive. Rebuilt on 3 occasions: in 1757 after fire damage, and after both world wars. See: Cathedral and Church of Notre-Dame (both basically 12C, linked by Gothic cloisters); Museum of Daily Life in the Vosges. Office de Tourisme: 31 rue Thiers. Several adequate hotels and restaurants. **Restaurant Tétras** (29.56.10.12) has modestly priced menus and a Michelin rosette.

Leave St. Dié on N420 (direction Épinal) but turn left after just 5km onto D31, a small valley road between wooded hills. At Corcieux turn left onto D60, which climbs up to meet much busier D8 at Col du Plafond, where turn right into **GÉRARDMER** (pronounced Gerarmé). A cool, agreeable hill resort, in the midst of ideal walking or cross-country skiing country (marked trails in forest), Gérardmer had the first tourist office in France (1875) and is still very popular. Retreating Germans destroyed the place, so it lost its original appearance, but the lakeside setting and refreshing unspoiled landscape of rock and woodland are delightful. Lots of good places to eat or spend the night at reasonable prices. The town's big hotel, quiet and a little pompous, is the **Bragard** (29.63.06.31) with its excellent restaurant **Au Grand Cerf**. By the lake, **La Réserve** (29.63.21.60), with equally good restaurant, is slightly cheaper. 4km out, modern chalet-style **Hôtel-Restaurant Les Bas-Rupts** (29.63.09.25) has a rosette and 2 toques.

D417 rises away from the town along the Vologne valley, through spectacular country via the Saut des Cuves waterfall, past Lac de Longemer, rather disfigured by campsites, equally popular little Lac de Retournemer, and Roche du Diable, with a good view over the two lakes. (An alternative route on this stretch, smaller but closer to the lakes, is D67a/D67.) A steep ascent brings the road to Col de la Schlucht (1,139m), former frontier post between France and Alsace. Hohneck, the green summit of the Vosges (1,362m), can be seen clearly to the south. By hairpin descents the road arrives at the old Alsatian spa town of **MUNSTER**, where the rivers Fecht and Petit-Fecht merge into one. Originally a monastery, another of those founded by Irish monks in 7C (Munster = monastery), ironically it became a centre of Protestantism in later centuries. There is an attractive Protestant church, built in the red stone of the region, a covered market, remnants of the abbey and other interesting buildings, and the town is above all a good base for walks or tours in the mountains or the Fecht valley. **Hôtel-Restaurant de la Cigogne** (89.77.32.27) is a 2-star Logis with low-priced rooms and *menu*.

Farm *auberges* along the valley do a roaring trade in *tourte*, the local pie in its various forms, and of course red-skinned tangy Munster cheese. On the Fecht's right bank D417 passes tiny spa **SOULTZBACH**, its waters most unusual in that they were reputed to cure mental problems, through **WINTZENHEIM** on the Route du Vin, and back into Colmar. Travelling instead on the left bank of the river, smaller D10 takes in several little villages, including **GUNSBACH**, where Albert Schweitzer lived (his house can be seen), and allows another look at Turckheim on the way back.

Franche-Comté

1–2 days/165km/from Lons-le-Saunier

Richly endowed with lakes and rivers, and forested with oak and beech at lower altitudes and pine on the higher slopes, the mountains and plateau of the Jura lie partly in France and partly in Switzerland. On both sides of the border a traditional, rustic way of life continues, mainly revolving around cheese-making, and little affected by tourism. Cheeses are made in local *fruitières*, as they are known, each one run for centuries under communal village ownership. Indeed the name 'Franche-Comté' given to the French Jura does not, of course, mean French but free and independent (as in *enfranchise*), just like the Franches-Montagnes on the Swiss

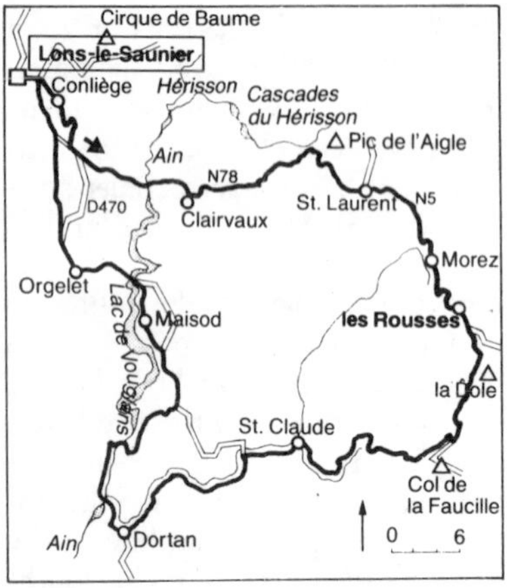

side of the frontier. For this is a region noted more than most for its love of liberty and local communalism. Yet despite the name, its inhabitants have been often subjugated: by Rome, Burgundy, Spain and, since the 17C, France. Nevertheless, Franche-Comté has produced many libertarians and political rebels — for example Victor Hugo, anarchist philosopher Proudhon, and his supporter the painter, Gustave Courbet — among several other great 'names' of science and art, such as Louis Pasteur, who came from Dole; and, from Belley, that most authoritative writer (indeed prophet) of French gastronomy, Brillat-Savarin. In both woods and meadows, delicate flowers, gentian, crocus, bloom all summer long. And surprisingly the Jura supports vineyards too, producing light, fresh vintages, both red and white, as well as one of the most curious and distinctive of all wines: *vin jaune* — rich and full flavoured, yellow in colour, and high in alcohol. Local cuisine makes much of its cheeses, and dishes like fondue (hot melted cheese-and-wine eaten from the pot with pieces of bread on long-handled forks) are favourites, while freshly-caught fish from the rivers and lakes are served in wine sauces. (Use Michelin map 70.)

LONS-LE-SAUNIER pop: 22,000 Likeable local capital among the vineyards; spa town with attractive 16–18C streets. See: rue du Commerce; 18C hospital (note: wrought iron grille; pharmacy). Good choice of hotels. First-class restaurant **Auberge de Chavannes** (84.47.05.52) at Courlans (6km west). SI: 1 rue Pasteur.

Before starting out on the route, first take a look, some 8km east of Lons just off D471, at the impressive rock formations, issuing water spectacularly, of the Cirque de Baume (remarkable view) and close by it, the picturesque but simple former abbey of Baume-les-Messieurs, founded in the 6C. It was a party of monks from Baume who established the great abbey at Cluny (p. 86). But Baume-les-Messieurs achieved its greatest, if more dubious, distinction as the seat of one of the most extraordinary characters ever to hold office in the Church — Jean de Watteville (1613–1702). Having killed first a fellow officer in the army, and then the abbot of a monastery which he entered in penance, he fled to Constantinople where he converted to Islam and entered the employ of the Grand Turk as a military commander. As such he made a fortune and lived as dissolute a life as possible for several years, before abandoning the Turks in the midst of victory, reconverting to Christianity and taking up the abbotship of Baume-les-Messieurs . . . where he spent his days not in prayer but as a richly rewarded military adviser to the King.

Start the route itself by heading east from Lons-le-Saunier on N78, which straight away reaches the vineyard village of **CONLIÈGE**, which has a lovely 14C church (note: 17C sculpture; wrought iron grille) and, shortly after, **Creux de Ravigny**, another of the several striking rock formations which have evolved in this limestone terrain: here, numerous caves eat into an amphitheatre of high cliffs. Continue on N78, which crosses the river Ain at Pont-de-Poitte and enters **CLAIRVAUX-LES-LACS**, a little holiday resort (beaches and watersports at nearby Grand Lac) with remnants of a feudal castle.

The road carries on through picturesque country to aptly named **BONLIEU**, near a pretty lake. There's a good 2-star Logis here, **La Poutre** (84.25.57.77), with an excellent, reasonably priced restaurant. The Jura is, not surprisingly, magnificent walking country, and several footpaths lead away from Bonlieu into the surrounding woods and hills. Indeed all this countryside and its sometimes quite spectacular scenery is best appreciated on foot. A little access road leads down from Bonlieu to the **Cascades du Hérisson**, a series of waterfalls on the little Hérisson river which flows rapidly down from Pic de l'Aigle (993m). Staying on N78, skirt past the Pic and join busier N5 at **ST. LAURENT-EN-GRANDVAUX**.

Les Rousses

This locality, Grandvaux, was always associated with its own breed of travellers, called *rouliers*, who transported local timber to the Atlantic coast for shipbuilding, and during the frozen winter months toured the lowlands selling the cheeses and other products of their region. St. Laurent is still a cheese-making centre in the traditional style, though it has been made less enticing by the replacement of the old-fashioned wooden roofs (which caused a terrible fire some 120 years ago) with safer metal sheeting. A little farther along the road is **MORBIER**, which gives its name to one of the Jura's more unusual cheeses — each 'round' has a horizontal layer of charcoal running through its middle. Nowadays it is Morbier's curiously situated neighbour **MOREZ**, lying like a ribbon at the bottom of a narrow gorge in the river Bienne, which makes most of the cheese. Nearby Rocher au Dade on the cliffs above gives a good view over the town, and a drive on the narrow road beside the gorge makes a superb outing from the town. (To shorten this route, it would be easy to continue along the Bienne gorge road all the way to St. Claude.)

Crossing one of the region's many *crêts*, 'crests', N5 continues to the pleasant little cross-country skiing resort of **LES ROUSSES**. Turn off the road left to go into the village centre. On a high plateau, very attractive with its woods and lake (the frozen surface of which is criss-crossed by ski-tracks in winter), outside the ski season les Rousses makes a delightful starting point for peaceful walks and drives in the Jura countryside. A particularly enjoyable trip is along the narrow lane D29^{e2}, which passes the Lac des Rousses and makes its way up to Bois d'Amont, where the convivial *restaurant avec chambres* **Auberge du Viviers** (84.60.03.40) can provide an excellent fondue and bottle of wine, a cheery *patron*, and pleasant atmosphere. There are four 2-star Logis in les Rousses (all with restaurants), and several other decent places to eat. **Hôtel de France** has the town's best restaurant (with rosette and 2 toques; 84.60.01.45).

Despite being a tourist centre (especially in winter), les Rousses is still as much as ever an agricultural village devoted to the traditions of cheese-making. At the local *fruitière* I was shown round — anybody will be made welcome if it is not too busy a moment — and was able to see the Morbier, Raclette and Comté cheeses, and others, being made, the unset wet cheese being scooped out of big vats with cheesecloth, and hand-pressed in wooden moulds. Ten farmers serve this village fromagerie, the farthest coming 7km each day with his milk. The largest producers bring 1,300 litres per day on average, although the smallest, an old lady with 3 unproductive cows, comes in with just 12 litres of milk. The most distinguished of the Jura's cheeses is Comté, a type of Gruyère. Each of the rounds of Comté cheese, weighing some 40kg, contains 500 or 600 litres of milk. The cheeses are aged for 8 to 12 months in cool cellars, after which time they are at their best. Comté made with summer milk (called *fruité*) is richer, sweeter and tastier than that made with the winter milk (*salée*).

Like wines, certain French cheeses have a pedigree deserving to be protected, and are required to meet strict standards and be approved by inspectors, who issue an *appellation d'origine*. To carry the name 'Comté', cheese must be made in a strictly defined area of Franche-Comté, using fresh unpasteurised cows' milk of a particular breed. Every Comté cheese has a mark of authentication and is stamped with the date on which it was made.

Just 2½km after les Rousses, N5 reaches the Swiss border at la Cure, but instead of crossing the frontier at this point (there is a turning here, however, if you do want to continue towards Lac Léman), swings round south and runs along beneath the lofty peak of la Dôle towards Col de la Faucille, where the frontier is again encountered. Our turning, D936 on the right, is 2½km *before* the Col, and leads sharply down to Mijoux. Here take D436 on the right. Rising and falling through this wild landscape of peaks, gorges and waterfalls, the road makes its way down, through the gorges of the river Flumen, into **ST. CLAUDE**.

A large mountain town (traditionally noted for pipe-making — see the pipe museum) in a beautiful setting of ridges and peaks typical of the Jura, St. Claude is in the midst of marvellous touring country whether on foot or by car. Particularly worthwhile is a walk to the Queue de Cheval (= horse's tail) waterfall (about 3hr round trip). The town itself, though not very charming architecturally, is built on a ridge above the confluence of the rushing Bienne and Tacon rivers and has spectacular views. Its 14–17C Cathedral, all that's left of an abbey founded here in the year 425, contains some fine, unusual 15C choirstalls.

D436 clings to the valley of the Bienne. The village of **DORTAN**, now rebuilt, was destroyed in July 1944 by German soldiers after they had tortured and killed many of the inhabitants. Here turn right onto D936, which follows the Bienne to **CHANCIA**, where it flows into the river Ain.

Travel north from Chancia (D60) to follow the picturesque and wooded Ain valley, much of it now transformed into long, narrow Lac de Vouglans. At places along the route, you'll find tall *belvederes*, lookout points, which give impressive views and, starting from almost every village, there are pleasant walks.

To follow Ain valley: 5km from Chancia, at Menouille, turn right onto D299. Turn left where it meets D470. Continue through Moirans. Take D301 on left to reach waterside **MAISOD**. Carry on north on the same little lakeside road to rejoin D470, where turn left and cross the lake at Pont de la Pyle.

Soon after, at **ORGELET**, with its interesting 13-16C church (note: Renaissance choirstalls) and 13C hospital (much changed, however, over the centuries), turn right and pick up D52 to return into Lons-le-Saunier.

*

For regional cuisine, see Alsace and Franche-Comté route introductions.

7 MASSIF CENTRAL

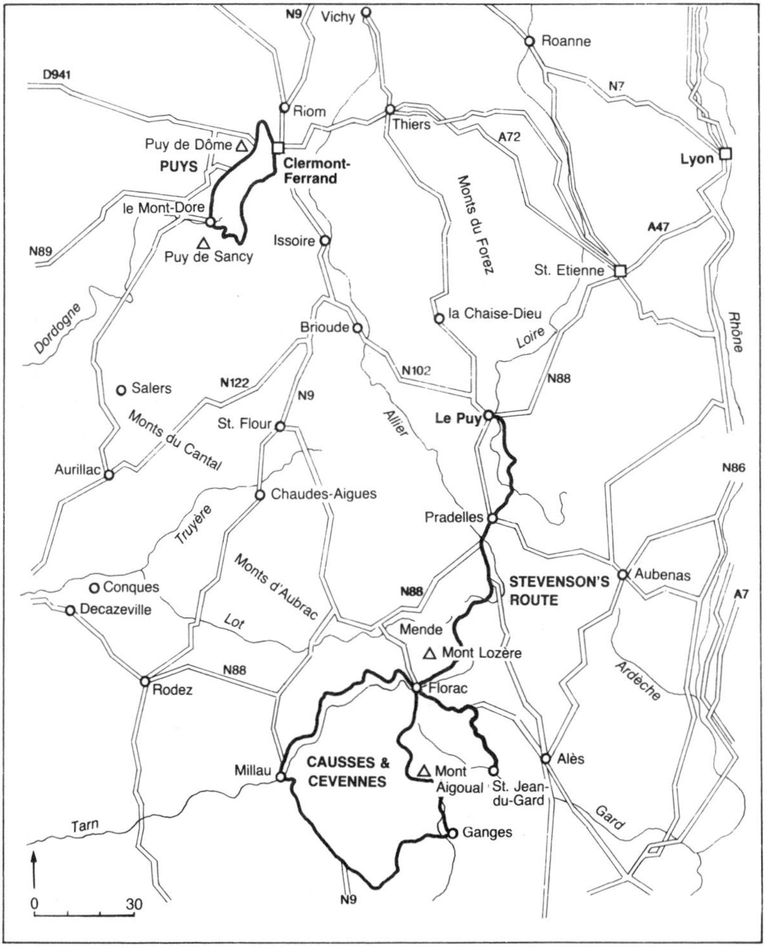

A vast highland area filling the middle of southern France, the Massif Central defies modernisation and development. In consequence the region is almost entirely rural, and one of the poorest in France. Staunchly conservative, deeply religious, and long cut off from the mainstream of French life, the people are tough, self-reliant and resistant to change. Nowhere is this more true than in the strange once-volcanic landscape of the Auvergne, heart of the region. For unlike the desolate crags of other ranges, these mountains are lived-in, they have a history, tradition and a culture of their own. In this steep and densely wooded hill country, cut through by numerous rivers and streams and with hundreds of lakes, barely half-a-dozen towns have any sort of urban lifestyle. In all of them, even in the capital Clermont-Ferrand, the surrounding countryside makes its presence strongly felt.

The *Puy* Region

1 day/122km/from Clermont-Ferrand

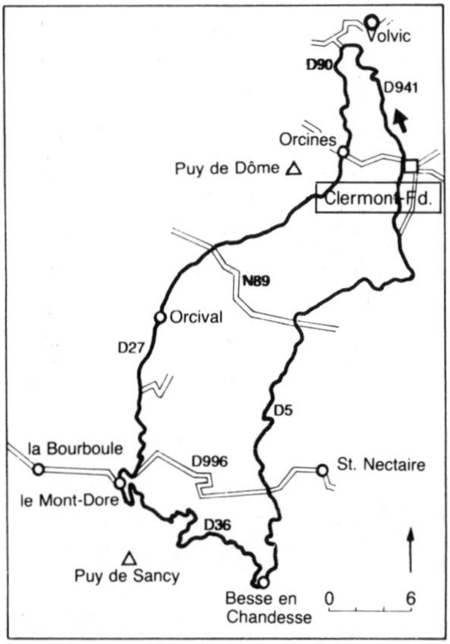

Most distinctive of the Auvergne's strange geological features are the *puys* (simply a local word for 'peaks'), abrupt, steep and sometimes curiously shaped hills. They are the weatherworn remnants of much larger mountains of lava and rock. Most have a crater at the summit, which often has become a lake. For this was a region of intense volcanic activity, the most recent — only 4,000 years ago — forming the 112 peaks of the Monts Dômes, west of Clermont-Ferrand, while just south of them, the starker pinnacles of the Monts Dores result from only three larger volcanoes, older and more eroded. The lofty Monts du Cantal, at the southern limits of the region and standing somewhat apart, are the last traces of a single primeval volcano of enormous dimensions. Some 3,600 km of this extraordinary landscape, together with its rustic villages, its spa towns and winter resorts, has been designated as the Parc Régional Naturel des Volcans d'Auvergne. Our route is a short — but, because of the terrain, not a fast — tour of the most spectacular of the *puy* country, lying surprisingly close to Clermont-Ferrand. (Use Michelin map 73.)

Leave **CLERMONT-FERRAND** (pop: 151,000; highly industrial, but with attractive old centre; see especially: 12C Notre-Dame du Port; 13C Cathedral) by heading west to pick up D941 (direction Volvic). On reaching D90, turn left and double-back on this small and unfrequented country road which has good views across Clermont. Continue straight through Orcines, crossing over D941b, until reaching D941a, where turn right. Immediately on the right a steep access road (toll) leads to the top of the **Puy de Dôme** (1,465m; highest of the Monts Dômes). At the summit the ruins of a Roman temple to Mercury are rather overwhelmed by more modern mercurial devices like the radio mast and observatory. But there is also a spectacular view across the chain of volcanic peaks, and on one of the (rare) clear days one can see into, so it is said, 11 départements.

On D941a continue to the junction at Les Quatre Routes, where take D216, and then left onto D27, a quiet lane which comes to **ORCIVAL**. After such a journey through unpopulated, even wild country, it comes as a surprise to find that this small village has the air almost of a holiday resort, with tour buses, souvenir shops and parties of visitors wandering around. The principle attraction is the 12C basilica of black volcanic stone, a superb example of the Auvergne Romanesque style. Inside sits one of the Black Virgins which command such reverence in the Auvergne: a stylised Madonna and Child in black, in stiff formal pose, the infant Jesus seeming more like a small adult than a child. Such a statue can be found in many of the old churches of the region, and is often credited with miraculous powers. At Orcival, the Madonna is thickly covered with silver and enamel. She was known in the Middle Ages as Our Lady of Iron and Chains, and worshipped by former convicts who had survived the gruelling conditions of imprisonment in those days. Today, it is Our Lady who is kept in high security under electronic surveillance, with an unseemly notice warning visitors not to approach. On Ascension Day the statue is carried through the village at the head of a traditional pilgrimage.

The drive on D27 and then D983 passes through marvellous, unusual country of pasture and rocks, giving some magnificent views all the way to **LE MONT-DORE**, a thriving spa dating back to before Roman times and now a winter resort built along the bank of the young and lively river Dordogne. It is also popular with walkers, and there are dozens of enjoyable footpaths starting from the town. The Syndicat d'Initiative, av Leclerc, has details of walks and drives in the area. Nearby **Puy de Sancy** (1,885m; highest point in Auvergne), 5km away, is almost too popular as an excursion for both walkers and motorists, but it does command a superb view over the surrounding Monts Dores.

D36 skirts Sancy and — a lovely drive — works its way through the hills to the pretty village of **BESSE-EN-CHANDESSE**, which has a number of 15/16C houses, a 9–12C Romanesque church, an interesting old marketplace and remnants of medieval fortifications. There's a good hotel here, too, with excellent and not terribly expensive restaurant, **Les Mouflons** (73.79.51.31; rosette and toque). St. Nectaire cheese is made in the village, and throughout this locality. D5 runs north from here to

MUROL, pleasant resort winter and summer. It has an unusual ruin of a 12-sided château made of reddish volcanic stone. Lac Chambon, 3km west along D996, is a large lake in a very attractive setting, while 6km in the opposite direction **ST. NECTAIRE** has two distinct centres: the old upper village has a fine 12C church, perfect example of Auvergnat Romanesque, while the lower village is a small spa resort. Disappointingly perhaps, St. Nectaire is no longer much concerned in the making of the delicious cheese to which it gave its name, although a few farms in the area do sell their own home-made whole uncut cheeses — look for the signs offering *fromage fermier*.

From Murol take D5 north (direction Clermont), through the heart of the Volcano Park, up to the junction with N89, where turn right, and follow signs to **ROYAT**, an agreeable spa on the outskirts of Clermont. From here return into the city.

Stevenson's Route

3–4 days/230km/from Le Puy to St. Jean du Gard

In September 1878, the Scottish writer Robert Louis Stevenson set off from Le Monastier, near le Puy, on a 12-day trek across the airy uplands of the Haute Loire and into the wooded hills of the Cévennes. To carry his luggage, which included, for example, a leg of lamb, an egg whisk, and a six-foot square fur-lined 'sleeping sack', he bought for 65 francs and a glass of brandy a wretched little donkey whom he christened (on account of her small size and price) Modestine.

It is not possible, of course, to retrace Stevenson's steps by car . . . the only way would be to get out and walk, and maybe, after all, that's not such a bad idea. Some of the tracks and paths he took are still not suitable for vehicles, while others have become such busy highways that their pace and character are altogether unlike that which Stevenson himself experienced. So instead of being *too* faithful to his footsteps we travel on pleasant minor roads which follow Stevenson's route as closely as possible.

Several strands in his life combined to bring the 28-year-old Stevenson to this region. First, he was lonely and disappointed in love, having fallen for a young American divorcée who, besides being declared by his father to be quite unsuitable for him, had in any case returned to her home in California. He had therefore decided to get away from it all and put his thoughts in order. He wanted, he said, 'to get down off this feather bed of civilisation and feel the globe granite underfoot and strewn with cutting flints', and to this end decided that he wanted to make an arduous trek somewhere far away from the 'drawing-room society' of his normal life. Secondly, he chose to start his walk at Le Monastier-sur-Gazeille because it was in the heart of a wild and unpopulated area vividly described in the books of one of his favourite writers, George Sand, for whom this was 'one of the loveliest spots on Earth'.

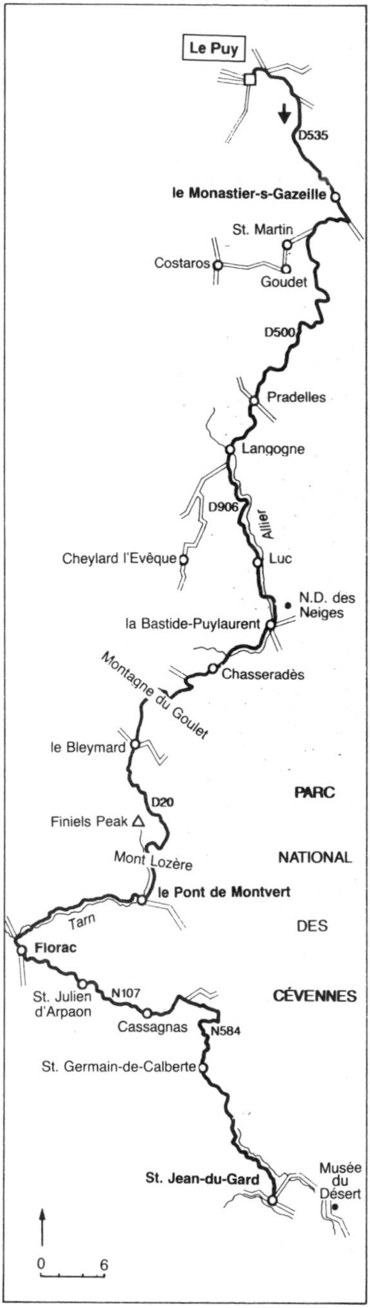

And thirdly, Stevenson especially wanted to get as far as the Cévennes because he was fascinated by the 18C Camisards, Protestant peasant-mystics of the region who prayed in the open air and who fought and died in their hills for the right to worship as they wished. With youthful romanticism — and rather mistakenly — he likened them to the Scottish Covenanters, and seemed eager as well to see similarities between the Cévennes and the highlands of Scotland, which perhaps did have a closer resemblance then than they do now. The creation of the Parc National des Cévennes, with its reforestation programmes, and the reintroduction of numerous native wild animals and birds, have given the Cévennes a quite different character since Stevenson's day. (Use Michelin maps 76 & 80.)

LE PUY EN VELAY pop: 26,000 Strangely located town, built on the slopes of a prominent *puy* called Rocher de Corneille — with massive red statue *Notre Dame de France* on summit, visible from afar. On the way up is the remarkable-looking cathedral (façade, frescoes, Black Virgin, cloisters). See also: curious 11C church of St. Michel d'Aiguilhe, perched on another tall *puy*; narrow streets of old centre, with lace-makers' workshops. Local speciality: digestif liqueurs made of *verveine*, verbena. Festival and pilgrimage to the town every 15 August. Syndicate d'Initiative in place Breuil. Hotels **Licorn** (71.02.46.22), **du Cygne** (71.09.32.36) and — slightly cheaper — **Le Val Vert** (71.09.09.30) are all reasonable 2-star Logis.

Take D535 to **LE MONASTIER**, a town both larger and yet less thriving than a century ago when Robert Louis Stevenson lodged here. The population is about half what it was. The people drink less too: in Stevenson's day there were 50 bars in the town, and he also remarked on the frequency with which stagecoaches in the area would stop at bars for passengers to drink a mug of wine. Now there are 10 bars in Le Monastier — one of them actually named in his honour, 'Le Stevenson'! He noted, too, several pretty fountains in the town, decorated with flowers, and many houses with ornately carved doorways, which still make the town attractive. But he was surprisingly unimpressed by the interesting and simple 11C Abbey Church. The Syndicat d'Initiative, in the Mairie (town hall), has an odd little Stevenson Museum, with photos of places along his route.

Setting out from the town on D500, he descended to the river Gazeille and climbed the other side of the valley. The road passes through simple hamlets — in one, milk churns were cooling in a drinking trough in the middle of the road as I went by — and continues, an attractive journey, to Pradelles. (Stevenson himself went by a different route through St. Martin de Fugères, Goudet, Ussel, Costaros and Le Bouchet-St. Nicholas. He spent the night in Le Bouchet, in the morning continuing on what is now the busy highway N88 to Pradelles.)

PRADELLES did not hold Stevenson's attention much, but deserved to. It's an interesting medieval town, with a curious church, the Chapelle de Notre Dame, which has murals and votive offerings to the lace-covered Our Lady of Pradelles who, according to a local woman who spoke to sceptical Stevenson, 'performs many miracles though she is made of wood'. He went on his way without investigating, eager to cross the boundary from Vélay to Gévaudan (now départements Haute-Loire and Lozère). He spent the night at **LANGOGNE**, busy modern town. Take D906 south along the charming valley of the Allier. Stevenson wandered by a more devious route, sometimes getting lost, on paths in the hills to the west of the road.

A century before Stevenson's visit, obscure rural district **Gévaudan** had become tremendously well known, its very name sending a chill down the spine of anyone who heard it. For during the 1760s the notorious Bête de Gévaudan roamed this area. Officially believed (without any evidence) to be a wolf, of whichever species, beast it certainly was, for in the course of three years over 50 people were attacked, killed and partly eaten . . . all of them women and children. Most of the killings took place between Langogne and Cheylard l'Evêque, the very area in which Stevenson chose to ramble on his way to **LUC** (on our road). The massive and unprepossessing white Madonna on the hillside above the village had just been erected as Stevenson passed by, as a date on the plinth confirms.

Continue beside the river to **LA BASTIDE-PUYLAURENT**, something of a miniature resort for, although no more than a village, it has a couple of good and inexpensive hotel-restaurants and is, besides, a stop on the main Paris-Nîmes railway — also new in Stevenson's day. He did

Le Pont de Montvert

not take a room here, but went up to the Trappist Monastery of **Notre-Dame des Neiges**, Our Lady of the Snows, some 4km east of the village (signposted), and was given lodging (they refused it to me).

Take D6 beside the Allier to **CHASSERADÈS**, where at the inn Stevenson was given accommodation in a stifling room full of other lodgers who were obliged to share beds. Because he was a gentleman he was allowed a bed to himself. After the village, in the shadow of a mighty railway viaduct, take D120 on the left to climb onto the Massif du Goulet. Follow the road round among the trees, turning left onto D20 to descend steeply into Le Bleymard, and up again to the top of **Mont Lozère**, which today is the boundary of the **Parc National des Cévennes**.

Stevenson, after sleeping on the cold turf just below the nearby Sommet de Finiels, highest point of the Lozère massif (1,699m: view extends to Alpilles in east, Mediterranean in southeast), rejoined D20 and walked down the hillside on this delightful, peaceful country road

LE PONT DE MONTVERT. There's something particularly cheerful and likeable about this lively Cevenol village through which the young river Tarn rushes and splashes noisily. Tributaries, too, pour in from north and south, watering the vegetable gardens. On a riverside embankment all the life of the village takes place, for here are post office, shops and café tables under the leafy branches of big *platanes*.

Stevenson lingered here for lunch and a rest at the **Hôtel des Cévennes**. A simple-enough auberge with considerable character, the hotel stands on the opposite bank of the river, reached by a graceful stone bridge, and still welcomes guests. When I spent the night, the four guests, together with the young proprietor and proprietress and two local peasants who had come in for their dinner, sat convivially to eat all at one table placed before a blazing fire in much the same manner as in Stevenson's day.

The austere Protestant faith of the peasants of the Cévennes was forbidden by the Catholic authorities and had to be practised in secret, usually in fields and caves. The name Camisard (Occitan* *camisa*, shirt — as opposed to the armour and uniforms of the soldiers they fought) started only after the outbreak of the guerrilla Camisard War. It was in le Pont de Montvert that the Camisards' war against Church and State began in 1702 with the slaughter of the monstrous local representative of Catholic authority, Abbé du Chayla, by a group of 52 men led by one Spirit Séguier. The Abbé was notorious for personally torturing Protestants whom he held captive in the cellars of his waterside house. The house has gone, but the cellars can be seen, and the Camisards are fervently remembered by the local people, who remain Protestant to this day. Many separatist slogans in Occitan are seen here, too, on walls and car stickers.

Stevenson set off later in the day on quiet D998, overhung with chestnut trees as it follows the Tarn. He slept on a terrace hidden above the road with his revolver by his side, and in the morning went down to bathe in the cool river water.

Passing through simple villages **COCURÈS** and **BÉDOUÈS** the road meets N106, where turn left into **FLORAC**, a delightful town, shaded with handsome mature trees. At its heart the lovely river Pecher descends by a series of terraces beside a medieval château (now an information and exhibition centre for the Parc National des Cévennes, with details of footpaths, accommodation, wildlife in the Parc area). Causse Méjean rises with grim majesty beside the town. Stevenson stayed overnight in rue Thérond, probably at 2-star **Grand Hôtel du Parc** (66.45.03.05) which now has its *back* entrance in that street.

The unfrequented mountain road which he then took above the valley of the Mimente has turned into today's rather busier N106. Stevenson turned off the road after **CASSAGNAS**, crossing the Mimente on a rickety wooden bridge (still there, still rickety, now overgrown with vegetation) and climbing through the wooded slopes of Mont Mars on a footpath, but travellers by car should continue to little D984 on right at

*The old language of southern France — see p. 155

Col de Jalcreste. Take this gorgeously quiet, rustic road as it meanders down to **ST. GERMAIN-DE-CALBERTE**. This village, oddly, always remained Catholic during the Wars of Religion; the Abbé du Chayla's body was brought here from Pont de Montvert, and he is buried inside the remarkably plain and simple village church. Despite everything, nowadays St. Germain is mainly Protestant.

Stay on this road through light, pleasant country all the way into **ST. JEAN-DU-GARD**, where Stevenson finished his walk, sold Modestine (for much less than he had paid), and caught the diligence to Alès where he hoped to have received a letter from the American, Fanny Osbourne. Whether or not there was a letter waiting, we do not know. Stevenson returned at once to Britain, where notes written during his walk were reworked and published as *Travels with a Donkey in the Cévennes*. His publisher gave Robert Louis Stevenson £30 for the book, which sum was sufficient to pay his fare to California, where he and Fanny were reunited.

St. Jean, with its ramparts and river Gardon de St. Jean (see the old bridge), is a bright and cheerful southern town. There are several good little hotel-restaurants here with low-priced menus (**L'Oronge** is a pleasant 2-star Logis: 66.85.30.34). The town's motto, in Occitan, is 'Al Sourel de la Liberta', in the sunlight of freedom, meaning of course religious freedom.

Near St. Jean: **MAS SOUBEYRAN**, just beyond Mialet (where inexpensive **Auberge du Fer à Cheval** has good food) on D50, the **Musée du Désert**, formerly the home of Camisard leader Pierre Laport, better known as Rolland, recaptures something of life at the time of the Camisards' struggle to achieve that liberty (Museum summer only: 66.85.32.72). *Désert* was how people formerly described this wild and uncultivated Cévennes countryside, the clandestine field preachers of the Protestants being known as Pastors of the Desert. Some of their meetings were held in the **Grotte de Trabuc**, 2km north on pretty access road, a large cave (with underground lake) inhabited from Neolithic times right up to the 18C.

Continuing along the narrow gorge of the Gardon de Mialet (all these little Gardons converge eventually to make up the river Gard), D50 reaches D129 at Générargues (beautifully situated, comfortable hotel-restaurant **Les Trois Barbus**: not cheap: 66.61.72.12), where turn left to **ALÈS** (industrial, pop: 44,000), 11km, or right through attractive **ANDUZE** and south into **Languedoc** (p. 155).

Causses and Cévennes

3 days/270km/from Florac (on N106 between Mende and Alès)

The gentle slopes of the Cévennes, where the southern hills of the Massif Central become Languedoc's northern uplands, are green with tough wild scrub, forests of sweet chestnut and pine, open heath and fields of pasture. Little rivers and streams rush through the meadows and woods.

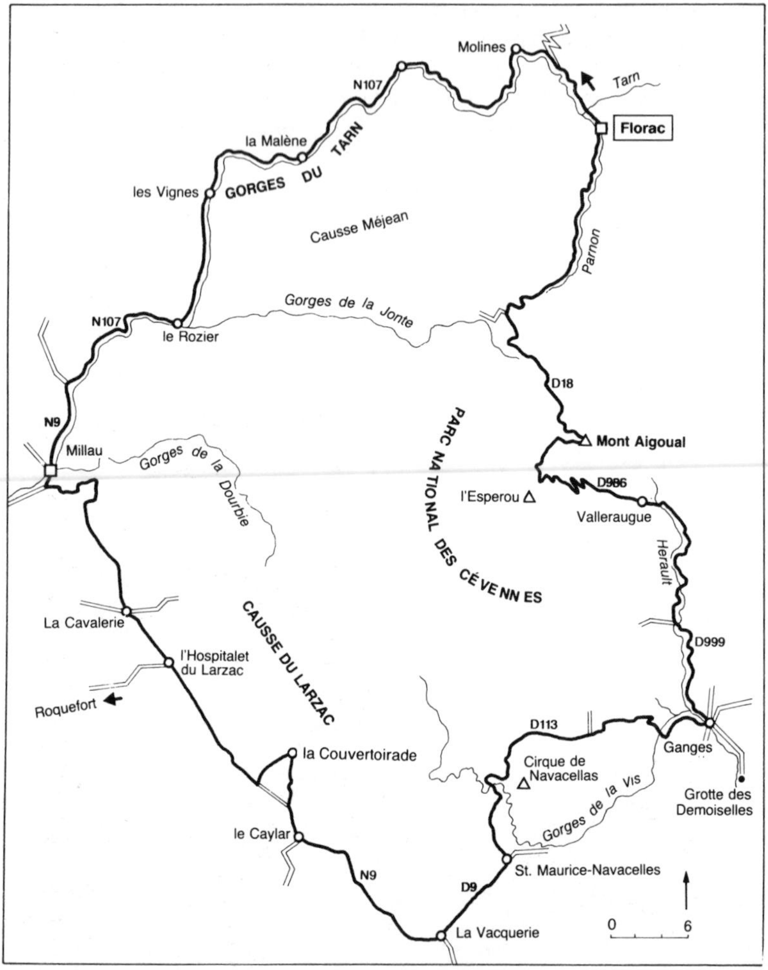

During the Wars of Religion the people of the Cévennes endured quite fantastic repression which they resisted with considerable violence, especially during the 18C Camisard War (see Stevenson's Route, p. 110). Rising away west of the hill country is the region of high plateaux, the *causses*, weatherworn limestone *massifs* divided one from the other by deep narrow river gorges. The whole region, *causses* and Cévennes, is marked by strange geological phenomena and honeycombed with curious grottoes and caverns. The great empty plateaux landscapes, impressively bleak, have a mysterious, compelling atmosphere. Living in simple villages, the few inhabitants are mostly shepherds with a ferocious pride and independence of spirit.

This is a route best tackled in summer. It can be difficult driving, in parts, at any time of year. As early as October, or as late as April, some of the roads become impassable. But the reward is scenery — landscapes as striking as any in France — and a profound feeling of remoteness from the rest of the country, and from the present day. (Use Michelin map 80.)

From **FLORAC** (see Stevenson's Route p. 110 for details) follow N106 north beside the Tarn river, turning left onto D907bis (direction Ste.

Gorges du Tarn

Énimie) to stay with the Tarn. After Molines, the valley walls rise to give the first inkling of the coming gorge. The **Gorges du Tarn** is a spectacular sight, well known to the French and to many foreign tourists. The narrow road twists through the plunging river canyon steeply enclosed by massive and overhanging rocks, fascinatingly coloured and over 500m high in places. Be prepared to meet quite a lot of traffic on this road during the summer-holiday months. The Tarn here carves its way between the Causse de Sauveterre and the Causse Méjean, altogether a journey of some 70km.

While the *causses* above are windswept and inhospitable, in the river valley there is striking alternation between areas whose grandeur defies human habitation and pockets of cultivation where old stone cottages cluster together: one wonders at the life that must have been led in these isolated villages, hemmed in by the overpowering might of the rocks, when the only access was on long and tortuous donkey tracks. Yet along the way are châteaux hidden among the trees, where presumably something resembling a lordly life was once led.

Main focus of the Gorges du Tarn's tourism is the attractive village **STE. ÉNIMIE**, at the entrance of the deeper part of the gorge. It offers canoe and bicycle hire, drives and walks (GR60 passes through the village) together with plenty of cheap accommodation and places to eat. A narrow road crosses the river from St.Énimie and threads up to **Cirque de St. Chély**, giving a tremendous view.

Just before **LA MALÈNE**, 15C **Château de la Caze** (66.48.51.01), standing in lovely gardens planted with 100-year-old trees, is one of the finest of the valley's old châteaux and now a rather grand, peaceful, terribly expensive hotel-restaurant. Farther along the Tarn at **LES VIGNES**, the **Gévaudan** (66.48.81.55) is a nice little hotel-restaurant with inexpensive rooms and generous low-priced menu (wonderful desserts!).

On the clifftop above Les Vignes there is a vantage point, a *point sublime*, accessible by a series of hairpins, with a breathtaking view across this section of the gorge and the facing *causse*. The river sweeps round in an immense bend along this stretch (best appreciated from the water: boat trips available). One exciting (and very popular) way to experience the Tarn ravine is to travel in a flat-bottomed boat from La Malène down to Les Vignes — arguably the most impressive section.

LE ROZIER makes another good base for more thorough exploration of the area. Here the Tarn is joined by the **Gorges de la Jonte**, an impressive drive (on D996) which gives access as well to the **Aven Armand**, certainly the most awesome of this region's underground caverns, and probably the best in France. Inside it consists mainly of a vast cathedral-like chamber filled with a stone 'forest' of some 400 stalagmites.

It's a short drive, too, from Le Rozier onto Causse Noir to see the weird rock 'chaos' called **Montpellier le Vieux** because of its supposed resemblance to a ruined city. Canoes can be hired at Le Rozier, and several rewarding and sometimes difficult footpaths, including long distance GR6, converge upon the village. From Le Rozier continue (on either side of the river) to Millau.

MILLAU pop: 22,500 Commercial centre for *causses* region. Lively, attractive town, beautifully located beneath the Causse Noir and Causse du Larzac at the confluence of the Tarn and Dourbie rivers. See: small old central area; octagonal belfry; fountain; 18C wash-house. Traditionally noted for glove-making and leather goods. SI: pl des Arcades. Several good inexpensive restaurants: **Buffet de la Gare** beside the railway station; **Restaurant Capion**, 3 rue J-F. Alméras (Gault Millau toque — mainly for the 'fresh, delicious desserts'); **La Mangeoire**, 8 bd de la Capelle. Comfortable inexpensive hotel with good restaurant: **International** (65.60.20.66) and, more expensive, **La Musardière** (quiet, gardens: 65.60.20.63) both with Michelin rosette and Gault Millau toque; and splendid **Château de Creissels** (65.60.16.59), genuine 12C château (with plumbing and creaky floorboards accordingly) in medieval village Creissels, 2km out of town on D592n (direction St. Affrique).

Take N9 (direction Montpellier) away from Millau; the road climbs in broad steep turns — giving superb views back across the town — onto the **Causse du Larzac**, largest of the region's plateaux. This ages-old highway, now incongruously wide, runs fast and straight as if eager to reach the other side of such strange terrain. First step on the journey is the Larzac's bleak little 'capital', **LA CAVALERIE**.

Larzac made news for a while, during the late 1970s, when the small army camp at La Cavalerie was greatly increased in size and importance. The local peasants, who had never much objected to the smaller barracks, suddenly exploded into a fury of opposition to the larger base. A federation called Paysans du Larzac was formed to organise resistance. Their tough anti-army demonstrations and sabotage attracted supporters from all over France; Larzac became the unlikely venue for huge rock concerts and festivals to raise money for the *paysans*. The word 'Larzac' became an often-seen graffiti painted on walls from here to Lyon, a slogan for opposition to the State, army, central Government and Paris bureaucrats, and in favour of all things southern and rural. Before his election victory of 1981, François Mitterrand made it part of his policy that he would restore the army camp to its original size. He did indeed carry out this promise, and calm has returned to La Cavalerie. Meanwhile, the army has moved its larger camp, with Mitterrand's blessing, to less hotheaded terrain in the backcountry of Provence.

N9 rushes from La Cavalerie to equally unprepossessing **L'HOSPITALET DU LARZAC**, its name a reminder of the Knights Templar and then Knights Hospitaller who once ruled Larzac — and much of the rest of this region. For an excursion away from our route, take D23 from l'Hospitalet to **ROQUEFORT-SUR-SOULZON**, a modest village with only one claim to fame; a fame which is, however, not inconsiderable. For in its extensive Cambalou caves all the world's Roquefort cheese is matured. A bacteria living in the air here turns the local sheeps' cheese into that distinctively rich, creamy and sharp blue cheese praised by Roman poets and emperors and everyone since, and served at all the best restaurants in the country. (The caves can be visited.)

After l'Hospitalet, minor turning D185 on left leads from N9 to **LA COUVERTOIRADE**, a walled town of the Knights Templar. It has changed little since the 12C neither in appearance, nor even, one suspects, in the manner of life carried on within its fortifications, though with a much smaller population. With barefaced effrontery, the remaining locals charge visitors money simply to enter the gates of their town! At La Couvertoirade there's an example of the interesting dewponds used all over the Larzac to collect drinking water for the large flocks of sheep. Because of its porosity, the plateau has no natural ponds or freshwater.

A narrow road returns to N9 close to **LE CAYLAR**. *Cay* means rock in the old Occitan language, and this simple village is named for strange, chaotic large rocks scattered on the earth nearby, visible from the road. Here leave N9, taking D9 to St. Pierre de la Fage and D25 to St. Maurice-Navacelles. Alternatively, travel to St. Maurice-Navacelles on very minor D152 (turning on left 3km out of Le Caylar).

At St. Maurice-Navacelles take D130 to **Cirque de Navacelles**. This is a marvellous spectacle — a geography lesson brought to life. For what we see, from the vantage point of high clifftops, is an incised meander in the plunging, tortuous gorge of the aptly named river Vis: that is, a bend which so extravagantly doubled back on itself that the river eventually bypassed it altogether. Steep hairpin bends descend to the former riverbed, now a strange and rather exotic environment, cultivated by the inhabitants of Navacelles village.

Climb out of the Vis ravine on a road as convoluted as the river itself to reach Blandas. Continue on D113 through Montdardier, at the very limit of the *causse* country. Stay on D113, the narrow backroad which eventually meets the river Vis again — running straight and peaceful now — and crosses it to join D25, where turn left to go into **GANGES**. This unpretentious little town is still known in the trade for its silk stockings, a centuries-old traditional local manufacture, although one imagines that sales must have fallen considerably in recent decades! (Worthwhile trip from Ganges: 5km south on D986, **Grotte des Demoiselles**, impressive network of caves and tunnels reached by underground funicular railway.)

Travel north from Ganges on D999 into the exquisite hill country around **Mont Aigoual** (Occitan *aiguilhe*, needle), itself usually shrouded in mist. At (industrial) Pont d'Hérault, turn right onto D986, a lovely road along the valley of the young river Hérault. (Le Rey, a few hundred metres beyond this junction, has a comfortable and peaceful hotel **Château du Rey**, with excellent restaurant, in restored 13C castle. Closed winter: 67.82.40.06.) At **VALLERAUGUE**, hardy walkers might brave the old and difficult footpath which goes direct from here to the summit of Aigoual (allow a full day). Drivers may feel that it might have been easier to take the footpath, for after Mas-Méjean (here entering the Parc National des Cévennes) the road becomes extremely winding as it climbs the Esperou *massif* before embarking on the final ascent to the top of Aigoual. In clear weather (infrequent) the view from Aigoual's summit (1,567m — highest point in the Cévennes) is astonishing, and takes in the Pyrenees, Alps and Mediterranean. There's a Meteorological Observatory up here, and an 'orientation table' to point out what is visible.

The descent on D18 is easier, though the road is narrow in places. Much of the route is heavily wooded with fir, beech and chestnut. At the foot of Causse Méjean D18 meets D996, where turn right to skirt the base of the plateau all the way back into Florac.

*

Products of the pig, seen in every farmyard throughout this most rural and traditional region, dominate the local cuisine. Pork, ham, bacon, sausages and all sorts of charcuterie feature in most dishes. Lard is the main cooking fat. Lentils, beans and cabbage are much-used, too — but usually in conjunction with pork or ham. The style of cooking is robust, unpretentious and simple. Slow-cooked meat-and-vegetable stews are a particular regional favourite. Of course, there's plenty of river fish, too, as well as sheep from the mountain pastures, and abundant wild produce such as mushrooms, chestnuts and — gathered in vast quantities — myrtilles *(bilberries or blueberries). Specialities include a rich chestnut soup (cousinat), a hearty pork-and-vegetable stew with lots of cabbage (potée auvergnate), stuffed sheep's feet (tripoux) and potato, ham and cheese omelette (omelette brayaude). But perhaps the main gastronomic treat in the Massif Central is cheese: scores of different sorts are produced, almost all using traditional farmhouse methods. Most often seen are Cantal (hard cheddar-like cows' milk cheese, either strong, mild, or 'entre-deux') and Roquefort (exquisite tangy but creamy ewes' milk blue cheese from the plateau of Larzac); there are other blues like Bleu d'Auvergne and Fourme d'Ambert, as well as Fourme de Laguiole (bitingly strong cows' milk cheese), little rounds of strong goats' milk cheese from every village, St. Nectaire (creamy and mild), Tomme d'Aligot (soft, sour, refreshing) and garlic-flavoured low fat Gaperon. Though not a great wine-producing region, a regional tradition is the distilling of strong aperitifs and liqueurs from local wild herbs and fruits: look out especially for potent spirits made from the herb verbena (verveine) and the mountain wildflower gentian (gentiane).*

8 THE DORDOGNE
(Périgord, Limousin, Quercy)

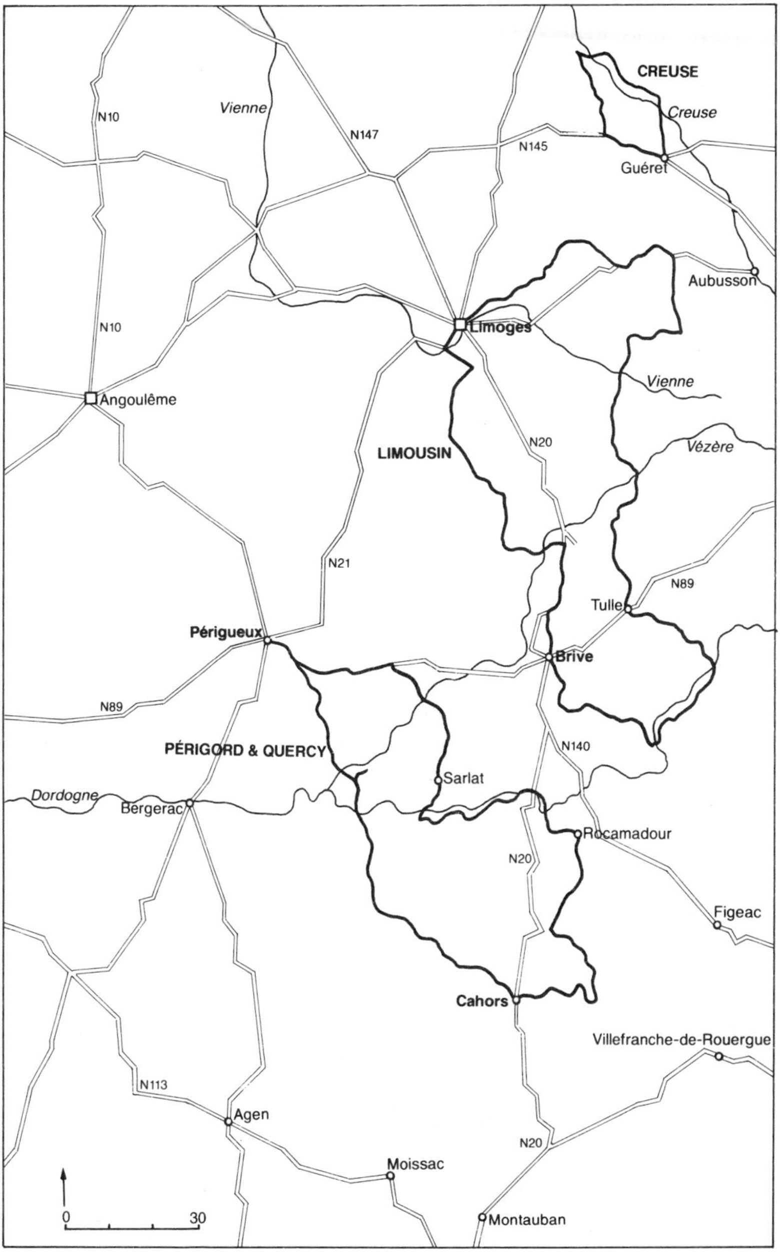

To the French, the Dordogne is simply a département; but to other Europeans and Americans the name conjures up a whole region, rustic and mellow, mild and beautiful, reaching the river Creuse in the north and as far as the Aveyron in the south and taking in all the départements between the western slopes of the Massif Central and the plains of the Atlantic and the Midi. Thus, with a foreigner's licence, we have effectively re-christened the former provinces of Périgord, Limousin and Quercy. Our Dordogne is characterised by its abrupt escarpments and hills, often topped by a castle, rising from gorgeous flowery meadows and magnificent valleys. Most beautiful of the rivers is the Dordogne itself, meandering lavishly and gently through the heart of the region. Narrow, secret country lanes give some wonderfully quiet picturesque drives. The region is noted, too, for its prehistoric sites, including caves with some of the oldest and best-preserved wall-paintings in the world. And not least of its attractions, the Dordogne has a long tradition of fine cooking and high-quality farm produce, abundantly displayed at colourful open-air markets in the backstreets and squares of almost every little town.

Périgord and Quercy

4 days/380km/from Périgueux

This is the tourists' Dordogne, and in a few places we shall make no effort to avoid them, because the sights everyone is flocking to see are well worth the inconvenience — marvellous traces of our prehistoric beginnings, feudal castles and fortifications, tremendous natural landscapes . . . and captivatingly pretty little country towns and villages. Note though that visitors to this region are somehow not quite the same as vacationers bound for Mediterranean beaches; their pace is slower, their interest in France greater, and clearly they have chosen this region because they appreciate gentle countryside and good restaurants — in both of which it excels. Nevertheless, along most of the route we shall discover that even in this popular touring area it is quite possible to leave the crowd far behind. (Use Michelin maps 75 & 79.)

PÉRIGUEUX pop: 35,400 Ancient capital of Périgord, now prosperous préfecture of Dordogne département. Old central area around river Isle has many interesting and attractive buildings, most striking of them being the unusual 12C Cathedral, with strong Byzantine influence (not benefited, however, by 19C 'restoration'). See also: 12C Romanesque Basilica of St. Front; Musée du Périgord containing what little survives of the city's Roman period; colourful street markets (Wednesdays and Saturdays). SI: av d'Aquitaine; Office de Tourisme: 16 rue Wilson.

Take D710 south from the town, through wooded hills, to **LE BUGUE** on the **Vézère river**. This valley has the most amazing concentration of prehistoric sites. Seemingly, along the length of the river as it passes

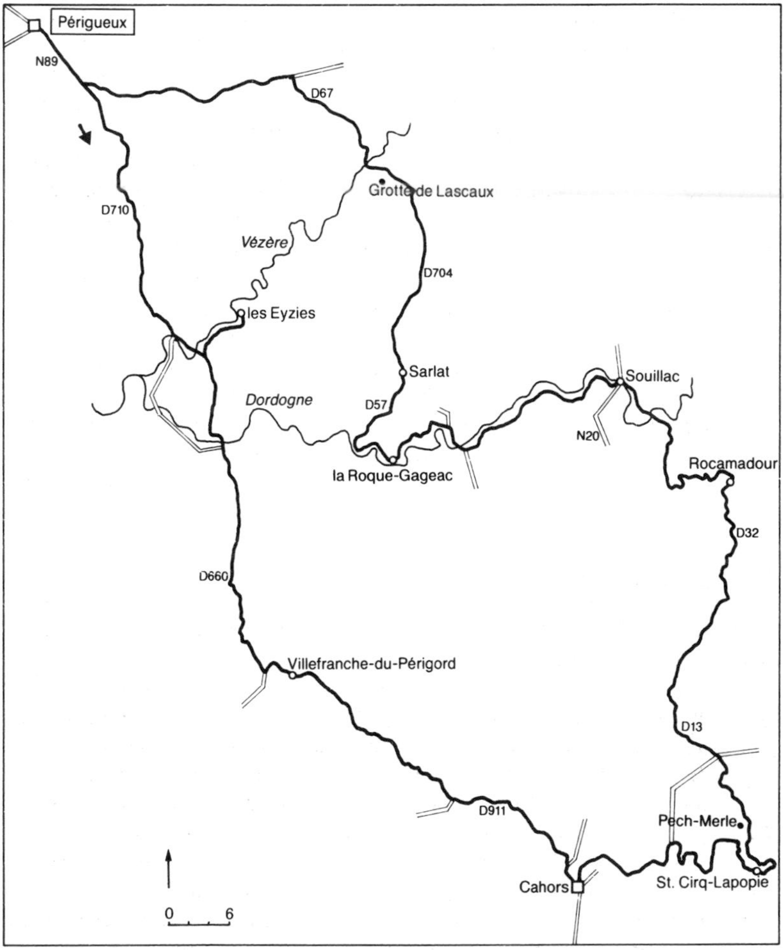

through this region, considerable numbers of people gathered together during the Palaeolithic (Stone Age) period, hunting mammoth, living in caves, where, on the walls, they painted pictures with a devastating elegance and simplicity, and, in effect, creating — 30,000 years ago — our human society. One is tempted to look around at the beauty and richness of the surroundings and say 'Stone Age Man was no fool to live here'. But in fact, although the Vézère flowed then as it does now, everything else looked quite different: these earlier men and women were living in the middle of an Ice Age. No fools though, to find, at such a time, a place abundant with water, shelter and game.

Le Bugue itself has the Grotte de Bara-Bahau (open summer only), with prehistoric engravings, but just 11km east along the river is **LES**

EYZIES-DE-TAYAC, around which are grouped several of the most impressive and important prehistoric cave dwelling sites in the world. Some of these cannot be visited, partly because they have no suitable paths for busloads of visitors, and partly because the temperature and content of the air inside the caves is altered, to the detriment of the wall-paintings, by the breath of so many people. It was the cool, never-changing conditions which allowed these pictures to remain undamaged by the passage of time. The best of the things which can be seen are: the National Prehistory Museum (a remarkably good overview of the subject, clearly showing the importance of the Vézère valley); the Font de Gaume cave (superb coloured wall-paintings); Combarelles cave (rock engravings).

Be warned that although the caves themselves will not disappoint, the coaches and crowds can make the visit a trying experience. Entrance to the caves is limited to 700 people per day, so for much of the year tickets have to be bought in advance. This can be very awkward, as the ticket office is only open for a couple of hours in the morning and a couple in the afternoon — a lengthy wait is almost unavoidable. Those lucky enough to get tickets are whisked rapidly round the caves in large groups. Remember too that, as usual, everything is closed on Tuesday. (If daunted by these obstacles at les Eyzies, bear in mind that there are other opportunities later in the route to see similar sights, for example at Pech-Merle.)

This whole area is packed with enticing family-run hotels and excellent, inexpensive restaurants. In les Eyzies, 2-star Logis **Le Centre** (53.06.97.13) offers a friendly welcome, pretty rooms and a shady garden, as well as superb food at very reasonable prices. More luxurious places include the well-equipped Relais et Château and 3-star Logis **Le Centenaire** (2 rosettes, 2 toques: 53.06.97.18); and, standing in 2-hectare grounds, the moderately priced **Cro-Magnon** hotel (1 rosette, 2 toques: 53.06.97.06).

Return along D706 as far as Campagne, where turn left onto D703. Cross the Dordogne river into Siorac-en-Périgord (hotel-restaurant **Scholly** is a quiet, civilised 3-star Logis: 53:31.60.02), where pick up the D710, and continue south on this road through **BELVÈS**, a fortified village with many medieval and Renaissance buildings. After another 20km across wooded country turn left (D660) into **VILLEFRANCHE-DU-PÉRIGORD**, a *bastide* with the arcaded main square and fine covered market typical of these fortified medieval 'new towns', as well as a pleasant woodland setting and good views. D660 continues winding through the trees towards Cahors. Pause at **FRAYSSINET-LE-GÉLAT**, a village tucked away in the crook of the hills; it has some well-placed café tables. There is a certain amount of logging here and at neighbouring Goujounac. D660 joins D911 (direction Cahors). At **MERCUÈS** the road reaches the river Lot (pronounce the *t*, both for the river and the *département*). Just here a broad weir breaks the flow of the river, overlooked by a château on a high hill. There's also some intriguing railway engineering which tags along beside the road all the way into Cahors!

CAHORS pop: 21,000 Capital of Quercy, now préfecture of the Lot département. Industrial at edges, but agreeable, rather southern atmosphere. Important local market (Wednesdays and Saturdays). Striking location on a bend in the river Lot, which is crossed by splendid 14C fortified Pont Valentré. See also: curious Divona spring (near Valentré bridge); interesting Cathedral (note: nave roof, north portal with Romanesque tympanum, 11C bell tower, 16C cloisters); medieval Badernes quarter. Syndicat d'Initiative is in pl A. Briand (and summer annexe by Pont Valentré).

(For a good one-day deviation from our route, follow the SI's marked drive through the Cahors wine area.) Cahors' historic vineyards, one of very few wine-producing districts in the Dordogne region, lie mainly west of the city, on both sides of the river. The wine itself is a rich, substantial red, full of flavour, and dark in colour. Romans sang its praises, and in the Middle Ages it was exported all over Europe. In the Eastern Orthodox Church, the Mass wine is called 'Cahors', because in the early days of Christianity it actually came from here.

Leave Cahors on D653 (direction Figeac), following the Lot upstream. After 15km stay with the river by turning right onto D662. Go through St. Géry and, soon after, cross the river into Bouziès. Take winding little D40 (great views across river) into **ST. CIRQ-LAPOPIE**. (Alternatively, find your way from Cahors on the D8, on the south side of the river).

St. Cirq truly is a place to savour, a wonderful medieval village of lanes and old houses built in steep, rambling terrain overhanging the Lot valley. There's nothing nicer to do here than stroll, admiring the old dwellings, restored and unrestored, or sit at a table outside the Auberge du Sombral by the main square, sipping a Fenelon, the local aperitif (Cahors wine with a dash of Crème de Cassis and Crème de Noix). Take a look, too, at the Renaissance church. St. Cirq can, however, become overcrowded with visitors at times: best plan is to arrive here in late afternoon when most of them have left, and stay overnight. **Le Sombral** (65.31.26.08) is a comfortable 1-star Logis in 'rustic' style, with excellent *menus* at reasonable prices. More expensive **Hôtel de la Pelissaria** (only 6 rooms, phone ahead: 65.31.25.14) is beautiful, unusual, the rooms with simple elegance and wonderful views.

Leave the village by crossing the Lot on a tiny bridge (D181), from which St. Cirq looks like a superb fairy-tale hamlet overhanging the valley. Once across the river, turn left (D662), and immediately right (D41), to follow the rocky escarpments of the lovely Célé valley into **CABRERETS**. This, too, is a village of great charm in a marvellous setting (with several good Logis and, 2km out on the Figeac road, an excellent, peaceful hotel-restaurant, **La Pescalerie**: 65.31.22.55). Right beside the village (on D13) are the caves of **Pech Merle**. Here, after *relatively* little waiting, groups are taken round by a guide in one of the most remarkable Stone Age sites. Some of the items pointed out by the guide are of doubtful interest, and others are mere natural phenomena, which — no matter how wonderful — cannot compare with the glorious sight of wall-paintings done 20,000 years ago by artists as great as any today.

Animals are shaped to the form of the rock on which they are painted, giving a vaguely three-dimensional quality — imagine them lit by flickering flamelight, instead of the guide's probing torch, and they almost leap off the walls. Ignore too the academics' theories about the 'function' or 'purpose' of this delicious art gallery: the truth is that no one knows why these pictures were painted. We do have some contact with their artists, though, for many of the works are signed, and in a most original way: with a handprint. This almost personal contact with another human being across such a chasm of centuries sharply reinforces a feeling that societies, behaviour, language, technology, everything may change but that we as people remain much the same.

Continue up D13 along the gorgeous valley of the Sagne. At D653 turn left, and carry on until D32 on the right, where turn for Labastide-Murat. All this is magnificent typical Dordogne landscape. At Labastide-Murat turn right onto D667; after 8km D32 reappears on the left: take this turning (direction Rocamadour). Stay with this road through woods and fields and lovely walking or picnicking country. After Couzou, the scenery becomes more dramatic, the road overhung by cliffs as it arrives at spectacular **ROCAMADOUR**.

Though crowded and popular this fortified medieval village deserves a visit. It is not yet thoroughly spoiled, and the setting is quite exceptional, the houses seemingly stuck onto the side of a sheer cliff face overlooking the deep Alzou valley. The place owes its existence and fame to a mysterious hermit called Amadour who supposedly lived in one of the caves in the rock face. At the very top of this vertiginous village, reached by going up 263 steps (which pilgrims climb on their knees), is a 12C Basilica. Enclosing a small, beautiful square or courtyard in front of the Basilica are 7 intriguing chapels, together with the cave in which St. Amadour's body was claimed to have been discovered here in 1166. It is well worth seeing inside the chapels if possible: there are guided visits at certain times. Tiny Chapelle St. Michelle is the most curious if not the most beautiful, with remarkable frescoes and with ceiling and wall made only by the bare rock. A path leads higher, from the Basilica to the clifftop castle and ramparts; originally 14C, it has been ridiculously over-restored but has marvellous views.

For an unhurried drive through lovely countryside, leave Rocamadour on D673 to **CALÈS**, where turn right onto D23, by-passing **LACAVE** (grottoes). Pass through little Belcastel with its storybook clifftop château. Takle D43 on the left, past the 14-17C **Château de la Treyne** (now a luxurious riverside hotel: 65.32.66.66), and cross the Dordogne river. Continue on D43 into **SOUILLAC**, a likeable small town with an old quarter (see: 12C Abbey Church; 15C tower) and, along the busy main street, a couple of good inexpensive restaurants and pleasant cafés with tables set well back from the traffic. **Hôtel des Ambassadeurs** (65.32.78.36) is a 2-star Logis with character, and reasonable restaurant, on the main road. The **Grand Hôtel** (65.32.78.30) occupies a most

La Roque-Gageac

unusual old building. There are also a couple of 3-star Logis; the **Renaissance** (excellent cheap menus: 65.32.78.04) and, quiet and peaceful, **les Granges Vieilles** (65.37.80.92).

Cross the river on main through-road N20, turning right at once onto exquisite minor road D43 (changes to D50), which follows the course of the Dordogne. Stay on this road through a succession of small villages until reaching D704, turn right to return to the Dordogne's right bank. On the other side of the river, take D703 on the left, passing the gorgeous village and castle of **MONTFORT**, perhaps popping over the river again (on D46) to visit the 'Cité Mediéval' of **DOMME**, a delightful, though touristy, wonderfully well preserved 13C French bastide. D703 soon reaches **LA ROQUE GAGEAC**. Here the village rising abruptly from the riverside clambers precariously up a steep cliff. Local builders must have a head for heights! A few km after the village, take D49 (changes to D57) into **SARLAT-LE-CANÉDA**, which has been called 'the most satisfying town in the Dordogne'.

Its location, close to many of the region's most interesting sights, is exceptional. And though rather commercialised, and rather sprawling at the edges, nevertheless the town retains at its centre a tremendous amount of medieval and Renaissance character. Its old alleyways and narrow streets deserve leisurely exploration, and numerous fine 17C buildings strike the eye, as well as several which are much older, such as 14C Hôtel Plamon. Make a point of strolling down impressive rue des Consuls, and too, the fascinating unrestored quarter west of rue de la République. Sarlat is an important local agricultural centre, with large weekly (Saturday) and monthly markets. The Office de Tourisme is in pl de la Liberté.

Travel north from the town on D704, which arrives eventually at **MONTIGNAC**, a handsome old village in the Vézère valley next to the **Lascaux Caves**, the walls of which are decorated with some 1,500 extraordinary and colourful pictures of animals drawn in Palaeolithic (i.e., Stone Age) times. Disturbances in the temperature and humidity caused by allowing visitors into the caves damaged the paintings, so they were closed to the public in 1963. Since then, working laboriously for 10 years, a group of artists using the same materials and techniques as were used to draw the original pictures have managed to create inside an artificial cave (modelled very precisely on the real one) an astonishingly faithful replica of Lascaux. Called Lascaux II, it stands 200m from the original (closed Tuesday).

Head out of Montignac on D704, turning left at once onto D67. At Thenon, this meets busier N89, where turn left and return into Périgueux.

Limousin

3 days/430km/from Brive

Limousin is a clean, fresh countryside of trees, rivers and lakes, green hills, small farms and quiet roads. Once powerful, it's a land of castles too. The conservative but wholehearted character of the local people is proverbial; prosperous small farmers, they are unostentatious, traditional, hard-working, and down-to-earth, with a liking for good food served in unstinting portion. And, in the towns, Limousin has long been noted for its ancient crafts: tapestry, enamelling and, more recently (since 18C), porcelain. Relative to the area to its south, this is the 'off-the-beaten track' part of the Dordogne region — yet just as well served with excellent restaurants and attractive little hotels. (Michelin maps 72 & 75.)

From **BRIVE-LA-GAILLARDE** (pop: 54,000; thriving regional industrial and agricultural centre) travel north on N20 to **UZERCHE**, a

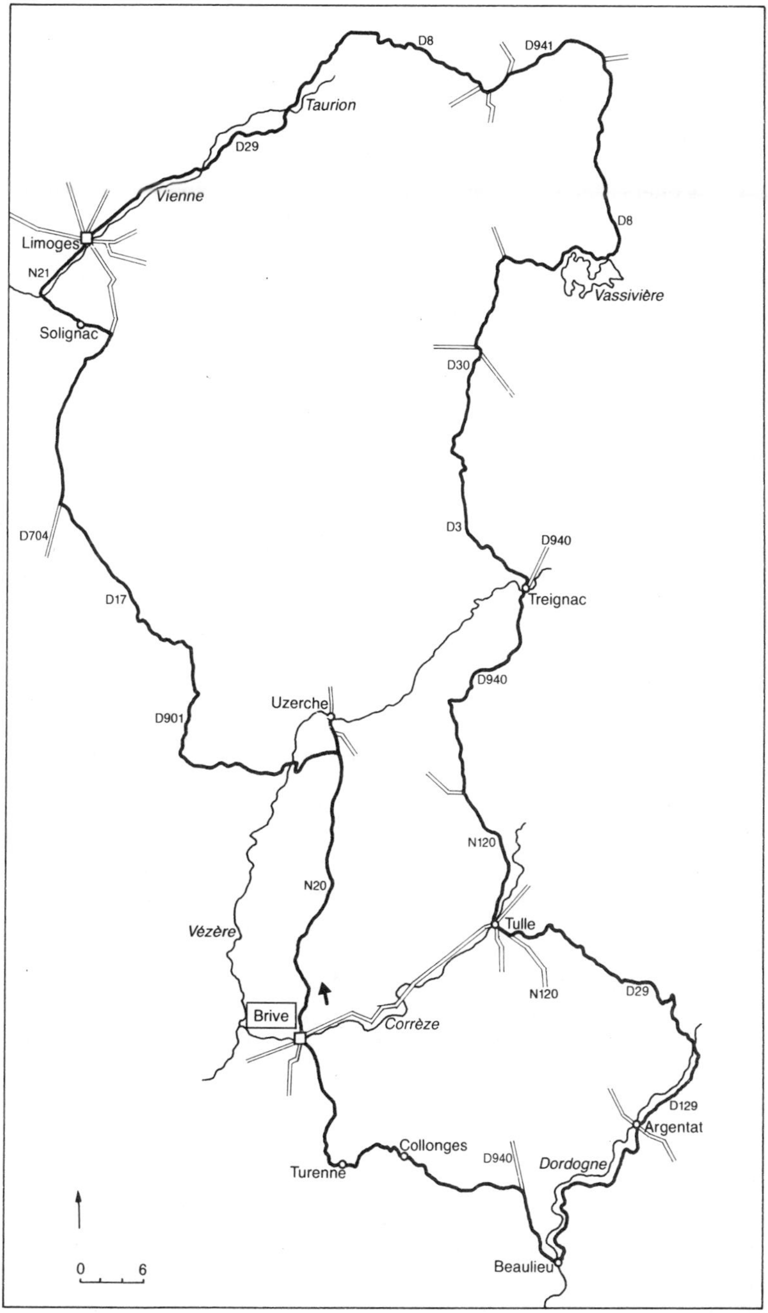
D8
D941
Taurion
D29
Vienne
Limoges
N21
Solignac
D8
Vassivière
D30
D704
D3
D940
Treignac
D17
D940
Uzerche
D901
N120
N20
Vézère
Tulle
N120
D29
Brive
Corrèze
D129
Argentat
Collonges
D940
Dordogne
Turenne
0
6
Beaulieu

suitably spectacular introduction to this overlooked region. The saying is, 'A house in Uzerche, a castle in Limousin.' For this country town, poised elegantly on a promontory above a great bend in the Vézère river, contains numerous fortified and turreted 15/16C mansions. So well-defended is the town by its location and its walls that it has confidently withstood attacks during every period of turmoil, and never once been taken by enemy forces — hence its maidenly motto 'Non Polluta' (never despoiled). That explains, too, why Uzerche has been so extraordinarily unaffected by the passage of centuries. See the 12C Romanesque Church of St. Pierre and the 14C gateway Porte Bécharie. Stroll along rue Pierre-Chalaud with its unusual old houses, and round to La Lunade Esplanade, from which the view across the Vézère is marvellous. Syndicat d'Initiative (summer only) is in pl Lunade.

Return 4km along N20 as far as D3 on the right, where turn to reach **POMPADOUR** (properly, Arnac-Pompadour), important to the French for two things, the 15C Château de Pompadour (never actually occupied by the famous 18C Marquise to whom Louis XV gave the title), and the adjacent stables of the National Stud. Both are open to the public on guided tours, and while neither commands quite the same interest to foreigners as to the French, they make an interesting excursion. The moated Château, with its mighty towers, is especially impressive from outside, and the stables are as enjoyable for the peaceful countryside setting as anything else. Small 2-star Logis **Auberge de la Marquise** (55.73.33.98) can provide straightforward rooms and an excellent meal.

Take D901 north from Pompadour, through **LUBERSAC** (château and Romanesque church), to **COUSSAC-BONNEVAL** (impressive 14–18C château; 12C lantern of the dead). Here turn right onto minor D17, which follow to **LA ROCHE-ABEILLE**. Just before entering this modest village you'll discover, in a 16C waterside mill, the marvellous hotel-restaurant **Moulin de la Gorce**. With just a handful of delightful rooms and first-rate (though not cheap) *menus*, 'this really is the most seductive halt in Limousin' according to Gault Millau (2 toques: 55.00.70.66). Continue on D17 to D704, where turn right (direction Limoges). After 18km turn left into **SOLIGNAC**. The abbey founded here in AD 632 was destroyed and rebuilt a number of times before the present interesting Romanesque abbey church was constructed in 1143. Despite many misfortunes, including being turned into a prison after the Revolution, it remains in surprisingly good condition. The interior is spacious, with a pleasing simplicity (note: 4 domes over nave; frescoes; 15C stalls). Close by, hidden among flowery meadows and fields down a lane on the bank of the Briance, **Restaurant Pradepont** (55.00.50.40) offers excellent meals in a tranquil setting. To find it, follow D32 (direction Pont-Rompu) for about 1½km out of Solignac; the restaurant (signposted) is down a track on the left.

Follow picturesque D32 to l'Aiguille, where cross the Vienne and turn right onto N21, which rushes into Limoges.

LIMOGES pop: 144,100 Capital of Limousin and busy préfecture of

Haute-Vienne département. Sprawling and unattractive at the edges, but with well-preserved old central area (many streets pedestrianised). Noted for fine enamel work, which can be bought from numerous small workshops, and also for porcelain. Formerly stained glass was another of the city's skills, as can be seen from some gorgeous windows in the impressive 12–16C Cathedral (and note: Gothic north entrance; Renaissance rood screen; 14C tombs). Several streets lined with interesting old houses, especially around rue du Temple and rue de la Boucherie, and tiny pl St. Aurelien (with amazing, lavishly decorated little chapel dedicated to patron saint of butchers, St. Aurelien). See also: Palais de l'Ancien Evêque, beside Cathedral; 14C St. Michel-des-Lions; Enamels Museum in Jardin de l'Évêché. Big daily markets at pl de la Motte and pl des Bancs. Syndicat d'initiative is in bd de Fleurus.

Unspoiled and beautiful countryside, green and hilly, extends in almost every direction from the city. Behind the cathedral at Limoges flows the Vienne river, and beside it, the D29, which escapes from the city streets along the exquisite valley. Take this road northeast to St. Priest-Taurion, where the Vienne is joined by the Taurion (or Thaurion). Stay on D29, which follows the Taurion valley. On meeting D5 turn left to reach the **Pont du Dognon**, a narrow iron suspension bridge. A dam farther down-river has created a lovely lake along this part of the Taurion. Just here are (despite their unprepossessing exteriors) two luxurious, utterly tranquil and inexpensive places to eat or to stay: **Le Chalet du Lac** (55.57.10.05)and, across the bridge, **Le Rallye** (55.56.56.11). Both have magnificent views across the water.

Soon after crossing the bridge, retrieve D29 on the right, and follow this meandering route (changes to D8) to **CHÂTELUS-LE-MARCHEIX**, well-sited above the Taurion. Continuing through the village, stay on D8 which twists and turns all the way into **BOURGANEUF**, where two 15C towers survive of a Knights Hospitaller castle. From here take D941, through Pontarion, shortly after which at St. Hilaire-le-Château is friendly, relaxed, moderately priced 3-star Logis **Hôtel du Thaurion** with well-equipped rooms and a first-rate restaurant (2 toques: 55.64.50.12).

Turn south at St. Hilaire, taking D34 (joins D8) across the countryside to the large (and quite resort-y) Lac de Vassivière. Turn right on meeting the lake, and drive around its north shore following signs (via D222/D13) to Peyrat-le-Château. At Peyrat, turn left onto D940, going through **EYMOUTIERS**, an ancient country town on the young river Vienne, and **TREIGNAC**, also very old, an attractive small town built rising up from the rushing Vézère (note: 15C houses; Gothic bridge; castle ruins; curious church). Away to the east rises the Plateau de Millevaches. There are not, incidentally, anything like a thousand cows on this great granite Limousin plateau; the name is said to be a corruption of local dialect from the more accurate title Thousand Streams. Stay on D940 into picturesque Tulle.

TULLE pop: 21,000 Préfecture of Corrèze département. The town threads along beside the river within the narrow and confined valley of the twisting Corrèze. Buildings climb up from the river in terraces. Unusual 12/13C Cathedral, around which small medieval *Enclos* quarter, with narrow alleys and steps, retains the best of the town's old houses. **La Toque Blanc** (55.26.75.41) is an excellent little *restaurant avec chambres* offering remarkable value for money. SI: quai Baluze.

Leave the town on N120 (direction Aurillac), soon turning left onto D978 and immediately right onto D29. Stay on this pretty and meandering minor road (watch signs carefully) via La Roche-Canillac and St. Martin-la-Méanne to the Chastang Dam in the **Dordogne Gorge**. Cross the river here, and at once turn right (D129) to follow the gorge closely, with some good views, all the way to **ARGENTAT**, entered by crossing the river on an old stone bridge. Its many interesting and picturesque old houses give this likeable waterside town great charm.

For a magnificent little journey along the river Dordogne, return across the bridge to the south bank, immediately turning right onto tiny D116, which threads its way peacefully to **BEAULIEU-SUR-DORDOGNE**.

Collonges-la-Rouge

Here cross again to the river's north bank to enter the town. Beaulieu's remarkable 12C Romanesque abbey church has a superb tympanum over the south doorway, and among other fine enamelled and gilt items in the Treasury there's a 12C silver-covered woodcarving of the Virgin. Facing the church's west doorway stands a Renaissance house, and all around are several other lovely old houses.

Take D940 north (direction Tulle) as far as D38 (direction Brive) on the left. Turn here and continue to **COLLONGES-LA-ROUGE**, which lies just off the road. Collonges is a curious place, with quite unusually fine buildings — and hardly a real village at all, because it has been so immaculately restored, and so snapped-up by wealthy outsiders, that there are almost no proper villagers left. Nevertheless, it is sheer delight to wander through its old gates into the traffic-free lanes of 15–17C red sandstone cottages decorated with turrets and spires and geraniums. There's a communal woodfired oven, still used on *fête* days and, next to the church (note tympanum), a tiny 10/11C Penitents' chapel with red walls and floor and beautifully vaulted ceiling. During the Wars of Religion, which tore at this region as much as any other, the church escaped destruction by dividing itself into two: half for Protestants and half for Catholics! Opposite the church entrance a strange statue faces into a wall; only its back can been seen. The tourist office says this represents a Bad Knight whose face is turned away from the church. A more popular view is that it symbolised a 'house of ill repute' — and that the church being so close was handy for those who wanted to confess afterwards. This seems equally improbable! Not only does Collonges manage to keep out all cars, but electricity cables are also hidden from view. The whole village has been declared a Monument Classé. Delightful little hotel-restaurant **Le Prieure** (55.25.41.00), in the village centre, offers a friendly atmosphere, good food and exceptional value for money.

Nearby **TURENNE** (continue on D38 for 5km; take D150 on the left) makes a striking contrast to Collonges, for its lofty ruined 14C fortress, and the 15/16C houses below, are all built of white limestone. The stern castle looks out far across a rich and peaceful countryside of little fields and hills and woods — all of which it commanded for centuries. The power of Turenne's lords was unquestionable, absolute, and extended over a considerable area of Limousin. However, it is said that their subjects (so long as they were obedient) were happy . . . and paid no tithes. The whole seigneurial court frequently moved to neighbouring Collonges (which is why that village has such splendid houses) as a summer outing. So great was their authority over the region that not until the 18C did the domain of the lords of Turenne become part of the Kingdom of France.

D8 returns from here through pleasing countryside into Brive.

Creuse Valley

1 day/100km/from Guéret (on N145 82km northeast of Limoges)

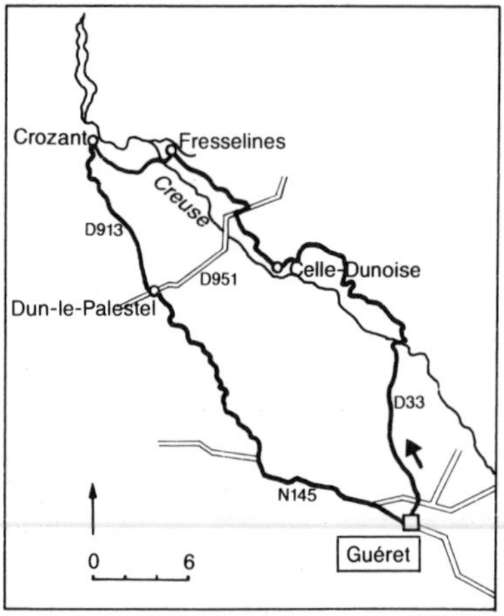

The river Creuse, flowing through its splendid valley in this tranquil corner of the Limousin, has a magnificence which strikes a contrast with the humble simplicity of the surrounding villages, quiet and industrious, where farmyards smell like farmyards, and incautious chickens cluck and wander in the roadways along which leisurely haycarts prevent any unseemly haste. (Michelin maps 68 & 72.)

GUÉRET, busy capital of the Creuse département, has an interesting old central area with an appealing produce market (Thursdays and Saturdays). Syndicat d'Initiative is at av Charles-de-Gaulle.

Take D33 out of town to delightful **ANZÊME**, with its leaning spire; cross the river (good view as road climbs on other side), soon veering left (D33) to **LE BOURG D'HEM**, which gives another good vantage point over the Creuse gorge.

Winding D48/D14 leads round to **LA CELLE-DUNOISE**; on a pleasant summer's evening I encountered no other tourists in this idyllic riverside village. Yet there are places to eat here, and places to stay, as well as a handsome Romanesque church.

A miniature lane runs from La Celle, through tiny Lavaud, to meet D951, where turn right and then immediately left (D78) to pass through la Buissière. Continue to **FRESSELINES**. Stop the car here and walk the short distance by footpath to the meeting point of the Creuse and Petite Creuse rivers — it's a lovely spot. From Fresselines take the road to **CROZANT**. On either side of the village are marvellous views from wooded heights over the river (in fact a lake, since it is dammed a few kilometres downstream), calm and wide in a green gorge. A modest hilltop ruin (11–15C) is the local 'sight' — but how unimportant it seems compared to the river and the valley! Several of the Impressionists came here, perhaps inspired by George Sand, who wrote 'Rien n'est plus beau que la Creuse en avril à cet endroit là' — Nothing is more beautiful than the Creuse in April at that spot. It was Crozant she was talking about. Sand's writings make it clear enough that she was especially affected by wild, natural scenery on the grand scale. Living at Nohant, which though so close by is in much tamer and milder country, Sand used often to make her way over here to walk or ride along the Creuse valley, or sit admiring it from one of the vantage points. The village has two inexpensive 1-star Logis. (A worthwhile excursion from Crozant is the journey along the right bank of the 'lake' to the dam at the other end.)

Joining D913, drive to **DUN-LE-PALESTEL**, the little main town of the area. It's bursting with flowers, and has a couple of 1-star Logis. Stay on D913 to St. Vaury, where turn left onto busier N145 and return into Guéret.

*

The goose and the truffle rule in the Dordogne region. Local specialities include that controversial food, pâté de foie gras (made by force-feeding geese with corn), as well as other pâtés, stuffed neck of goose (cou farci), wild cèpes (mushrooms) and, of course, that other curious wild fungus, growing underground and sniffed out by specially trained dogs, the truffle. Look out for omelettes made with either of the above; ducks or geese cooked in their own fat (confit); potatoes cooked in goose fat (pommes sarladaises); walnut salad (salade aux noix). To follow, try clafoutis, a delicious moist cake with cherries sunk into it. In the Limousin area, sausages and black pudding, freshly caught river fish, and chestnuts from the extensive woodlands, make a frequent appearance on menus. The Bordeaux region is right next door, but local wines come from Bergerac and, better, from Cahors — both are robust, full-flavoured reds.

9 ATLANTIC

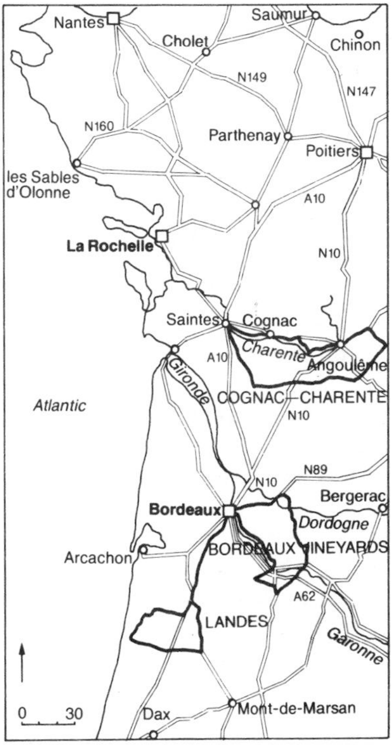

The story of the Atlantic region, ancient Aquitaine, shows more clearly than that of any other how French and English history are intertwined. When Eleanor of Aquitaine married Henry II of England in 1152, all her possessions became his. They included almost the whole of western France. It should be remembered though that Henry was himself no Englishman: a Plantagenet, he came from Anjou. And the language which he and Eleanor spoke was neither French nor English, but a French dialect, Gascon. Thus the union between Aquitaine and England does not seem so strange after all. For two centuries, the region lived peacefully as part of England, the population enjoying freedoms not known to the neighbouring French. But in time the tensions began to show, finally sparking off the bloody and divisive Hundred Years War (1356-1453) during which the Kingdom of France tried, and finally managed, to bring back this region into its domain. Attracted to Protestantism, the area suffered again during the Wars of Religion, which led to large-scale emigration of Huguenots to England. This part of France is mainly low-lying, crossed by numerous great rivers reaching down to the ocean. Yet it has astonishing variations in landscape, people and agriculture, ranging from extensive marshland, to long ocean-washed sandy beaches, to lush pasture, to the vast Landes pine forest. And though not, on the face of it, ideal grape-growing country, the Atlantic region produces not only enormous quantities of wine and spirits, but also some of the finest in the world.

Cognac-Charente

3 days/245km/from Saintes

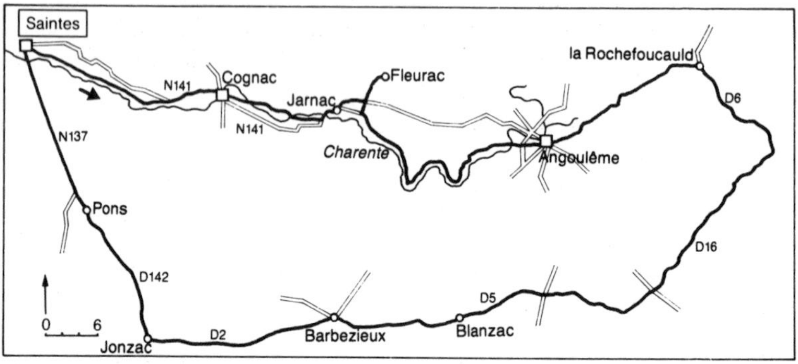

Cognac distillers reckon that the equivalent of 23 million bottles of their golden brew evaporates each year into the air over the green Charente countryside. Generously (though perhaps impiously) they call this the Angels' Share. The art of making the best brandy in the world developed and grew in this region alone because of a unique conjunction of circumstances: the right grapes, sharp and not too strongly flavoured; the ideal climate, mild and warm; the forests of Tronçonnais and Limousin not far away producing the perfect old oak wood in which to mature the brandy; and, of course, crucial to the whole operation, the broad Charente river, essential for carrying the wood and the filled casks. In the riverside villages and towns, the walls — inside and out — of cellars and distilleries are streaked black by a mould which lives exclusively on a little percentage taken from the Angels' Share. In the countryside all around, every farm beckons with signs offering home-made cognac and that other local concoction, Pineau de Charente, an aperitif with something of an acquired taste, made by maturing a mixture of cognac and grape pressings. Cheap they may be, but these farmhouse versions cannot be compared with the fine product which emerges from the great household-name cognac houses (which welcome visitors). Of course there's more to the Charente than its famous fiery *digestif*. Somehow it remains undiscovered, a connoisseur's region, a quiet undramatic land, simple and unpretentious, marvellous for peaceful drives and walks along country lanes and beside streams. Most fascinating of all, some combination of latitude and humidity gives to the sunlight over the Charente a curious pearly brightness, a gentle hazy brilliance. (Use Michelin map 72.)

SAINTES (formerly Xaintes) pop: 27,500 Industrialised market town on the Charente river with many remnants of a past going back well beyond Roman days. The medieval *vieille ville* surrounds 12–17C St. Pierre Cathedral on the river's south bank, and this was also the site of the

Roman city; the Roman bridge across the river (demolished as recently as 1842) reached over to the Arch of Germanicus (AD19), still standing. Close by is impressive Abbaye aux Dames, of which the best part is 11C Eglise Ste. Marie (note: doorways, curious domes, façade). Performances are given in the abbey during the town's summer Music Festival. See also: remnants of 1C Roman amphitheatre; the Archaeological Museum. Cruises on the Charente make an enjoyable excursion. Syndicat d'Initiative at Esplanade A. Malraux.

Leave Saintes towards Cognac, but instead of taking main road N141, travel beside the river on minor D24 through **PORT-HUBLÉ** (so called because it was once a river port on this important trading river), **CHANIERS** (Romanesque church), **MERPINS** (former Roman spa) and **ST. LAURENT** (mill).

COGNAC pop: 21,000 This town, which has given its name to the Charente's best-known product, is large enough and busy enough to have many other activities besides distilling. Yet it is the Cognac distilleries (*chais*) which give the town its character and aura of importance. Cognac houses based here include Camus, Hennessy, Martell. There's an interesting *vieille ville* with old timbered houses. See also: the Museum of Cognac (local life and traditions). Syndicat d'Initiative is at 16 rue du 14 juillet. Just out of town on N141 is the enticing (though not very expensive) hotel-restaurant **Logis de Beaulieu** (45.82.30.50).

Head east from Cognac beside the Charente's north bank; there are several small lanes, some not marked on the map, with glimpses of the wide river across neat vineyards. Take C7 if you can find it. At **BOURG-CHARENTE** (12C church; good restaurant **La Ribaudère**: 45.81.30.54) cross the water and continue on the south bank before returning over the river again to enter picturesque **JARNAC** (President Mitterrand's hometown). Park in the main square (just at north end of bridge) of this small town and explore on foot. Market days at this agreeable spot are Tuesday and Sunday.

Cognac cellar master

The Courvoisier cognac distillers, at one side of the square, give guided tours which are perhaps more leisurely and less known-about than those in Cognac. Here you will be told about the 100- to 250-year old oak needed to make the barrels in which to mature the new cognac;

the fact that local air humidity averages the exact percentage required to produce the best cognac; that tasters are a special breed who have to be trained for *20 years*: their palate and memory make and continue the unique style made by each of the cognac Houses (for each is different). The guide will take you into the cool dark cellars, with the heady atmosphere of the Angels' Share, where row upon row of barrels wait during long years to reach perfection. You will be shown the curious-looking contraption in which the wine is first distilled. And the all-important distinction between the different Charente grape-growing localities will be explained — with the Bois Ordinaires districts at the bottom, going through 3 more gradations before attaining the Petite Champagne and, at the top, the Grand Champagne area (just to the south-east of the town of Cognac).

For a wonderful overnight stop and first-rate dinner, from Jarnac take N141 (direction Angoulême), soon turning left on D157 to **FLEURAC**. Here the **Château de la Domaine de Fleurac** (45.81.78.22), a superb little restored castle with spacious and elegant bedrooms looking out over private gardens and woods, has become an unusual and utterly tranquil hotel-restaurant with surprisingly moderate prices. Ask for a cognac after dinner and they bring a 6-page list of them to choose from.

Return directly to the river from Fleurac on D157, crossing straight over main road N141, to reach the hamlet Triac, where turn left onto D22. Pass through **BASSAC** with its old Romanesque abbey, to Châteauneuf-sur-Charente, and on to (D84) **ST. SIMIEUX**, a lovely old village right on the waterside. Follow the road (becomes D7, D72) through Sireuil and eventually into Angoulême.

ANGOULÊME pop: 50,200 Préfecture of the Charente département. The busy newer parts of town encircle the raised-up and fortified older centre. From these quieter heights there are good views across the surrounding country, best seen by walking around the ramparts. A great bend in the Charente river below the town is impressive. There are many interesting old buildings: Renaissance houses, 2 towers of the former château, 12C cathedral (note: façade; bell tower), and more. The Syndicat d'Initiative is in the Hôtel de Ville, rebuilt in 19C in former 13C style.

Take N141 across the Branconne woods to **LA ROCHEFOUCAULD**, a small old town on the Tardoire river. Here stands 11/16C Château de Rochefoucauld, the decaying pile of the ancient Rochefoucauld family, former rulers of much of Charente, who still own the castle but have clearly given up any interest in the building. It's now terribly decrepit but still striking and romantic with its spired turrets, high walls, and pretty riverside location above a broad brushing weir. Small modestly priced hotel-restaurant **La Vieille Auberge** (45.62.02.72), a grand old stone building with dark beams, fine woodwork and antique furniture, has character.

This is the edge of the cognac-producing region; if not distilled, the local wines are drunk 'green', that is, very young. In this area, much troubled during the Hundred Years War and the Wars of Religion, many of the isolated older farmhouses are heavily fortified. Some are walled and turreted, and look almost like miniature castles. There are walled hamlets too.

From La Rochefoucauld, take D6 along the valley of the Tardoire, to **MONTBRON** (12/15C château). Turn right onto D16, crossing rolling farmland and woodland to **MARTHON**. This village, with its narrow old streets, little river, 12C church and small ivy-covered château, makes a very pleasant pause. Beyond Marthon the country becomes wilder and more wooded. Carry on to Villebois-Lavalette, where turn right onto D5. Stay on this road to **BLANZAC** village (note: interesting and unusual interior of 12/13C Romanesque church), and on to **BARBEZIEUX**, capital of the cognac's Grande Champagne grape-growing area. This is a likeable agricultural town, with interesting 11/18C church and remnants of another medieval Rochefoucauld château. Excellent 2-star Logis **La Boule d'Or** (45.78.22.72) has good food and modest prices.

D3 (changes to D2) runs to agreeable local market town **JONZAC**, capital of the Petite Champagne vine area, and a centre as well for Charente dairy farming. There's a 13/15C castle, prehistoric sites, and an interesting partly Romanesque church. D142 leads into handsome **PONS** (pronounced Pon), with its feudal castle and riverside setting.

Return to Saintes on N137 (or to Cognac on D732).

Bordeaux Vineyards

2 days/200km/from Bordeaux

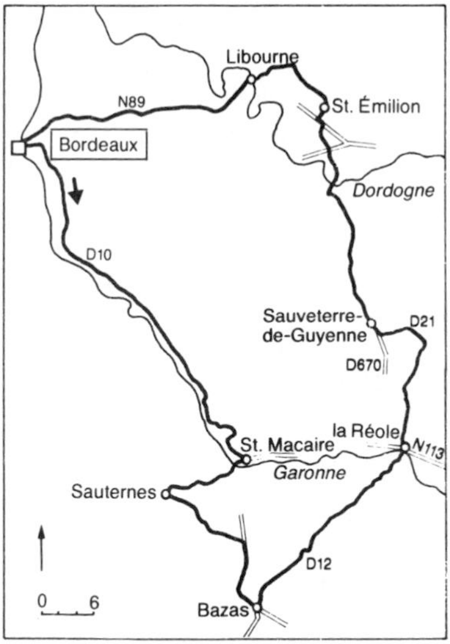

The warm gentle countryside around the great city of Bordeaux has a long history of wine-making. Today, it produces around 400 million bottles annually (half the total French output of appellation contrôlée wines) and, unlike most other wine areas, excels in several quite different types of wine: full-bodied reds, lighter reds, sweet whites and dry whites. During three centuries that Aquitaine was ruled by the English Crown, Bordeaux's red *clairet* (hence the modern name claret for Bordeaux reds) achieved tremendous popularity among the English nobility. So much so that the region's entire wine production was shipped to England in a special fleet of some

300 ships. English families, long established in the area, still dominate the local wine trade. But, though highly praised even then, the wine did not attain the quality for which it is now renowned until mass-production of bottles and corks, which permitted aging in the bottle, began in the 17/18C. (Previously all wines were drunk young — hence the Classical custom of adding resin to wine to help conserve it.) Appellations contrôlées in the Bordeaux wine region cover districts within which there may be several châteaux, producing wines of different quality. Signboards proclaim 'Dégustation', tasting, at farms where one is welcome to try, and perhaps buy, their wine. A 'château', in the Bordeaux region, incidentally, means only a farm where grapes are grown for making into an appellation contrôlée wine; it may indeed be a château in some cases, but in others could be a simple modern house surrounded by vines. Always pleasing, the region is at its best for touring during September and October, at harvest time, when the leaves of the millions of grape bushes covering the countryside turn to their extraordinarily vivid autumn colours. (Use Michelin maps 75 & 79.)

BORDEAUX pop: 211,300 Préfecture of Gironde département, largest in France. A long tradition of liberalism and local freedom resulted from the period of English rule, when rights were granted to encourage local loyalty to the English Crown. Standing on the broad tidal Garonne, the city has since Roman times been a busy port. Modern Bordeaux retains a pleasant central old quarter and very attractive 18C river frontage. The wide shopping boulevards and squares with 18C buildings are impressive. See also: Grand Théâtre; Esplanade des Quinconces and the Girondins Monument; remains of Roman amphitheatre; mainly 12C church of St. Seurin; 12–15C Cathedral; several good museums; and much more. Dozens of first-class restaurants and hotels. SI: 12 cours du 30-juillet.

Leave the city on D10, the quiet and shady road which runs along the north bank of the Gironde. This stretch carries the appellation Premières Côtes de Bordeaux. Along the length of the road are mansions called *chartreuses* — grand 18C bungalows. Each riverside village has something to interest or delight. **RIONS** has narrow medieval streets and 2 towers surviving of its old fortifications. The 17C château at **CADILLAC** is the only Renaissance (i.e., Loire-style) château in the Bordeaux region; on Saturdays local peasants come here to sell fruit, cheese, flowers in the attractive covered market square. At **LOUPIAC** some sweet wines are produced, and this commune has an appellation of its own. The village was built on the ruins of a spacious 3C Roman villa standing in the midst of its vineyards. At **STE. CROIX-DU-MONT** (another separate appellation) take D229 to go into the village and climb up the strange 'mont' — actually a hill made of prehistoric oysters. The whole hill is riddled with caves and grottoes. Caves dug into the hill below the church on the summit show that the earth is entirely made of these ancient shells. There's a fine view from the top of the hill: Château d'Yquem can be seen on a crest in the distance, and farther away stretches the immense Landes forest. Take D117 through rustic **VERDELAS**, then return on D120 to retrieve D10.

Continue to walled **ST. MACAIRE**, a tranquil old *bastide* of honey-coloured stone, and capital of another small appellation, Côtes de Bordeaux St. Macaire. Within the walls the village is marvellously quiet, with swallows darting about; there's a beautifully arcaded market square (pl du Mercadier) and an unusual postal museum here. Cross the river into Langon, which itself comes within the Graves appellation, but take D8 (direction Villandraut) into the vineyards of the prestigious Sauternes district. Go only as far as D116^{e1} on the right, where turn for the **Château d'Yquem**, that awe-inspiring name on the labels of the most expensive and sought-after of sweet wines. The château dates from medieval times, but has had many later additions. It is not lived-in; anyone may park here and walk around the grounds and courtyard — but to visit the *caves* is next to impossible. There are good views from the vineyards back across the river to St. Croix-du-Mont.

On average, a square metre of vineyard at Château d'Yquem produces a single glass of wine. The secret of its concentrated sweetness is *la pourriture noble*, noble rot, a fungus which lives on the grapes' skins, drying out the moisture from the fruit but leaving the fruit sugar intact. The all-important fungus results from the daily early morning dense mist caused by the meeting of the cold Ciron river with the warm Garonne. Ideal harvesting conditions are mist until noon and a warm dry afternoon in which to gather the grapes. Noble rot makes the fruit difficult and unpleasant to handle, and harvesting is very slow — it can last 2 months (as opposed to the usual 3 weeks); only old women, because they are not so strong and are more patient, are employed to gather the fragile Sauternes grapes.

An unfrequented little road leads the short distance into tiny **SAUTERNES** village. Two restaurants in the heart of the village: **Les Vignes** (56.63.60.06), charming and friendly with inexpensive menus and, more expensive, **Le Sauternais** (56.63.67.13), with its large covered outdoor dining area standing in the midst of the green fields and vineyards. Both sell exquisite Sauternes by the glass (better as an aperitif than as a dessert wine).

Drive along D125 to **ROAILLIN** (Romanesque church), just after which, 14C **Château de Roquetaillade** is a handsome little fortress, the palatial interior (frescoes) of which was restored by Viollet-le-Duc. Continue on D125 to D932, where turn right, crossing countryside in which grapes give way to tobacco, another important local crop, and soon reach into **BAZAS**. This is another *bastide*; its lovely spacious arcaded square has 16–18C houses in front of a beautiful 13C Gothic cathedral (note: portals; stained glass). Big, splendid son et lumière performances are put on in the square on high-summer weekends. For the rest of the year it serves as a marketplace every Saturday.

Take D12 directly to **LA RÉOLE**, an unusual old town with good views and plenty of character. High up at its centre there's a Romanesque town hall and, close by, interesting former abbey church St. Pierre. Most of the triangle of land between the rivers Garonne and Dordogne, as far east as the limits of the département, belongs to the well-known dry white wine appellation Entre-Deux-Mers, 'between two seas': not such a bad name, because both rivers are tidal far inland — the Garonne as far as la Réole, the Dordogne as far as Libourne.

St. Émilion

Crossing the Entre-Deux-Mers district, take D21 north from la Réole to **CASTELMORON-D'ALBERT**, a fortified 12C village now cleaned up and supremely picturesque, with narrow, flowery lanes, small church, pretty post office, school and medieval *lavoir* (wash-house). Turn onto D230 to enter the gate of handsome 13C *bastide* **SAUVETERRE-DE-GUYENNE**. From here head north on D670, cross the Dordogne river at St. Jean-de-Blaignac into the St. Émilion appellation district, and so continue into the extraordinary town of **ST. ÉMILION**.

Unfortunately rather crowded with tourists (unlike most of the route so far), St. Émilion deserves a thorough exploration. Built of pale golden local stone, its streets cobbled with darker stone imported from Cornwall, this was formerly the fortified frontier town between French and English territories. It is strikingly situated on two levels, one towering above the other. The town has a tremendous sense of occasion and pageantry: each spring, for example, the Fête des Fleurs marks the first flowering of the grape vines, and in autumn, the start of the harvest is announced with a fanfare from the top of what remains of the old ramparts, after which a procession descends to the strange Eglise Monolithe, a large underground church literally carved out of the interior of one enormous rock (guided tours). What makes it all the more curious is that its spire projects above the ground quite separately. 'Monolithe', because (apart from the spire) the church consists of a single piece of stone — no building materials have been used. Apart from the underground church, St. Émilion has its gloomy moist labyrinth of catacombs, occupied in past ages by Benedictine monks and by Templar knights.

Standing on top of the Eglise Monolithe is the more ordinary 12C church — with delightful Gothic cloisters alongside — which St. Émilion residents use nowadays. There's much else to see in the town: an 18C winepress in the Office de Tourisme; a timbered house dating from the year 1150; and more.

On D243 and (turning on the right) D245, travel through some of the most famous vineyards in the world to **POMEROL**, with its own appellation, a tiny village tightly enclosed by its vines. Take one of the lanes which runs into the attractive but busy former *bastide* and still-active Dordogne river port **LIBOURNE**, a major commercial centre of the Bordeaux wine trade. Its ramparts have been replaced by a pleasant shady walkway.

Cross the Dordogne here and return into Bordeaux on N89.

The Landes

2 days/225km/from Bordeaux

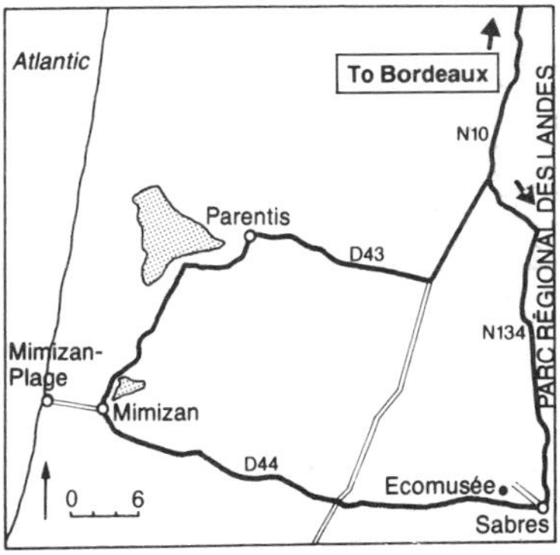

Extending from the Gironde estuary to the foothills of the Pyrenees, les Landes today consists almost entirely of a huge artificial pine forest, planted in the last century. Before that time it was a poor and bleak area of marshes and shifting sand dunes. It remains rather a monotonous region for touring, but the coastline, a single long and straight sandy beach backed with *étangs* (shallow lakes) and pines, attracts great numbers of visitors. (Use Michelin map 78.)

From **BORDEAUX** (see p. 139) travel into the Landes region on N10. After some 50km, take N134 through Pissos to **SABRES**. Here, park the car and, after pausing to see the church (Renaissance doorway; arcaded bell tower), catch the little train to the **Ecomusée de Marquèze**, an interesting museum of the Landes region, including a reconstruction of farm life in the area before the creation of the forest.

From Sabres take D44, past Solférino and Escourse, the forest at times breaking to allow fields of corn, to lakeside **MIMIZAN**. Now 6km inland from the coastal resort Mimizan-Plage, this was from Roman times until 17C a busy seaport. The harbour was swallowed up by sand, but several interesting relics of a 12C Benedictine Abbey survive. There's also in Mimizan, looking out over the lake, an unusually good little 2-star Logis, **Au Bon Coin du Lac** (58.09.01.55), with an exceptional restaurant (rosette, 2 toques); rooms are quite expensive but *menus* reasonably priced.

D652 passes the lake and makes its way, through the area known as Born, to **PARENTIS-EN-BORN**, which is surrounded by intriguing old oil wells. In Parentis, Esso has an exhibition about the Landes oil drilling.

Turn right in town onto D43 which turns 16km directly to N10, where turn left to return to Bordeaux.

*

Fish and shellfish fresh from the sea are popular in this coastal region. Specialities include mussels in white wine sauce (mouclade), mussels flambées on pine needles (éclade), eel soup (bouilliture) and fish soup (chaudrée). Eels and river fish, too, are abundant and, from the inland farms, chickens, pâtés and dairy products. Wine, grapes or grape juice feature in many local dishes. Among the possibilities for the cheese course, try chabichou — a hot goats' cheese served with toast (or variations on the theme!). For dessert look out for clafoutis (cherries sunk into delicious moist cake) or cheese pastries. To drink? A cool Pineau de Charente before the meal, good Bordeaux wine with the food and a fine cognac to follow.

10 PYRENEES

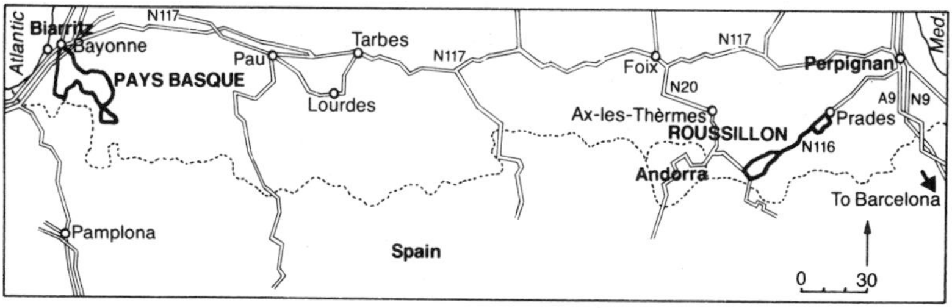

The southern range of mountains which separates France from Spain is relatively little known to foreign visitors. Achieving high and inhospitable peaks only in the middle of the chain, the Atlantic and Mediterranean extremities offer a magnificently beautiful landscape of high, airy green pastures and clean, rushing rivers and streams. These mountains have given rise to, and provide refuge for, two peoples and cultures each standing with one foot in France and the other in Spain while belonging truly to neither: the Basques in the west and the Catalans in the east.

Pays Basque

2-3 days/150km/from Bayonne

An ancient people, speaking an ancient (and astonishing!) language, the Basques (or Euskadi, in their own tongue*) are known as a strong, fine-looking people, with a taciturn but strong-willed, resourceful and emotional nature. Communal life plays a vital role in their society, and the fascinating traditional folk dances (many for men only) and fêtes remain tremendously popular. Among many other distinctive characteristics is the Basque national game *pelota*, played by two teams of three players. Every village has its *fronton*, the wall against which the game is

*The intials of their separatist organisation ETA stands for Euskadi Ta Azkatasuna (i.e. Basque Freedom).

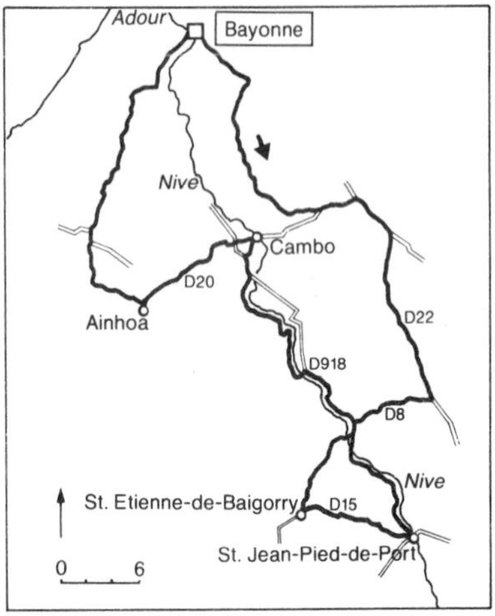

played. (It's a bit like, let's say, playing squash against a single wall.) *Pelota* has several variations, and Basques also happen to be fanatical about rugby.

Basque food draws its inspiration almost entirely from the rivers and the sea; seasoning has been developed to a fine art; and the red pepper rules over other vegetables. From the high pastures come lamb and delicate little sheeps' cheeses. Local specialities include ttoro (fish stew) and piperade (a preparation of tomatoes and hot peppers, either in an omelette or as a sauce for other dishes).

The hill villages are attractive with whitewashed and timbered houses. However, almost all Basques live, not in such traditional mountain cottages, but along the crowded and commercialised strip of coast between the hills and the Atlantic. Although their land is divided by the Spanish frontier, it is interesting that only on the Spanish side of the border is there an active independence movement. On the French side there seems little wish to escape from the civilised and tolerant embrace of the far-away Parisian Government. The green mountains and numerous streams and rivers twisting and dashing through exquisite valleys make this an idyllic countryside for leisurely touring; the climate, too, is excellent, warm and sunny without scorching heat, refreshed by periodic showers rather than the usual sudden southern downpours. Be warned that in high summer, certainly, you won't be alone here, not even on the minor back roads; the gentle, warm spring months, before everybody else arrives, or the balmy days of late autumn, are the best time in this region. (Use Michelin map 78 or 85.)

BIARRITZ (pop: 26,600) and **BAYONNE** (pop: 43,000) nowadays form a single conurbation, yet something of the former distinction between them can still be felt. Biarritz was a simple but prosperous fishing village which became a seaside resort. Bayonne was capital of the Basque country. At its heart (around the confluence of the Nive and Adour) it preserves a certain dignity, and with its old streets and quays, and powerful fortifications, it has much charm despite the modern industries which are established here. See also: 13C Gothic Cathedral; Bonnat Museum; Basque Museum. SI: pl de la Liberté.

Start simply enough by going only as far as **la Croix de Mouguerre**, a high point on the edge of Bayonne giving a good clear view over town, river, coast and hills. Via **MOUGUERRE** village (and exceptionally

St. Jean-Pied-de-Port

steep little D257), join D22 — the grandly, but not unjustly, named 'Route Imperiale des Cimes' (Imperial Summits Highway), a beautiful road which in places gives magnificent mountain views. Stay with D22 as it goes in one side of industrial **HASPARREN** and straight out of the other.

The road veers off into steep and attractive hills, rising steeply as it travels towards the modest summit of Moiné Mendia (374m), then re-descending. At Celay turn right onto D8, which at Ossés (strange octagonal tower) reaches busier D918.

Here turn left and press on into **ST. JEAN-PIED-DE-PORT**. This agreeable little resort (summer and winter) on the river Nive is well used to receiving visitors, for, during the Middle Ages, Compostela pilgrims (the tourists of their era) used to flood through the town. This was their last halt before climbing up to the Roncevaux Pass, the historic gateway into Spain. They did not use the route followed by D963 up the valley of the Petite Nive, but climbed a much more ancient footpath, now GR65, which goes steeply and directly from St. Jean to the Pass. St. Jean's medieval walls, pierced by its gateways, encircle the old centre with the river running through the middle. Many of the town's attractive houses, made of russet-coloured sandstone and with sculpted doorways, date from 16C. The Vieux Pont (good view) links the two sides of the Nive, with the Ville Haute (Upper Town) and old fortified 17C Citadel on the right bank. Beside the bridge an interesting pelota museum occupies a former old charity hospital. The neighbouring village of **ST. JEAN-LE-VIEUX**, obviously a much older community, has a lovely old church in the warm colour of the local sandstone.

For an excellent *restaurant avec chambres* at St. Jean-Pied-de-Port, **Les Pyrénées** has magnificent food at very reasonable prices considering the quality, and small but comfortable rooms also most moderately priced (2 rosettes, 3 toques 59.37.01.01).

D15 (good views) goes to **ST. ÉTIENNE-DE-BAÏGORRY**, small town in the attractive **Vallée des Aldudes**. The river itself is called, a little oddly, Nive des Aldudes, and where it flows through St. Étienne is crossed by an old hump-backed bridge. See too the Basque-style church with galleries, and 16C château. There's another marvellously located, quiet, pretty and inexpensive hotel-restaurant here, the **Hôtel Arcé** and its restaurant **Le Trinquet** (1 rosette, 1 toque: 59.37.40.14).

Using D948, return to D918 in the Nive valley, where turn left towards Cambo-les-Bains. Instead of staying on the main road, turn left at Bidarray, crossing the river by a medieval bridge onto narrow, steep, winding and picturesque D349. This clings to the left bank of the Nive, eventually reaching the Pas (pass) de Rolland and descending into the village of **ITXASSOU**, with its cherry orchards and pretty church (note: galleries). Here rejoin D918 and head into **CAMBO-LES-BAINS**. (If this circuitous route into Cambo seems too steep and slow, leave out D349 and stay on faster D918.) Cambo's Basque-style church gives a fine view over this pleasant leafy spa town (now also a winter resort). The upper part of town, more modern and prosperous, looks down grandly onto the Nive. The village-y older area, with old-fashioned Basque character and appearance, clusters by the riverside.

D918 passes through **ESPELETTE**, a pleasing village with traditional Basque houses and church (in graveyard note 200- and 300-year-old tombs with carved circular headstone — a former Basque custom). Espelette attracts visitors each winter for its annual horse fair at which *pottoks*, the small Basque ponies, are sold. Shortly after the village, head off left on D20 to **AINHOA**, another extremely attractive Basque village with delightful old whitewashed, timbered houses and interesting Romanesque church (galleries). This out-of-the-way spot is by no means undiscovered, and there are several enticing hotels and restaurants. 2-star Logis **Ohantzea** (59.29.90.50) and **Hôtel-Restaurant Ithurria** (toque; 59.29.92.11) are both in lovely 17C Basque houses.

Turn back from Ainhoa to find narrow D305, just outside the village on the left, and follow this road (joins D4, then D3) to **ST. PÉE-SUR-NIVELLE**. Here take D755 or, for a more scenic alternative, D3 (turn right soon after leaving St. Pée), back to Bayonne.

Roussillon

1–2 days/151km/from Prades (43km from Perpignan on N116)

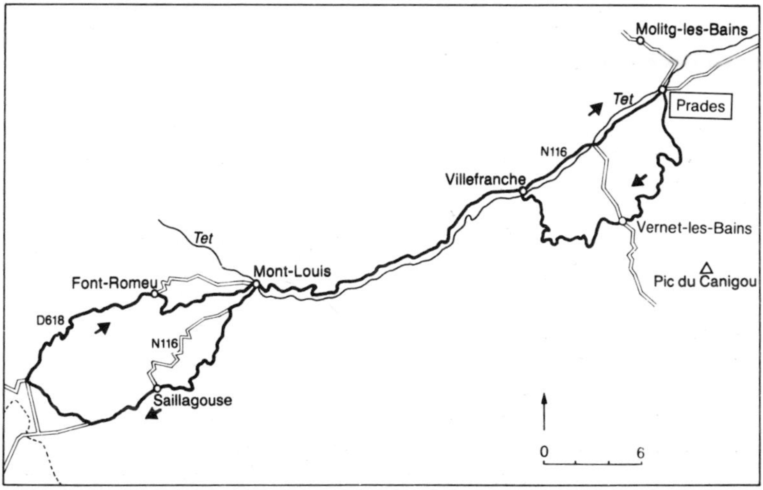

Roussillon, now the département of Pyrénées Oriéntales, at one time considered not French enough to be part of France, was signed over to Spanish rule in 1258. But the people of Roussillon, Catalans like their neighbours on the other side of the Pyrenees, proved a problem to Madrid. They were recalcitrant and rebellious, didn't speak Spanish and constantly demanded independence. Certainly they were a weak point in Spain's border with France. Finally, in 1659, the whole region was transferred back to French rule, although as was revealed when soldiers were being conscripted here in World War I, two-and-a-half centuries later much of the rural population of Roussillon still did not know which country they were living in. Today, as with the Basques, it is mainly on the Spanish side of the frontier that Catalans aspire to a self-governing state of their own. On the northern side of the Pyrenees, with their customs, traditions and language respected, Catalans seem quite happy with their position in a rather remote and overlooked corner of France. Their small region embraces a tremendous variety, with rustic hill villages cut off in winter, and the teeming urban life of its historic capital, Perpignan. In landscape, too, it extends from a hot, sunny Mediterranean coast, in some places fringed with broad sand beaches, in others with magnificent rocky crags rising straight from the sea, through cool, pleasant green mountain pasture — which is Roussillon's most typical aspect — and up into the lonely Pyreneean summits. Catalan life brims with energy and feeling: there are numerous colourful time-honoured fêtes throughout the year, often reflecting a fervent devotion to the

Church; the Catalan language* is still widely spoken alongside both Spanish and French; the popular *sardana* (done by any number simply forming a circle) and other folk dances are readily performed to their traditional music; and from civic buildings fly the gay colours of the Catalan flag. Not least of the local customs is Catalan cuisine, based on olive oil, garlic, plentiful fish, and charcuterie from the mountains. Tomatoes and peppers are much used, and bitter oranges feature among the seasonings together with the abundant wild herbs. Specialities include fish stew (boullinade), snails (cargolade), creamy mayonnaise-type sauces flavoured with garlic and sweet biscuity pastries. The region flows with cheap, drinkable local wines both red and white, as well as producing some excellent fortified sweet wines. (Use Michelin map 86.)

N116 runs up the fertile valley of the river Tet from Perpignan to **PRADES**. This is a cheerful little town, centred around its large Catalan-style church, typical with its simple exterior of rounded stones and a highly ornate interior with gaudy retable. Beside the church, the pleasant main square becomes the town's marketplace every Tuesday. The Massif du Canigou, dominating the landscape, rises to the south of the town, and Prades makes a good base for walkers intent on making the difficult climb from here on GR36 to its summit, the **Pic du Canigou** (2,784m: panoramic view extends to the Cévennes and to the coast).

3km south of Prades on D27 is one of the most striking of Roussillon's many Romanesque churches, the **Abbey of St. Michel-de-Cuxa**. The annual music festival organised by Spanish-Catalan cellist Pablo Casals (1876–1973) is still held here each summer. Founded in 9C, the present church dating from 10C, the abbey has been well restored by the Cistercians now in residence. What remains of its cloisters is especially impressive: tragically, much of the rest of the cloisters was appropriated for display in the Cloisters Museum in New York. Stay on D27 as it meanders over the foot of the Canigou massif, reaching **VERNET-LES-BAINS**, a spa below an older area with Romanesque church and restored castle. Rather surprisingly, considering the difficult access at that time, in the early years of this century many English visitors, among them Rudyard Kipling, frequented Vernet's sulphur-rich spa baths. It still has several good hotels and restaurants, including one modest establishment called **Angleterre**. Another English devotee was Hilaire Belloc, who was so pleased by the Canigou that he described it as 'the mountain which many who have never heard the name have been looking for all their lives'. From Vernet there is an easier approach to the Pic for walkers (on the way up, see the waterfall called the Cascade des Anglais!). Apart from the view, Canigou's other great interest is the superbly remote and dignified 11/12C Romanesque monastery **St. Martin-du-Canigou**, reached by a steep 45min walk from Casteil, Vernet's neighbour on D116.

Tiny D27 now struggles from Vernet to **SAHORRE** (interesting

*When reading place names, note that Catalan x is pronounced sh, ch as k, u as oo, and final g is tch.

Vernet-les-Bains

Romanesque church) and back down to the Tet valley and N116. Turn left onto the main road (ignoring Villefranche until the return journey) and proceed up between the wild, steep, *garrigue*-covered slopes of the Tet gorges to fortified **MONT-LOUIS**. It's curious to reflect that in the 17C (when Vauban built the ramparts) this quiet and agreeable mountain town was an active military base, vital in France's defences against the Spanish. It thrives today as a winter resort, but the beautiful setting — the walled town poised above the valleys of the Cerdagne, Capcir and Tet rivers — clearly had strategic advantages. It still has an army barracks.

France's researches into the uses of solar energy are largely concentrated in the Roussillon Pyrenees, which in general have exceptionally clear and fine weather throughout the year. Near Mont-Louis a 'solar oven' — rather a misleading name — has been set up: in fact it is a concave arrangement of mirrors directing sunlight onto a single point, which reaches a temperature of 6000°C. The area around Font-Romeu, farther along our route, has another (more visitable) 'solar oven' and a solar power station.

From Mont-Louis carry on along N116 up to the Col de la Perche (great views; 1,579m), at which point D35 leads off left to picturesque villages **EYNE** and dramatically located **LLO**, at the foot of the spectacular river Ségre gorge. A 2km journey leads back to N116 at **SAILLAGOUSE**. There are quiet, comfortable and enchanting *auberges* at Llo (**Atalaya**: 68.04.70.04) and Eyne (**Auberge d'Eyne**: 68.04.71.12) and a good inexpensive hotel-restaurant at Saillagouse (**les Planes**: 68.04.72.08).

From Saillagouse all sorts of alternative routes present themselves. Just 5km west lies the Spanish enclave of **LLIVIA**, a town and a territory, most decidedly Catalan, which somehow remained Spanish when the rest of Roussillon was tranferred to France. If you want to go this way, note that on reaching the border of Llivia there is a No Entry sign and an unmanned border post. Apparently it is *not* forbidden to cross this point (I have done so without suffering any ill effect!); drive across Llivia, pausing to explore the small Spanish town, and exit onto D30 (do not take the flyover which goes straight from Llivia into the rest of Spain). At D30 turn right and go to the village of Ur. Another possibility is to continue on N116 to the D30 turning on the right, and reach Ur that way. Thirdly, if you want to visit the once disreputable smugglers' outpost, now respectable border town, of **BOURG-MADAME**, simply stay on N116, picking up N20 at Bourg-Madame, and continue to Ur on the main road.

UR itself is nothing special, except for an interesting 10C Romanesque church. The main road (N20) to Andorra, the tiny state in the heights of the Pyrenees (with Catalan as its official first language), heads away to the west, while our route turns east on D618. D10 on the left leads up to tiny **DORRES**, which has curious Black Virgin statues in the church and, beside the village, a sulphur-rich hot spring. Back on D618, press on through **ANGOUSTRINES** (12C church) up to the strange granite rock formations called the Chaos of Targassonne. Soon after, accessible by a track, is the curious-looking Targassonne Solar Power Station (sign-posted).

At a fork in the road, take the left-hand into **FONT-ROMEU**, a modern and unappealing spa and major Pyreneean summer and winter resort with a phenomenal sunshine record (hence the solar power station). From the Calvaire (Calvary) of Font-Romeu (1,857m) there are fine views. The 17C Baroque chapel of adjacent **ERMITAGE**, where the original *font roméu* (Catalan, pilgrim spring) is located, is the summer home of a 12C statue of the Virgin, Our Lady of Font-Romeu. On 8 September she is carried in solemn procession down to the church at Odeillo, there to remain until the following June.

Take the road which she takes, to **ODEILLO**, a distance of 3km, and see another experimental 'solar oven', a fascinating arrangement of mirrors which concentrate the sun's light (and heat). With a 1,000 kilowatt capability, it is at present used commercially for ultra high temperature chemical applications. Inside the control building there's an intriguing permanent exhibition (with space-age-y video). From Odeillo take D10, a minor and picturesque road, through the village of Bolquère and resort Super-Bolquère, back into Mont-Louis.

Here pick up N116 again, and return towards Prades. Stop at **VILLEFRANCHE-DE-CONFLENT**, which was by-passed on the way up. Villefranche is a superb fortified village on the banks of the river Cady where it pours into the Tet. Though very popular with visitors, the town deserves a look. Entered grandly through an impressive gate, the town's ramparts enclose narrow medieval streets of tremendous atmosphere. No cars are allowed. See the old citadel and interesting 12C church. Nearby **CORNEILLA-DE-CONFLENT** (D116 — close to Sahorre and Vernet which were visited earlier in the route) has another most unusual Romanesque church, one of the oldest in Roussillon (note: painted wooden statues).

From Villefranche it's 6km on N116 back to Prades.

*

For regional cuisine see Pays Basque and Roussillon route introductions.

11 LANGUEDOC

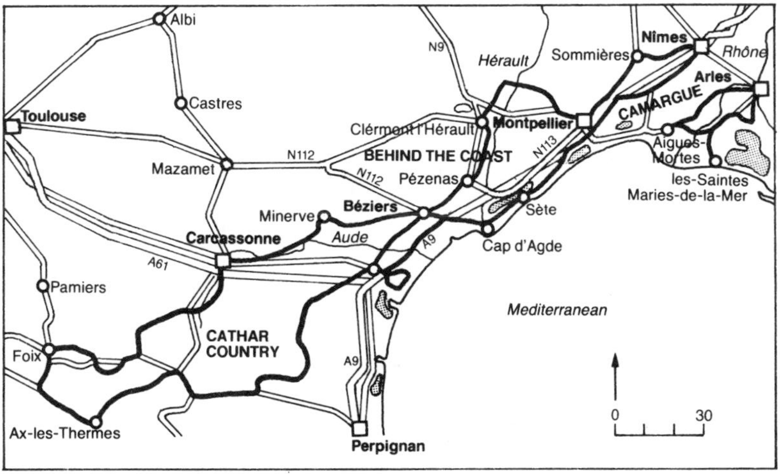

Languedoc was a melting pot of the ancient world, settled by Greeks, Levantines, Romans, Moors. The region, in which was spoken the old Provençal tongue — the Romance language Occitan, called the *langue d'oc* — extended at its farthest across southern France from Bordeaux to Lyon, taking in the whole of Rome's Provincia. As generations passed, the South fragmented into independent dukedoms and counties: most powerful of them was the County of Languedoc, controlling most of the land west of the Rhône. The South was all too conscious of its cultural differences from the Frankish kingdom to the north. The Catharism which swept southern Languedoc, and the Protestantism which followed it in the hills farther north, were simply ways of continuing to be separate from the Catholic French — who willingly met the challenge by launching a crushing military defeat of the South and its way of life. The population was halved by emigration and war, and eventually the Occitan language itself was forbidden. The old tongue has withdrawn into isolated rural areas and degenerated into a patois. Occitan has become 'folklore', and the long drawn out conquest of the South is complete. Or not quite, perhaps — for the sense of separateness, of a longer, a larger history persists even today.

The region's sunny plains are swathed by endless vineyards and the inland hills by wild *garrigue* (tough evergreen scrub, holm oak and fragrant herbs). The traditional stone villages and market towns remain satisfyingly ill-equipped for tourism, while old cities matter-of-factly offer a chance to see superb antiquities. On the coast new resorts have sprung up but between them stretch broad sandy beaches still hardly touched.

The Country of the Cathars

4 days/500km/from Béziers (or Narbonne)

There is not one God in the Universe, but two equal powers; one evil, whose domain is the physical world and everything in it, and the other good, who rules the spiritual sphere. That at least was the belief of the Cathars, who maintained that they were the true followers of Jesus Christ, repudiating the materialism of the Catholic Church and its priests, and condemning the close relationship between Church and State. In place of an institutionalised priesthood, Cathars had their self-appointed *parfaits*, perfects, who ritually renounced the material world and lived on charity. Their principal rite was the *consolamentum*, given to the sick or dying, who were then supposed to starve themselves to death. Known as Albigensianism to is enemies, the movement had some appeal to the poor because it gave a justification for refusing to pay tithes. In the 12C Catharism was widely taken up in southern and western Languedoc, by the nobility as well, though there is evidence enough (see *Montaillou* by Emmanuel le Roy Ladurie) that neither they nor the peasants really believed the natural world to be evil.

In the early 13C the Pope authorised a crusade of northern barons — the Albigensian Crusade (named after the town of Albi) — to stamp out this heresy which threatened to destroy the political power of the Church in Languedoc. All sins committed by the Crusaders were pardoned in advance, and in some towns and villages the entire population, Catholic as well as Cathar, was wiped out by the zealous Papal forces. The leaders were permitted to keep whatever they could seize; in due course the overall commander Simon de Montfort (whose son became Earl of Leicester) took possession of almost all of the County of Languedoc.

The Crusade lasted 20 years (de Montfort died before its completion), during which time Cathar communities barricaded themselves into lofty, inaccessible hilltop castles. But one after another these refuges were starved into submission, and their occupants, if unrepentant, burned alive. In 1229 the King of France declared at the Treaty of Meaux that the Crusade was over and that Languedoc had been annexed to his kingdom. Royal troops then took over where the Crusade had left off, continuing to root out heretics until well into the 1300s. The Cathars'

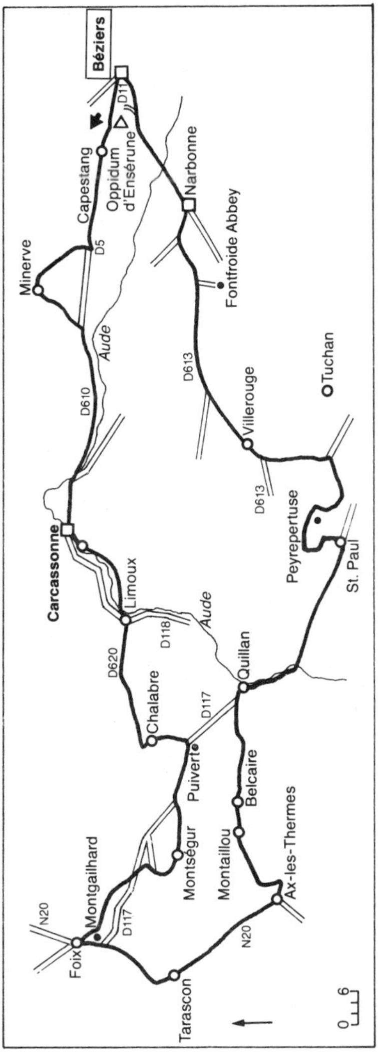

gaunt castles, now half-ruined, still stand like very symbols of resolute and hopeless defiance. (Use Michelin maps 83 & 86.)

BÉZIERS (see p. 165) was the first place reached by the Crusaders, on 22 July 1209. The population of the city numbered probably 60,000 at that time, including some hundreds of Cathars. Met by a refusal when he asked the local people to hand over their Cathars, the Crusade's ecclesiastical leader, Arnauld-Amaury, Abbot of Cîteaux, gave his famous order to the Papal troops: 'Kill them all. The Lord will know his own.' The evidence is that few citizens survived the ensuing attack, although the Abbot's own account shows that 'we were only able to slay twenty thousand'. Much of the city, including the Cathedral, together with hundreds who were sheltering inside, was burnt to the ground. Béziers was subsequently rebuilt — it is now largely in florid but attractive 18C Renaissance style — yet it remains firmly regionalist and anti-Paris, and something of those events of 700 years ago still haunts the town.

From Béziers, following much the same route as the anti-Cathar mercenaries, take D11 (changes to D5; direction Carcassonne), through **CAPESTANG** with its huge — but incomplete — church (many large fortified churches were built after the Albigensian Crusade to intimidate the local populace), turning right after 30km onto D607 which winds through wild *garrigue* and tiny vineyards to **MINERVE**: as soon as it comes into view one can see that Minerve was a good place for a stronghold.

Nowadays noted for one of Languedoc's best red wines, this small fortified village is strikingly situated on a promontory in a strange and beautiful rocky landscape carved by the confluence of two twisting narrow rivers. De Montfort's army must have had a difficult job here, for to reach the village in those days involved first a difficult descent and then a steep climb. Yet the Cathars, despite their magnificently unassailable fortress, soon surrendered because de Montfort worked out how to cut off their water supply. When the pyres were lit to burn the 180 unrepentant heretics, they apparently 'did not have to be pushed but, obstinate in their error, threw themselves into the flames'. Within Minerve's old walls, the Romanesque church has an altar dating from AD465, and the village museum tells the story of the local Cathars, of whose fortress only ruins remain. It's intriguing to explore the footpaths near the village, and to discover the two curious '*ponts naturels*', natural tunnels, which run under the road.

Taking D10 return to the Carcassonne road (D11) via **AZILLANET** and **OLONZAC**. This whole area, the Minervois, makes extremely pleasant touring. As the road reaches the outskirts of Carcassonne, follow signs to La Cité, the oldest and most interesting part of town.

CARCASSONNE pop: 42,500 Préfecture of the Aude. La Cité, standing apart from the later Ville Basse, is a medieval city powerfully fortified with dry moat and double bastion of walls, oldest parts dating back to Roman times. Taken by the Albigensian Crusade in 1209. France's most southerly town until Roussillon (formerly Spanish) annexed in 1659. Spectacularly restored to its original state (with some inaccuracies now being corrected) by Viollet-le-Duc in 19C; the original buildings have continued to be fully occupied as both residential and commercial premises. Small enough to explore thoroughly on foot. See: 12C Château Comtal; 11/13C Eglise St-Nazaire (de Montfort's tomb; body later removed). Ville Basse, its centre a hexagonal 14C *bastide*, is the larger, more important part of modern Carcassonne and much less appealing. Tourist Office: 15 bd Camille-Pelletan. Hotel-restaurants: **Terminus** (68.25.25.00); **Trencavel** (68.71.09.53).

Minerve

To avoid the busy route nationale, leave Carcassonne on the right bank of the Aude (Cité side) taking hilly little rte de St. Hilaire (D204; changes to D104) south from the Cité, via the hamlet of **AURIAC** (excellent, tranquil but expensive 4-star Relais et Château in 19C **Domaine d'Auriac**: 68.25.72.22) and **ST. HILAIRE** to **LIMOUX**. The village of **PIEUSSE** just before Limoux was a Cathar community. This is picturesque country producing good inexpensive wines: Blanquette de Limoux is a *méthode champenoise* sparkling white, Limoux a crisp white and Anne des Joyeuses a rich red. Limoux itself is attractive with decorated old wooden-fronted houses, arcaded square and 15C bridge.

Take N620 west from Limoux across steep hills to Chalabre, turning there onto D12 down to **PUIVERT**, overlooked by the ruins of its castle, a Cathar refuge defeated in 1210. (Longer and busier alternative, but faster: Limoux to Puivert via Quillan on N118 and N117.) On N117 take direction Lavelanet; at Bélesta turn left onto D5/D9, the minor road which goes to **MONTSÉGUR**.

The château at Montségur was effectively the last great Cathar stronghold to fall to the Crusaders. Perched impregnably on top of a steep and treacherous pinnacle of rock, it was besieged unsuccessfully several times during 35 years, the Crusaders being unable to discover its sources of food or water. Finally, after a continuous year-long seige, in March 1244 the 1,000 heretics who had been living in this small castle gave themselves up; 205 refused to renounce their beliefs and died in the *bucher*, the pyre, of Montségur. Legend and wishful thinking has it that a vast Cathar treasure was concealed here, but if anyone has found something so far they have managed to keep their good fortune awfully quiet. During the day a small charge is made to walk up the rough and dangerous path to the château. It takes about half an hour to reach the top. The cold and bare stone castle, open to the winter winds and clouds (rolling in low as we stood there one chill autumn evening), feels a grim place to spend a full year of confinement. Strange that on the strength of that suffering, Montségur now flourishes as a small centre of tourism.

Continue on D9, which turns left at Villeneuve d'Olmes; at D117n turn left, soon retrieving D9 on the right. (This route avoids uninteresting Lavelanet.) The land is getting steeper here, the air bearing a hint of Pyreneean freshness. Pass the Cathar fortress at **ROQUEFIXADE** from which bonfire messages were sent to the other strongholds at Puivert, Montségur and, a few km farther along this road, **MONT GAILHARD**, near Foix.

Although a workaday town, and préfecture of the Ariège, the old heart of **FOIX** has many 15/16C timbered houses, 2 fine covered markets (Wed and Fri), and is made especially dramatic by its magnificent setting at the meeting of the Arget and Ariège rivers overlooked by a feudal castle of 3 tall towers. Daunted by its defensive position, Simon de Montfort's northern army did not tackle this particular southern stronghold. It was successfully taken much later though, in 1272, when it no longer harboured Cathars but continued to deny the sovereignty of France. Office de Tourism: 45 cours G.-Fauré. **Hôtel Audoye**

(61.65.52.44) is an agreeable, inexpensive 2-star Logis with low-priced *menus*.

Follow the Ariège valley south on N20, rather a busy road but beautiful none the less with wooded slopes and glacial rock deposits and views of the Pyrenees. Pass again near ruined Montgailhard château by the hill known as Pain de Sucre and, farther on, impressive 13C Pont du Diable across the Ariège. Continue into **TARASCON**, now industrial, once at the heart of a staunchly Cathar district. Nearby are extensive underground caverns in which the heretics gathered to listen to their speakers. In some, strange mystical graffiti decorates the walls. The **Grotte de Niaux**, up a narrow hill road, has other well-preserved wall-paintings dating from 20,000BC. Adjacent to **USSAT-LES-BAINS**, the Grotte de Lombrive is the focus of another 'lost Cathar treasure' legend, the truth probably being that their treasure was spiritual. It was in this cavern that several hundred Cathars were cornered, walled-in, and thus perished from starvation.

Follow the river south. At **UNAC**, just off the road (cross the river) 8km before Ax, **L'Oustal** (61.64.48.44) is a peaceful, comfortable, inexpensive little hotel-restaurant. In Ax itself there are three 2-star Logis, but these are usually fully booked well in advance. **AX-LES-THERMES**, a thriving spa resort today, was just as popular as a Roman holiday place. An excess of hotels taints the intrinsic charm of this town at the meeting point of 3 rivers hemmed in by wooded mountains. Several natural hot springs in the town include an open-air public footbath, and a smaller open-air bath of water steaming away at 90°C. During my visit, an elderly man with a complexion all too similar to a stewed prune was perched beside this hot pool for some six or seven hours each day. He swore it was what kept him so young-looking. Water for washing pours from a public fountain at 77°C.

Twisting D613n climbs steeply away from Ax to reach Col de Chioula (1,431m), after which the landscape becomes more open and unpopulated. Soon after the simple village of Prades a small turning on the right leads to **MONTAILLOU**, a hamlet 2km off the road in a magnificent rural setting above a fertiel valley. This village, as it was in the 14C, is the subject of Emmanuel le Roy Ladurie's book *Montaillou*, which is based on the records of the Inquisition of Bishop Fournier (later Pope Benedict XII) at Carcassonne and at Pamiers. The Fournier Register, as these records are called, is today kept in the Vatican. In the 1300s there was a popular revival of Catharism in the Comté de Foix, centred on Montaillou. Fournier interrogated the villagers at great length and in great detail to discover exactly which of them were heretics. Most were. Sentences ranged from wearing a smock bearing a yellow cross, to having the tongue cut out, life imprisonment in fetters on a diet of bread and water, or being burned alive. A few families — either by being loyal Catholics or, more often, through double-dealing and having the right friends — managed to survive the Inquisition, and survive to this day in Montaillou. At **BELCAIRE**, 7km away on the main road, **Hôtel du Bayle** (68.20.31.05) is a small Logis with basic rooms and delicious, inexpensive and unpretentious meals. Tall snow posts mark the edge of the road as it crosses a bleak plateau before the descent into **QUILLAN**.

At this busy little town rejoin the Aude valley, following it south on N117. In the Défile de Pierre-Lys the river cuts deeply between forested cliffs. Soon after, above the village of Lapradelle, the gaunt ruins of 11/13C château of Puilaurens, once an important outpost of France's southern defences, stand on a rocky summit. At St. Paul-de-Fenouillet turn left onto narrow D7, which climbs through the Gorges de Galamus to Cubières, where turn right onto D14. The village of **ROUFFIAC-DES-CORBIÈRES** is splendidly overlooked by the 11–16C **Château de Peyrepertuse** (accessible by car from Duilhac, a little farther along the road), finest of the numerous severe, lofty fortresses hereabouts: it sheltered Cathar and Catholic alike from the Papal army. The last of the Cathar fortresses to be taken, despite the greater importance and drama of Montségur, was in fact the Cháteau de Quéribus (now restored) which stands high up not far off the road south of **CUCUGNAN**. It surrendered to the anti-Cathar forces in 1255. A little access road leads up to the château. At **PADERN** turn left onto D123 to enter the gorges of the Torgan (or continue on D14 into busy **TUCHAN**, at the centre of the wine-producing region known as Corbières, and itself within the appellation of Fitou, an excellent rich red wine, certainly one of Languedoc's best).

Keep on this road (changes to D410), through Maisons and past Davejean, as far as N613, where turn right to enter **VILLEROUGE-TERMENÈS**, an exceptionally picturesque medieval village. For some 12km to St. Laurent de la Cabrerisse the road continues winding and hilly, after which it becomes a faster, easier drive 30km (via beautiful 12/13C cloisters and chapterhouse of the Cistercian Abbey of Fontfroide, 2km off road on the right, signposted) into ancient **NARBONNE** (see p. 165), badly damaged by the Alibgensian Crusaders. Take D9 back to Béziers, perhaps stopping to see the strange view from Oppidum d'Ensérune (D162e on the left; see p. 165) on the way.

Behind the Coast

3 days/325km/from Nîmes

The Languedoc coastal plain is remarkably agreeable, interesting and easy to explore. For most of the year the weather stays perfectly warm and dry, if windy sometimes (especially in winter when the Mistral and the Tramontane blow their hardest). Although utterly peaceful now — hardly disturbed even by tourism — this region has seen great upheaval and violence in the past, especially during the bitter wars between Protestants (Huguenots) and Catholics. The population is almost entirely Catholic today. Our route touches upon fragrant, hilly *garrigue*, vineyards in their neat rows, old towns and villages with shady *platanes*, and finally returns (on busier roads) along the edge of Mediterranean beaches. (Michelin map 83.)

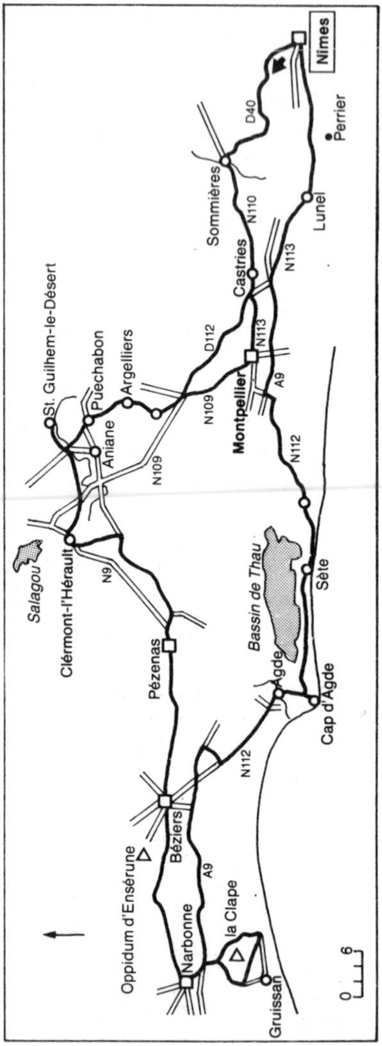

Leave the centre of **NÎMES** (pop: 130,000. Industrial. Outstanding Roman remains. See especially: Arena; Maison Carrée, SI: 6 rue Auguste) by following direction Montpellier but at the edge of the city look for signs to Sommières, D40 on the right. Take this pleasant country road which by-passes a succession of old villages to reach **SOMMIÈRES**. Despite a traffic problem caused by the narrowness of the main streets, this is an attractive and likeable small town. Part of the centre is still walled, and entered through an old gateway. The town is handsomely located on the banks of the river Vidourle, broad at this point, with a weir at which gypsy women can often be seen doing their washing on the far side. The author Lawrence Durrell, although closely associated with Greece in readers' minds, has lived here in a house on the other side of the river for the last 30 years.

Cross the river to take picturesque N110 (direction Montpellier) through miles of *garrigue* and vineyards. Pause at **CASTRIES**, with interesting 11C church and, overlooking the village, a little château (with good furniture and enjoyable woods and gardens), which has belonged to the noble Castries family since 1495. An aqueduct specially designed for the family in the 18C by Paul Riquet, builder of the Canal du Midi, marches 6km across the countryside to bring water to the château!

To avoid Montpellier, shortly after Castries at Vendargues, take D112 on the right; take direction first to Clapiers, then on D65 to La Paillade, then to Grabels on D102. At Grabels take D102 (direction Montarnaud) to rejoin the route. Otherwise continue on N110 into **MONTPELLIER** (pop: 201,000. Large university, founded before AD1000. Pleasant atmosphere. See: extensive old centre of narrow streets; 18C Promenade du Peyrou with view to Cévennes. SI: 6 rue Maguelone).

Leave Montpellier on the Route de Lodève (N109), staying on this road until the turning right (D27e) to Montarnaud. The junction is on a bend in the main road at hamlet Bel-Air, and can easily be missed. Immediately one is plunged into marvellously undeveloped country, alternating vineyards and *garrigue*. At **MONTARNAUD** follow D27e round to the right in the village, continuing through beautiful and increasingly wooded country to **ARGELLIERS** (good view), where turn left to **PUECHABON**, a very old and unspoiled village, picturesque yet rarely visited. (Recommended hotel nearby: the **Clamouse** inexpensive 1-star Logis with good restaurant, 5km away at Aniane; 67.57.71.63.)

Turn left at Puechabon onto D32, soon regaining D27e on the right. This descends sharply to the Pont du Diable, as it is called, which crosses the river Hérault just at the point where the narrow and rushing Gorge de l'Hérault opens out onto the plain (popular swimming place). Beside the present bridge a humbler older (11C) structure still spans the river. On the other side, turn right onto narrow D4 which clings to the riverside. Passing the **Grotte de Clamouse**, an impressive network of large underground caverns and tunnels (guided visits), after 4km the road reaches

ST. GUILHEM-LE-DÉSERT

It is rather a pity that pretty little St. Guilhem has become a focus for visitors to the region, since it cannot really absorb more than a small number of people. The village is strikingly situated along the sides of the

St. Guilhem-le-Désert

Verdus, a rushing stream passing beneath houses and diverted into tiny vegetable gardens. Opening off the main square is a magnificent Abbey Church, mainly 10-11C, still belonging to a religious order. Tragically, and stupidly, the Cloisters have been sold and removed to the Cloisters Museum, New York. The pieces which remain show that it was worth keeping. Today, as always, this is a tightknit community, the houses bearing crosses and religious insignia. None the less, a lively Midsummer Festival on 19 June, though called Fête de St. Jean, involves such pre-Christian rites as jumping the bonfire! Footpath GR74 (to Larzac) goes through the village up an ancient cobbled bridleway — for centuries the only access to St. Guilhem — past a ruined seigneurial château, and climbs the hillside to give a fine view over the lush and peaceful enclosed valley called the Bout du Monde, End of the World.

Return on D4 (not crossing the Pont du Diable) past St. Jean de Fos with its green-glazed square church spire, and follow the signs, through Lagamas, to St. André-de-Sangonis, where pick up signs to **CLERMONT L'HÉRAULT** (situated beside N9), pleasant and busy market town (Wednesday till noon) and local capital. It has a fine 14C fortified church, and an unspoiled old quarter of narrow alleyways and steps. (Nearby, Lac du Salagou has become a popular recreation area; an attractive road encircles the southern and western sides of the lake, passing through delightful villages. One of these is curious **MOURÈZE**, surrounded by hundreds of weird rock formations known as the Cirque de Mourèze.)

N9 is the busy direct road from Clérmont to Pézenas; for a more relaxing alternative, take D2 — signposted for Canet and Sète — out of Clérmont, turning right after Canet onto straight, tree-lined D32. Where this meets the N113, turn right for **PÉZENAS**.

This small market town, so ordinary-looking from the main road, comes as a surprise. For at one time it was far from ordinary: Pézenas, from 1456 to 1700, was the seat of the Estates of Languedoc, a wealthy, aristocratic town noted for elegant social life. The appearance of its *vieille ville* has hardly altered since those days, and is now a protected area. It has not been 'prettified'. Remarkable 16/17C houses, many with courtyards open to the public, line the narrow streets, with hardly a souvenir shop in sight. Fascinating rues Litanie and Juiverie, unchanged since the 14C, formed a miniature Jewish ghetto for centuries. Molière, with his theatre company, visited the town several times. He would put up with a friend at Maison du Barbier Gely (today the Syndicat d'Initiative), in pl Gambetta. The États de Languedoc councils were held in the ornate Maison Consulaire opposite. Molière's plays were performed at Hôtel Alphonse, 32 rue Conti (now with a pricey little snack bar/*salon de thé* on its vaulted ground floor). 'Les Amis de Pézenas' have signposted a tour of the town centre and fixed up explanatory plaques along the way; a guide to the tour is sold at the SI. Lively market all day Saturday. **Hôtel Genieys** (67.98.13.99) is a reliable 2-star Logis with good substantial menus and very modest prices. From Pézenas take the main road N113/N9 to Béziers.

BÉZIERS pop: 78,500 Commercial centre of the region's wine trade. A lively, dynamic southern city with a dramatic history. Originally a Celtic/Greek town, it has twice been destroyed — by the Romans (who built Julia-Beterae on the site), and in 1209 by the Albigensian Crusaders (see Country of the Cathars route, p. 156). Now noted for its Spanish-style bullfights and its rugby football team. See: Magnificent main esplanade Allée Paul Riquet; attractive old quarter; Musée du Vieux Biterrois. SI: Hôtel Dulac, 27 rue du 4 septembre.

Take N113/N9 (direction Narbonne). At Nissan-lèz-Ensérune, 7km out of Béziers, a little turning right (D162e) leads to the **Oppidum d'Ensérune**, an exceptionally well-preserved fortified Greek/Celtic town of 6CBC–AD1C, and for archaeologists one of the most important sites in France. Signs of dwellings can be seen clearly, and in the site's museum numerous everyday objects of the town — a remarkable quantity having come from Greece — are on display. The oppidum runs strategically along the top of a hill, and a visit is worthwhile if only for the startling view of the Ancienne Étang de Montady. This inland salt lake was drained in the early 13C using water channels radiating from the centre: the fields which have been cultivated on the land ever since follow the same unconventional pattern. Returning to N113/N9 turn right to Narbonne.

NARBONNE pop: 43,000 Gallic Narbo founded in 600BC, colonised by Rome 11BC, became the first capital city of Provincia. Cosmopolitan, important, wealthy seaport (coast now 12km away) for 1,500 years until Albigensian Crusade dealt it a critical blow in 1209/1210. With the expulsion of the Jewish community in 1306 its prosperity (and the university which they had founded) went into sudden decline: within 50 years the great harbour silted up. A canal divides the town centre into Bourg (medieval backstreets — some restored, some squalid) and Cité (grander historic city). See: immense northern Gothic 13/14C Cathédrale St. Just (strangely shaped inside because despite its size this is only the choir of an unfinished structure), displaying fine old tapestries, sculpture, ceramic artwork; also 14C cloisters; Archbishop's Palace (interesting archaeological museum); other good archaeology museums; 13C tower Donjon Gilles Aycelin. SI: pl Roger Salengro (beside cathedral). **Restaurant le Réverbère**, 4 pl des Jacobins (68.32.29.18), has excellent food, good service, acceptable prices for such high quality (Michelin rosette; 2 Gault Millau toques). Much cheaper, but good, is **Restaurant Alsace** in av Paul Sémard. **Hotel du Lion d'Or** (also in av P. Sémard, at the northern end of the Cité: 68.32.06.92) and, cheaper, **Hotel du Midi** (close to the Bourg: 68.41.04.62) are both reasonable 2-star Logis.

On the seaward side of Narbonne, the **Montagne de la Clape**, an area of weatherworn rocky hills of *garrigue* and vineyard (robust red wines), has a tremendous atmosphere and provides some excellent walks and drives. By its summit a Sailors' Cemetery looks seaward; above it stands the chapel

Notre-Dame des Auzïls. To reach it, leave Narbonne following signs to Gruissan all the way to the small road on the left (signposted N.D. des Auzils) which climbs to the cemetery. The coast road itself is very disappointing, so continue from the cemetery down in the direction of Narbonne-Plage (use map carefully, rough, winding road without signposts — don't attempt this near nightfall). On reaching D168 turn left to Narbonne.

Our next step is to return to Béziers, heading from there on N112 to the ancient town of Agde. For variety (and greater speed), autoroute A9 (on-ramp as you return to Narbonne from Montagne de la Clape) provides an alternative route: leave it at the Agde-Pézenas exit or the Béziers-Est exit and follow signs into **AGDE**.

Little remains of Agde's long history. 4km inland, and now catering to large numbers of tourists, the town was founded in about 600BC by Phocaeans (i.e. Greeks), who called it Agathé Tyché. Despite ceaseless attacks, against which it was well defended, it prospered for centuries as a commercial seaport. Later the Romans found it equally useful. From AD400 almost until the year 1800 it was even the seat of a bishop, although after 12/13C it had become overshadowed as a port by Sète and gradually degenerated into a sleazy fishing harbour, which it remained until the recent growth of tourism. **Mont St. Loup**, between the town and the sea, is an extinct volcano, the dark stone of which was the traditional local building material, giving Agde's old town — particularly its ugly, heavily fortified 12C cathedral — a distinctive appearance. Hotel-restaurant **La Tamarissière** (2 toques: 67.94.20.87) stands out, for both quality and price, from the multitude of uninspiring pizzerias and tourist eateries. Syndicat d'Initiative is under the town hall arcade in av de Vias, near the cathedral, while behind the cathedral the Hérault flows between black stone embankments to the Mediterranean at **CAP D'AGDE**, largest and most successful of the new Languedoc resorts. The Cap itself is a large volcanic mound, but along the coast in both directions are good beaches of find golden sand backed by modern blocks 'in the traditional style of the region' (that at least is the theory). There's a vast **Quartier Naturiste** (tollgate access), which has the best of the beaches and accommodation for 20,000, as well as its own restaurants and supermarkets full of naked people.

A single coast road (N112), rather busy in summer, travels along the narrow 20km strip of land which connects Agde with Sète. On one side the sea breaks onto an endless sandy beach, while from the other stretches the still water of the large Bassin de Thau, one of several *étangs*, 'lagoons', along the Languedoc coast. Once detested as the breeding ground of mosquitoes, these inland lakes are now more associated with the magnificent flocks of pink flamingos which find the shallow waters such a congenial home. The Bassin de Thau yields a rich harvest of oysters and mussels, while some *étangs* consist mainly of rice paddies, and others support less picturesque industrial development. Meanwhile the mosquitoes, for the most part, have gone.

SÈTE (spelt Cette until this century) pop: 40,500 Lively, attractive, popular harbour town, with scores of small boats moored at busy quaysides lined with seafood restaurants (recommended: **La Marine**, **La Palangrotte**, **La Rascasse** — all above average, with low prices). Became important as the terminus of Canal du Midi and Canal du Rhône à Sète with their construction 300 years ago. Town rises up **Mont St. Clair**, 180m (good views). See also: Cimetière Marin (sailors' cemetery), where poet Paul Valéry is buried, near the old port; Musée Paul Valéry, above the cemetery, has rooms dedicated to Valéry and to Georges Brassens, radical singer, another Sète native; Brassens' grave in Cimetière le Py, on the other side of Mont St. Clair, overlooks the Bassin de Thau (contrary to his wish to be 'buried on the beach at Sète'); Vauban's waterside fortifications. In summer, especially 14 July, see traditional water-jousting on the canal. The Syndicat d'Initiative is inconveniently located at 22 quai d'Alger.

The admittedly charmless journey from here back to Montpellier (N112; inland alternative N113 is perhaps preferable) does have one consolation: industrial **FRONTIGNAN**, Sète's neighbour, unexpectedly produces a superb Muscat wine, rich and sweet, slightly fortified: a *vin doux naturel*, as they call it in these parts. Drink it as an aperitif, like sherry. To by-pass Montpellier, it's not a bad idea to take the autoroute from the Montpellier-Ouest entrance as far as the Vendargues exit, where join N113 (direction Nîmes). Otherwise, pass through Montpellier following signs to Nîmes. Stay on N113, which passes through another little Muscat-producing town, **LUNEL**. Soon after, near **CODOGNAN**, the massive bottling plant of **Perrier**, built over the famous spring, can be seen off the road to the right. Return to Nîmes on N113.

The Camargue

1–2 days/125km/from Arles

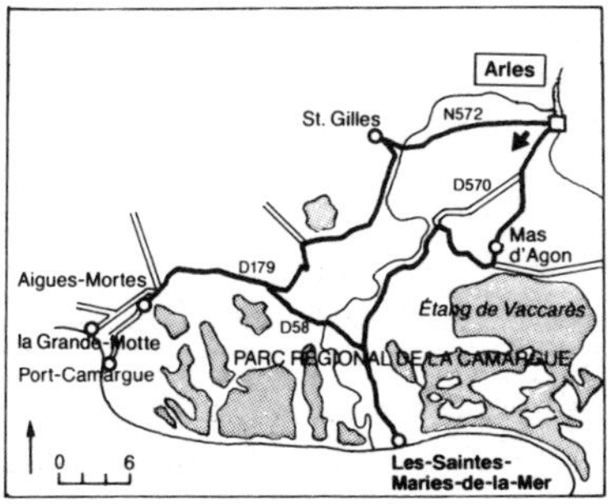

The Camargue, flat windy marshland lying across the immense Rhône delta between Languedoc and Provence, is an extraordinary, haunting, indeed a unique landscape — the only wild wetland remaining in Europe. Seawater makes its way up the labyrinth of channels descending from the river, and the 'soil' between the multitude of watercourses contains great concentrations of salt as well as alluvial mud. *Étangs*, shallow salty lakes, break up the land, providing a refuge for great numbers of birds, including magnificent flocks of graceful pink flamingos. Most of the area falls within the Parc Régional de Camargue, one-third being an enclosed wildlife (especially bird) sanctuary not open to the public, the Reserve Naturelle Zoologique et Biologique. Outside the reserve, much of the land is farmed as rice-paddies. The black bulls of the Camargue, bred for the bullfights of Provence and Languedoc, can sometimes be glimpsed in the distance wandering on vast ranches called *manades*. More often seen are the region's famous troops of handsome half-wild white horses. The bulls are herded, and the white horses tamed and ridden, by *gardians* (in dress which bears a striking similarity to that of the cowboys in Wild West films!). Camarguais *manadiers* live in spacious old farmhouses built around a large yard; *gardians* and peasants make their homes in low whitewashed cottages, *mas*, isolated or in primitive villages. One other resident of these watery terrains deserves a mention — the mosquito, horribly prolific all summer long. To avoid its attentions, visit the Camargue in autumn. (Michelin map 83.)

ARLES pop: 51,000 Founded by Greeks 600BC, subsequently a major Roman city and port (Emperor Constantine born here), today attractive, pleasing, rather Bohemian market town on the Rhône's left bank (the Provençal side). See: remarkably intact Roman Arena, still used for bullfights; adjacent Roman Theatre, not so well preserved but still used for open-air plays; medieval cathedral St. Trophime and cloisters; several interesting museums, especially fine arts Musée Reattu containing a surprising collection of rough sketches (each one dated but not signed or named) by Picasso, a frequent visitor to the town. Retrace the haunts of Vincent van Gogh who lived here during his most prolific and disturbed period. **Hôtel Calendal** is simple, inexpensive, quiet and central, with shady courtyard (90.96.11.89). Pricier, more luxurious, equally well-placed, is **Hôtel d'Arlatan** (90.93.43.20). Best restaurants in town: **Lou Marquès**, bd des Lices and **Vaccarès**, pl Forum. Syndicat d'Initiative in Esplanade des Lices.

Leave town on D570 (direction Les-Saintes-Maries-de-la-Mer). After the junction with D36, look out for minor turn on the left to Mas d'Agon. Take this deserted road across the heart of the Camargue, through minute hamlet Mas Ste. Cecile, to tiny Mas d'Agon, and on to meet D37, where turn right. This road runs beside the Camargue's largest *étang*, le Vaccarès, on the edge of the prohibited area of the Nature Reserve. Stay on D37 until it rejoins the main road D570, where turn left and continue to the small and ancient coastal town **LES-SAINTES-MARIES-DE-LA-MER**.

Known as Les-Saintes-Maries, 'the Holy Maries', for short, this bright and picturesque harbour, to which van Gogh made frequent visits, takes its name from one of the Catholic faith's more incredible legends. The story is that a boat carrying Mary Magdelene, a sister of the Virgin Mary who was also called Mary, the mother of the apostles John and James whose name was also Mary, and their Ethiopian maidservant Sarah, together with Martha, Lazarus, Maximinus and Sidonius, put to sea from the shores of Israel after Christ's crucifixion and landed at this spot on the Camargue coast.

On landing, the group separated, Mary Magdalene and Maximinus going to St. Maximin in Provence (see p. 178) where, according to the legend, they are buried in the church. Martha went to Tarascon to kill a mythical dragon, while the other Maries and their servant Sarah stayed at Les-Saintes-Maries. The gypsies long ago decided that Sarah was their patron saint and aver that she was in fact Egyptian. The impressive and atmospheric 12C fortified church of Les-Saintes-Maries, built on the site of a pagan temple, contains dark, powerful-looking wooden statues, reliquaries of Sarah and the saints Mary, lavishly dressed in white lace and silk. Each year on 24–25 May, thousands of gypsies from all over Europe make a pilgrimage to the town to pay homage to Sarah. On the first day a Mass is said in honour of the Travellers; on the second day, the statue of Sarah is carried into the sea at the head of a big procession of gypsies, local people in traditional dress and, of course, quite a large number of tourists. **Hostellerie du Pont de Gau** (90.47.81.53) is a small and simple 2-star Logis with excellent cheap menus. SI: av van Gogh.

Return along the Arles road to the Aigues-Mortes turning D38 on the left. Take this road (joins D58) to the perfectly preserved fortified medieval town, **AIGUES-MORTES**, 'dead waters'. Dead, because it stands in the midst of stark and unlovely salt-flats, in which nothing can grow. The town was constructed as a seaport in 13C specifically for use by Crusaders. Constant efforts to control the silting-up of its ship channels, together with ceaseless battles to defend it from invaders, exhausted the various factions who at different times siezed and held the town. Principal landmark is the Tour de Constance, used as a prison for Camisard women during the 18C (see p. 110). Starting from this tower, a walk around the ramparts takes about 30min. The streets are in the grid pattern typical of the many fortified 'new towns', *bastides*, of the Middle Ages. Despite its impressive ramparts, the town's charm is much diminished by modern housing outside the walls, and by the surrounding Salins du Midi industrial area extracting and refining the salt.

Return along D58 as far as D179 on the left. Take this very unfrequented backroute across the marshes, via Mas des Iscles, all the way to **ST. GILLES**. Originally the site of the hermitage of this 8C mystic, the town kept its religious importance over the centuries, and is now best known for the beautiful and unusual surviving west front of its 12C Abbey Church, the rest of which has been destroyed. An agreeable town today, surrounded by its vineyards, it was also a favourite place of the Counts of Languedoc, especially Count Raymond IV of Toulouse, who preferred to call himself Raymond of St. Gilles.

Return to Arles on N572.

*

*Olive Oil, wild herbs (thyme, rosemary, sage), and plenty of garlic characterise the flavours of Languedoc's dishes. In general the local cuisine is filling and tasty, coming from a peasant tradition. Sausages and charcuterie are popular. Specialities include a stew of beans and meat with slices of sausages (cassoulet), fish stews, and lamb or mutton from the nearby uplands and plateaux. Daube, often seen, is a meat stew cooked long and slow. Along the coast, fish predominates. Anything which can be hunted or gathered from the wild is especially popular: wild boar (sanglier), small game, birds, snails, leeks, mushrooms, herbs and, for dessert, bilberries (*myrtilles*), which are usually made into a tasty flan. Among the vegetables, delicious tomatoes, green peppers, courgettes and aubergines are most abundant. Local wines are mostly unpretentious reds, with a handful of distinguished names (Minervois, Fitou, . . .); but excellent sweet Muscat wines too (Frontignan, Lunel, . . .) come from a few towns on the coastal plain.*

12 PROVENCE

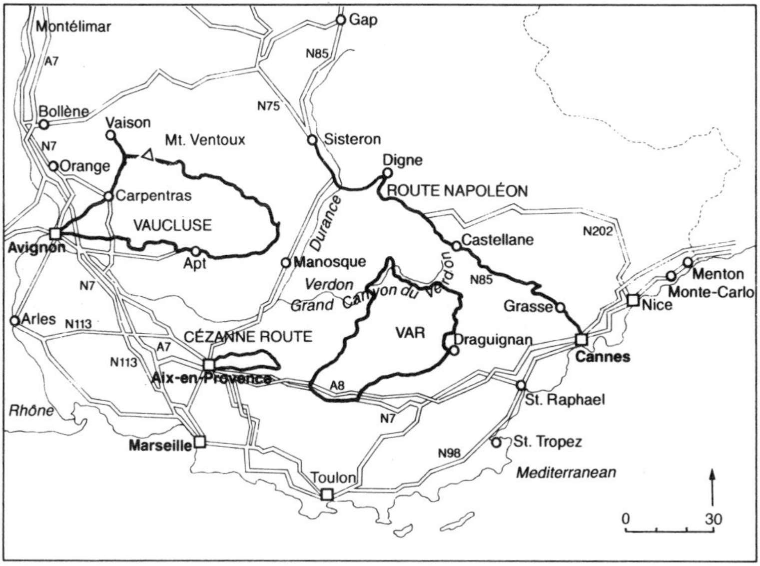

Somewhere well south of Lyon the traveller passes through an invisible frontier into Provence, slipping gently into another landscape, a warmer, more comfortable climate, and a way of life more leisurely yet more vibrant. The most fascinating quality of this new country is *sunlight*. Everything is vivid, brilliantly illuminated. The rocky hills look scoured clean.

In about 150BC, ancient Greek settlements on Gaul's Mediterranean coast called upon Rome to help fight off the unruly local tribesmen. The Romans obliged, then took over the Greek colonies as well, and turned the whole region (including neighbouring Languedoc) into a wealthy province of Rome — hence the name, and hence, too, the astonishing number of Roman arenas and theatres, temples and monuments, preserved by good weather and sturdy construction in amazingly good condition. After the 5C Roman withdrawal, Provence broke up into independent principalities, counties and duchies. Through the complexities of inheritance, the largest of them, the County of Provence, fell into the possession of the French Crown in 1481, and in 1539, after a military conquest, French was made the official language.

In the end it was the Revolution which truly united France and Provence, although the South, the Midi, has continued to chafe against the domination of the North; and Provence, with its leafy *platanes*, its open-air life, men sitting chatting at outdoor tables with their glasses of *pastis*, or playing *boules* in a quiet square, is still visibly a different country from the rest of France. The brilliant light and colours have produced, and attracted, the greatest of modern artists, Picasso, Cézanne, van Gogh and others. Its old towns, at peace after a long and turbulent history, remain cultured and civilised, with festivals of music, drama and dance throughout the summer months.

Cézanne Country

½-1 day/60km/from Aix-en-Provence

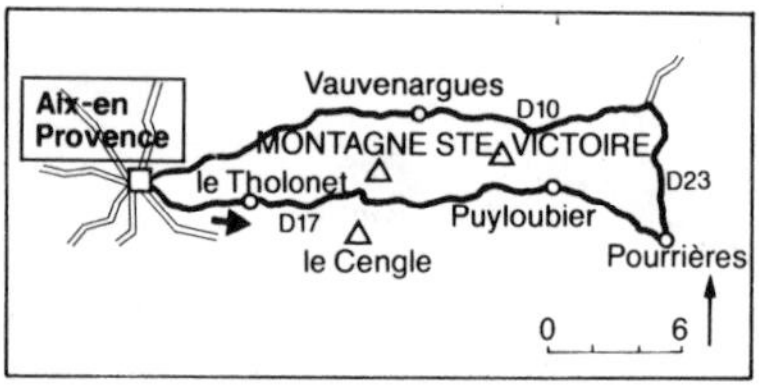

A native of the beautiful city of Aix-en-Provence, Paul Cézanne (1839-1906) was not only unsuccessful in the Paris salons until late in life but was also very much unappreciated in his own land. Local children, he wrote, threw stones at him as he made his way to and from his studio. And although Aix makes much of Cézanne now (too much: hotels, restaurants, even garages are named after him), it was only in 1984 that the city purchased any of his paintings. Paul Cézanne frequently wandered with his painting gear in the rustic country to the east of Aix, attempting to capture images of the Provençal light itself, which so fascinated him. 'The great Classical landscapes, our Provence, and Greece, and Italy,' he said, 'are those where light is spiritualised.' Travelling through gentle greenery and roadside flowers and strongly-scented firs, this route encircles the massive shape of Mont Ste. Victoire, which dominates this countryside and was often at the centre of Cézanne's canvas. (Use Michelin map 81.)

From **AIX-EN-PROVENCE** (pop: 125,000. SI: pl Gen. de Gaulle. See: Cours Mirabeau; old town; Musée Granet) peaceful D17 runs along the southern edge of the mountain through exquisite country. After **LE THOLONET** (Roman quarries; 18C château), the first village on the way, a number of footpaths climb up Mont Ste. Victoire on one side of the road and Montagne du Cengle on the other.

Continue on D17 through **PUYLOUBIER**, whose modern touches do not destroy its charm, and take D57d to curiously named **POURRIÈRES** (rottenness — said to be because the Romans left great numbers of corpses to rot after a battle here with the Celts in 102BC). Turn north on D25 through wild but pretty country. Take D223 on the left (direction Vauvenargues, changes to D10), to drive along the northern edge of the mountain. The road clambers up quite steeply then down to the wooded valley of the Infernet.

Behind the village of **VAUVENARGUES**, the 16/17C hilltop château was Picasso's home for the last 15 years of his life. The interior walls have frescoes which he painted, but there is no admission to the public. Picasso died here in 1973 and is buried in the grounds.

A footpath heads up from Vauvenargues to Pic des Mouches, highest point of the Ste. Victoire massif (1,011m panoramic view). An easier and shorter path (part of GR9) from **LES CABASSOLS** climbs to another peak, La Croix de Provence (969m, superb panoramic view).

Continuing on D10, a little turning on the left (D10f) leads to the Bimont Dam at the head of a large picturesque lake on the Infernet. The view of Mont Ste. Victoire from here is impressive. Return on D10 into Aix.

Route Napoléon

1-2 days/175km/from Cannes to Sisteron

In 1815 Napoleon Bonaparte escaped from exile on the island of Elba and made his way under cover of darkness to the French coast, landing on 1 March at Golfe-Juan. With a band of supporters he made his way inland from Cannes, going from town to town, meeting little resistance from local authorities and gathering ever more support from the population. Of his systematic and triumphant progress towards Paris, Napoleon said 'The eagle will fly from steeple to steeple as far as the towers of Notre-Dame'. (All this triumph was of course temporary — Napoleon was to meet his Waterloo a matter of weeks later.) The sign of the eagle marks the route he took along an ancient Alpine highway, now N85.

Towns and villages along this very popular touring road are much too dependent on tourism to be exactly rural, but nevertheless this makes a splendid drive through the mountainous backcountry of Provence. It especially should be considered as part of a longer through-route on the way to or from the Côte d'Azur. (Michelin maps 84 & 81.)

From **CANNES** (pop: 73,000. SI: Palais de Congrès, La Croisette) take N85, following signs to Grasse. Soon after the road has left the town and passed the autoroute, high on the right rises **MOUGINS**, little town with a fortified medieval village at its centre; it has some *half-dozen* outstanding — but pricey — restaurants. Two of them are **Le Rélais du Mougins** (Michelin rosette, 2 Gault Millau toques: 93.90.03.47) and **l'Amandier de Mougins** (2 rosettes; 93.90.00.91). For something even more excep-

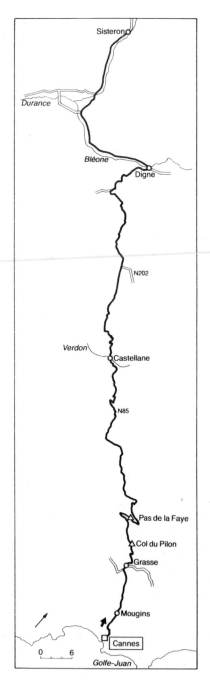

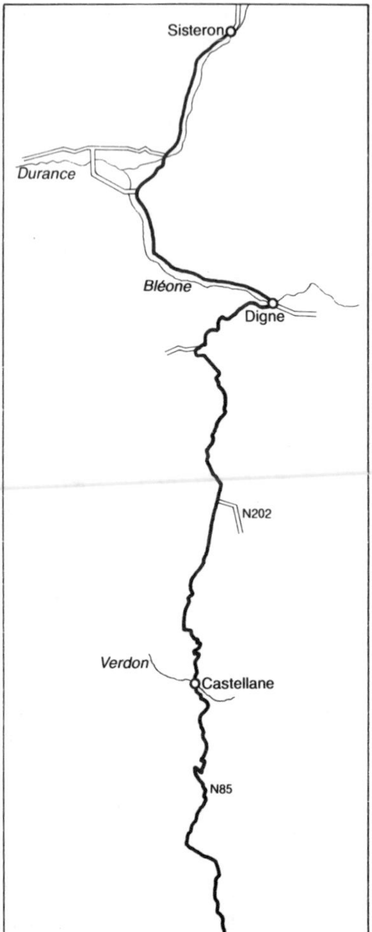

tional, and even more expensive, approach Mougins via Notre-Dame-de Vie, on D3, where you'll find one of the best little hotel-restaurants in the whole of France, **Moulin de Mougins** (3 rosettes, 4 toques: 93.75.78.24). Skirting **MOUANS-SARTOUX**, overlooked by its 16C château, N85 continues towards Grasse, climbing steeply to enter the town.

GRASSE Pop: 38,000 Industrial and largely unattractive, but with some good views onto plain below. World's 'Capital of Perfume' — 75 per cent of bottles use Grasse essences. See: perfume factories; old town centre with Arab atmosphere. SI: pl de la Foux.

Shortly after leaving Grasse, N85 reaches some of its most spectacular points, the Col du Pilon (786m) and a few km farther, after **ST. VALLIER-DE-THIEY** (excellent, peaceful and wonderfully inexpensive hotel-restaurant **Le Préjoly**, 93.42.60.86), climbs in great sweeps up to the Pas de la Faye (981m); all the way up — and down the other side — there are marvellous views.

The next little town, **CASTELLANE**, is compellingly attractive and has a superb location, but is tragically overcrowded. In the main square, where local men play *boules* obliviously, there are parked cars from everywhere in Europe. This is probably the most popular point on the Route Napoléon, standing across the banks of the Verdon just 12km from the start of the drive along the river's spectacular canyon (see Var route, p. 179). There's a good deal left of the old part of town together with its original 14C ramparts. Most striking of all, though, is a soaring limestone cliff which dominates the town. High on this pillar stands a small chapel, Notre-Dame du Roc. It's a half-hour walk to the top.

N85 rises circuitously to Col des Leques and Clue de Taulanne, then falls away to follow the valley of the Asse between the rocky *massifs*, their slopes covered with acacia, Mediterranean pine and wild *garrigue*. Most of the road has been considerably improved since Napoleon passed this way, but even so some of the bends are hair-raising.

Just before Digne, the Alexandra David Neel Foundation is a Tibetan Centre created in the home of this remarkable woman traveller who during her long life (1868–1969) 'always chose the longest route and the slowest means of locomotion'. **DIGNE**, always an important stopover on this highway, is a bright, clean, prosperous town, refreshing and airy, dominated by green surrounding hills. Many visitors come to take the waters at its thriving *Établissement Thermal* (3km out on D20). In the attractive main square there are frequent outdoor events on summer evenings. The quasi-Classical Great Fountain shows clearly enough how much calcium there is in the town's spring water: barely a century and a half old, the fountain is already choked by an amorphous mass of 'fur' deposits. The narrow streets and tall houses of the interesting *vieille ville* cluster around a hill with a distinctive church poised on the summit. SI: next to bus station at end of main street av Gassendi. Best hotel and restaurant in town: **Le Grand Paris** (1 rosette, 2 toques; book ahead: 92.31.11.15).

From Digne to Sisteron the route is flatter and straighter, running first along the valley of the Bléone, and then of the broad island-filled river Durance, once considered, because of its unpredictability and flooding, one of the 'Three Scourges of Provence' (the other two were the *mistral* and the Parlement de Provence based in Aix). The waters of the Durance are now held very much in esteem and, properly controlled, have been turned from a scourge into a blessing, for they provide much of the irrigation which has in this century made the region so much more prosperous. The confluence of Bléone and Durance is also the meeting point of N85 with N96, which heads back down through lavender fields towards Aix-en-Provence. (At this convergence of ways the village of **CHÂTEAU-ARNOUX** offers a 'good stopover' at pretty, charming, but not cheap hotel-restaurant **La Bonne Étape** (rosette and 3 toques: 92.64.00.0).)

At **SISTERON**, just below the confluence of the Durance and the Buëch, the valley narrows, the mountains closing in as if to stem the river altogether. It flows between two sheer and monumental faces of rock, each scored with the lines of vertical strata, and seeming to stand guard between Provence to the south and Dauphiné to the north. Indeed Sisteron was long known, in Occitan, as La Clau de Provenco — the Key to Provence. The town, standing dramatically above the river, today has only the 5 sturdy towers of its former ramparts which enclosed the *vieille ville*. A walk in the old quarter, a maze of narrow streets, stairways and curious covered alleys (known locally as *andrones*), is fascinating. 12C

Sisteron

Eglise Notre-Dame is a satisfying, unsophisticated building; its few (mostly later) attempts at frivolity are subdued by the massive simplicity of the structure. Little survives of the town's medieval Citadelle except the angular and intricate outer walls, perched eagle-like on a crag of rock high above the river valley. It is well worth a visit if only for the view. Office de Tourisme: in the Mairie, av de la Libération.

Napoleon continued from Sisteron via Gap to Grenoble. For anyone who, like him, is heading north, this makes a good cross-country route through the mountains to Lyon. Alternatively, take the magnificent drive via Die and Crest down to Valence in the Rhône Valley.

The Var

2 days/235km/from Draguignan

Probably no other French département is quite so endowed with a sense of physical well-being, nor so perfectly designed for leisurely, unhurried enjoyment of life, as the Var. It rises from the beautiful *corniches* of the Mediterranean into a quiet, warm, rustic hinterland of peaceful, basking villages, terraced hills and woods of parasol pine. This route must certainly be one of the most pleasing, satisfying and, in places, most spectacular drives to be made in the south of France. (Michelin map 84.)

DRAGUIGNAN pop: 28,300 Agreeable market town with extensive medieval quarters. See: façade of 13C synagogue; 17C clocktower; American military cemetery on edge of town. Syndicat d'Initiative at 9 bd Clémenceau.

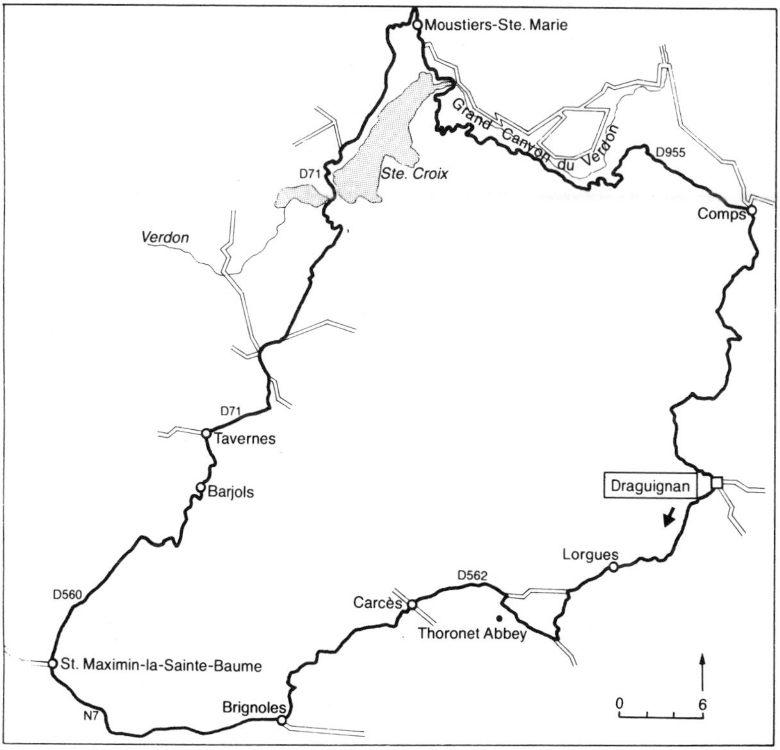

Travel west out of town on the route de Lorgues (D567; changes to D562) through rough, hilly, delightful country of Mediterranean pines, wild flowers, abandoned terraces and tiny vineyards. **LORGUES** itself is an old leafy, unpretentious, small town with many pretty corners. Travelling between masses of roadside flowers and pine woods, stay on D562, shortly turning left onto D17 to reach, via the village of le Thoronet (where turn right onto D84), the **Abbey of Thoronet**, buried in peaceful seclusion in the midst of the woods. This church, mainly in 12C Provençal Romanesque style, together with 3-level cloisters, chapter house, tithebarn and outbuildings, have survived remarkably unharmed. The church, sturdy and austere in keeping with Cistercian principles, is beautifully simple and unadorned inside. The monks' polygonal communal bathroom is also delightful. Together with Silvacane (near Cadenet) and Sénanque (near Gordes, see p. 181), Thoronet was known as one of the 'Three Cistercian Sisters of Provence'.

Continue on D84 to rejoin D562, where turn left to enter **CARCÈS**, a medieval small town attractively bordered with vineyards and vegetable gardens. Follow D562 (and D554) to **BRIGNOLES** a small, but once rather important town on the ancient Provençal highway, N7. This was the Via Aurelia, which went from Rome, through Nice, Fréjus and Aix, to Arles: one of the busiest roads in the Roman Empire. Some local country people I have spoken to still known it as *lou camin aurelien* (Occitan, le chemin aurelian).

Travel west on this road to **ST. MAXIMIN-LA-SAINTE-BAUME**. Leading off the handsome tree-shaded esplanade on the main road, narrow lanes and streets redolent of the Middle Ages, and lined with curious 14/15C houses, make their way up to a strange Basilica which dominates the town. Its exterior doors are superb, rough and huge. Inside, there's a tremendous amount of artwork, traces of frescoes and a massive ornate organ. Note especially the 16C painted wooden statue of St. John the Baptist and a fascinating 16C retable, in gold-painted frame, of the crucifixion. At the same time, there's some appalling 17C and later decoration.

Down below is the Roman crypt of the Basilica, where a skull, said to be that of Mary Magdelene, is set into a gold statue. (You look at it through a metal gate, and press a button to get five minutes of light.) Catholics believe that after the crucifixion, a party of Jesus' companions set sail from the shores of Israel and landed on the Camargue coast (see Camargue route, p. 168). Two of them, Mary Magdelene and St. Maximinus, came inland to the small Gallo-Roman town of Villa Latta, where both died. As long afterwards as the year 1279, Charles of Anjou improbably declared that he had discovered the sarcophagi of the two saints. The

St. Maximin-la-Sainte-Baume

Basilica was built over them and became a great centre of pilgrimage for centuries. (See also: Vézelay, p. 77.) A decent restaurant in town on the main road is **Chez Nous** (94.78.02.57).

Take D560 north through attractive country to **BARJOLS**, a well located town, very pleasing with its shady squares and numerous old fountains and warm, relaxed atmosphere. Many traditional customs have survived in the locality — such as the making of tambourines and *galoubets* (3-holed flutes) to play at ancient festivals like the 2-day Fête des Tripettes (every 4 years in January: 1989, 1993), when an ox heads a procession of butchers through the town, only (of course) to be slaughtered, roasted on a spit and distributed to the townspeople amidst much revelry.

Round about, there are many other little country towns and villages of great charm and sunny atmosphere — Varages, Le Verdière and Tavernes for example. D71 (changing to D13, then D11) continues from Barjols in rich farmland through Tavernes and Montmeyan, where turn right onto D30 and left onto D71 to Baudinard. (Alternatively, for a nice, quiet hotel with restaurant, in a lovely village overlooking the pines of the valley of the Aups, go 10km farther to Moissac-Bellevue, where **Le Calalou** has pretty, simple rooms: 94.70.17.91.)

Carry on through Baudinard down to Ste. Croix dam, which has created the beautiful Lac de Ste. Croix on the Verdon River. Here, cross the river onto D111 and travel beside the lake, passing by the village Ste. Croix de Verdon and continuing all the way — beside brilliant lavender fields in places — to **MOUSTIERS-STE. MARIE**, which is so crowded and popular that it may come as quite a shock after such a tranquil drive!

A marvellously picturesque village of narrow streets and stairways, and attractive old houses, built precariously on the slopes of a spectacular ravine, it's not surprising that Moustiers attracts visitors. Most curious of all the 'sights' is the gilded star on a chain hanging right across the ravine. Exactly who put it there and why has almost been forgotten — but it's said to be a votive offering made by a Crusader after he was freed from captivity. **Les Santons** (booking essential: 92.74.66.48) is an excellent little restaurant. (*Santons*, by the way, or *santouns* in Occitan, are an odd Provençal tradition — carved tableaux of the nativity, with figurines of biblical personages and typical Provençal characters assembled round the crib.)

Moustiers is good, too, as a base for visitors to the nearby **Grand Canyon du Verdon**. Grand indeed, for along the canyon of the Verdon river sheer rock face plunges sometimes 700m on both sides of the valley down to the twisting ribbon of water below. On the sinuous clifftop road a succession of *Points Sublime* offer amazing views into and across the most impressive river gorge in Europe. It is possible to make a round trip, seeing the gorge from both the north and south sides; however, the canyon is a long and slow drive — some 75km — and, magnificent as it is, one side should be enough. Take D957 south from Moustiers; for the north bank route take D952 on left, but I prefer the south bank drive (the 'Corniche Sublime') for which stay on D957, cross the river next to the lake, and take D19 on the left (becomes D71).

Stay on D71 all the way to Comps-sur-Artuby, where turn south onto D955 and return across the hills to Draguignan.

The Vaucluse

2 days/300km/from Avignon

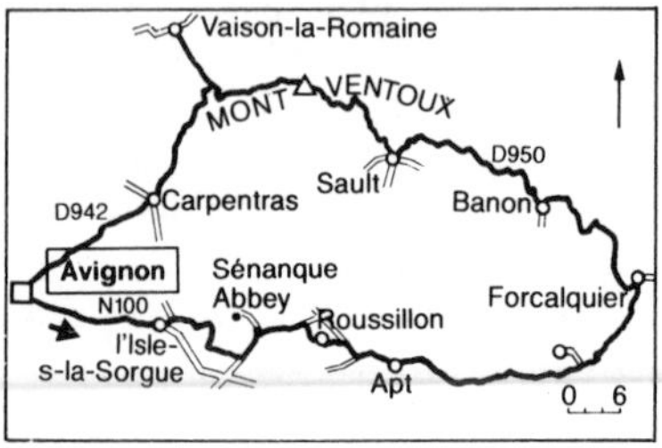

The département of Vaucluse, set well back from the coast, is alternately wild and gentle, cultivated and uncultivable, and has a sense of being almost submerged, subdued, by millennia of history and sunlight. This tranquil, rustic, often hilly countryside of ancient olive groves, soporific villages, farmyards, peach orchards and vineyards lies between majestic borders: the might of Mont Ventoux in the north, the great river highway of the Rhône along the west, the Lubéron Massif and the unpredictable waters of the broad Durance in the south. To the east rise the Provençal Alps, into which our route wanders briefly before returning to the drystone villages and terraced fields of the Vaucluse. The whole region is packed with first-class hotels and restaurants of character. (Use Michelin map 81.)

AVIGNON pop: 91,500 Capital of Vaucluse. Lively fortified city on Rhône near confluence with Durance. Makes much of brief period (14C) as the Papal capital. Lowering mass of ugly Papal Palace dominates from a distance, but within the walls the tangled labyrinth of sleazy, atmospheric backstreets is more striking. See also: truncated *pont d'Avignon* (Pont St-Bénézet), where *on y danse*; Petit Palais; Musée Calvet; Rocher des Doms (public gardens with impressive views). Noted one-month music and theatre Festival July-August. Many outstanding restaurants. If funds allow stay at luxurious 16C **Hôtel de l'Europe**, pl Crillon (90.82.66.92) — former guests include Charles Dickens, the Barrett Brownings, John Stuart Mill, Henry James and all wealthy 19C Britons *en route* to the Riviera. Départemental tourist office: pl Campana (off main square pl de l'Horloge); SI: rue de la République.

Take N100 east out of the city to **L'ISLE-SUR-LA-SORGUE**. This interesting little town, standing on an island in the Sorgue (as its name suggests!), is pleasant with tree-lined streets, and has a 17C church with an extremely ornate interior, an 18C Hôtel-Dieu (Hospital) with its original pharmacy, waterwheels on the Sorgue, and some delightful inexpensive places to eat (or stay), e.g.: **Mas du Cure Bourse** (90.38.16.58) and unpretentious 1-star Logis **Le Pescadou** (90.38.09.69).

Take D938, then D175 on the left (good views) through the *garrigue* to reach nearby **Fontaine-de-Vaucluse**, one of the outlets for the complex system of underground rivers beneath the Vaucluse Plateau. In springtime up to 12,000 cubic metres of water per minute gush from the spring at the foot of an impressive cliff — making this one of the world's most powerful natural sources of fresh water. However, in summer the water supply is disappointing, and there are also far too many visitors here for comfort at that time. Apart from the Fontaine, this is also where 14C poet Petrarch lived in peaceful but painful isolation, writing about the mysterious and beautiful Laura with whom, after one glimpse in an Avignon church, he had fallen desperately in love. Laura was no imaginary fiction: it is thought that she was a member of the noble de Sade family — and already married.

Use tiny backroads D100a, D100, D110 to reach **GORDES**, built curiously, one house almost on top of another, on the sides of a steep hill with a proud château at the summit. All around Gordes are settlements of bories, primitive stone huts dating from 200BC — and lived in, by poor peasants and labourers, from then until the 19C! Not at all in the same category, however, is **Restaurant Les Bories**, a dry-stone dwelling in open country on the Sénanque road (Michelin rosette, 2 Gault Millau toques: 90.72.00.51). Farther along this road, hidden away in the Sénancole valley, 12C **Sénanque Abbey**, last of the 'Three Cistercian Sisters of Provence' (the others were Silvacane and Thoronet) was extensively restored while temporarily reoccupied by monks of the Order earlier this century. It has an exquisite simplicity and grace. See the fireplace in the Monks' Hall. Today, the Abbey buildings contain a cultural centre and, more surprisingly, an institute (with museum) devoted to the Sahara desert.

Follow D2, turning right onto D102 (if you miss it, there are alternative roads) to the amazing village of **ROUSSILLON**. It is poised on a ridge — all that's left of a landscape eaten away over the centuries — in the middle of brilliant ochre quarries. You can walk through tunnels and climb cliffs of dazzling red and yellow sand which clings and stains like watercolours. A 2-hr walk on GR6 leads to the wonderful Rustrel Colorado quarry. After this experience, the everyday colours of nature, when next you see them, are put to shame. All Roussillon's village houses, too, are made of tinted sandstone. An excellent little restaurant here is **La Tarasque** (book ahead: 90.75.63.86).

Return via lovely D104 and D4 to N100, where turn left to enter **APT**, one of those small attractive old country towns — of which there are so many in Provence — with plane trees, fountains, and a square with men playing *boules*. It has a big local market every Saturday.

N100 climbs east through attractive country. At Reillanne, just off the road, **Auberge de Reillan** is a Provençal farm cleverly converted into a lovely small quiet hotel-restaurant (92.76.45.95). The road continues up to **FORCALQUIER**, a modest little place which nowadays seems like the middle of nowhere, yet once was a great political and cultural centre. But that was centuries ago ... For this used to be the capital of Haute-

Provence. It still has a cathedral (12–17C) and numerous medieval buildings in its narrow and picturesque old lanes; there's a former Jewish quarter and a few traces of the town's once-powerful castle. Today, Forcalquier is just a peaceful agricultural centre, with important monthly trading fairs and weekly sheep markets. Its location gives magnificent views over the surrounding country. There's a very good 2-star Logis with delicious inexpensive *menus*, **Hostellerie des Deux Lions** (92.75.25.30).

Take D950 onto the Vaucluse Plateau to **BANON**, a pleasing hill village, the old fortified centre with its arcaded pavements standing high on a rock. Banon gives its name to a distinctive goats' cheese wrapped in chestnut leaves for which it has long been noted. This whole high undulating terrain is tunnelled with scores of strange natural caves, underground rivers and potholes. The Gouffre du Caladaire, close to Banon, is one of the more extraordinary examples, nearly 500m in depth, and containing a system of prehistoric 'canals'.

Continue on D950 across the plateau to medieval **SAULT**, around which are several more *avens* (potholes). Strikingly situated with views over the Nesque river gorges, Sault also has an interesting 12–14C church and a small museum of local Gallo-Roman finds. (To foreshorten the route, D942 goes straight from Sault to Carpentras along the spectacular Nesque gorge.)

Northwest of the little town rises a great Provençal landmark, the pale conical mass of **Mont Ventoux** (1,909m). The name means windy, and it is, with temperatures substantially lower at the summit than at the foot (usually the drop is about 11°C, 20°F), but the view from the top is quite amazing on a clear day, taking in the Alps, Rhône Valley and Vaucluse Plateau. D974 from Sault goes right over the summit. Stay on this road as it runs along the crest of the *massif*, descending to join D938. Here turn right and soon enter **VAISON-LA-ROMAINE**.

Vaison, on the Ouvèze river which runs round the northern edges of Ventoux, is an agreeable small town with an important local produce market (Tuesday morning). In fact it's 3 towns, all of them interesting, the newest lying partly on top of the oldest. On the north bank of the Ouvèze was the Gallo-Roman city Vasio Vocantiorum. In the Middle Ages the town moved over to the better defended hill south of the river, where in the 12C the Counts of Toulouse built the castle. And in the modern era, until 1907, life extended back onto the north bank, and many of the Roman ruins were built over. The original Roman bridge still links the medieval *ville haute* with the north bank. Since 1907, in a succession of excavations, the Roman town has been partly uncovered again, the best feature being the mosaic floors of the villas. The town's museum has an impressive collection of Roman sculpture, while the Theatre has been well restored and is used throughout the annual Summer Festival of drama, music and dance (early July to mid-August). Every 3 years, in August, there is an International Festival of Choral Music, les Choralies. Vaison has rather too many tourists and, in addition, tickets for festival performanes, or to visit monuments, are expensive, as are the hotels. Syndicat d'Initiative in pl Sautel.

Vaison-la-Romaine

Double back along D938, continuing on this road into **CARPENTRAS**. Once the capital of the Pope's Comtat Venaissin territory, it's now just a typical warm Provençal town. On Fridays it comes to life for a big street market. There are masses of interesting things to see here, especially the richly decorated 15C synagogue, believed to be the oldest surviving in France. The local *confiseurs* specialise in stripy triangular sweetmeats called berlingots. From 14 July to 15 August there's an arts festival, with open-air music, dance and drama. SI is at 170 Allées Jean-Jaurès.

D942 returns across the Vaucluse Plain into Avignon.

*

Abundant olive oil, garlic and aromatic wild herbs from the Provençal hills are the hallmark of cooking in this sunlit southern countryside. Tomatoes, green peppers, aubergines and courgettes are the commonest vegetables and generously used. Succulent, highly seasoned stews — meats, fish or vegetable — are the region's favourite dishes. Specialities include bourride and bouillabaisse (both difficult-to-prepare fish stews), ratatouille (a highly seasoned stew of Provençal vegetables) and meat 'en daube' (seasoned and cooked in rich stew). Piquant sauces are popular too: aïoli (garlic mayonnaise) and pistou (basil and garlic sauce) come into numerous dishes. Almost alone among French regions, Provence has several traditional snack dishes: look out especially for pan bagna (a salad-with-anchovies bread roll) and pissaladière (like a small pizza — open tart with tomato, garlic, olive and anchovy topping). There are plenty more to discover. Small disc-shaped sheep's and goats' cheeses — particularly Banon, which is wrapped in chestnut leaves — are made by peasant farmers and sold in markets. And there's no shortage of palatable wines. There are dozens of appellations in the region, ranging from plentiful cheap-and-cheerful table wines to first-rank red (Côte du Rhône, Châteauneuf-du-Pape, Gigondas), rosé (Tavel, Côtes de Provence) and fortified sweet Muscat wines (Beaumes de Venise).

13 CORSICA

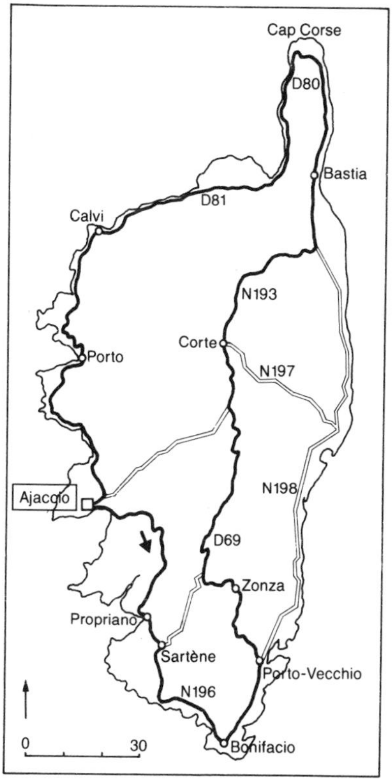

Most visitors touring France do not include Corsica (about 5–7 hours from Provence by car ferry, or 45 minutes by plane) on their itinerary, and equally, most visitors to Corsica fly direct and do not consider that they are in France at all. It's certainly true that this French Mediterranean island has remarkably little in common with the mainland. When sold to the French for hard cash by its former rules the Genoese, in 1768, the island's long struggle for self-government had almost come to fruition. But the French were better able to deal with the patriotic Corsicans, and soon crushed the independence movement. Yet the fight to free themselves from foreign rule has gone on right up to the present day. Food, culture, way of life, even language (the local patois, widely spoken, comes from an old Genoese dialect), are far removed from the French. The rugged mountainous interior with its covering of pine, chestnut and tough, fragrant *maquis*, largely uncultivated (indeed, uncultivable), and the widely indented rocky coastline, are astonishingly beautiful. Roads are circuitous and narrow, making driving slow. Life in some of the inland villages remains startlingly primitive. Agriculture — and local cuisine — revolve around the island's abundance of chestnut trees, goats and wild pigs.

Accommodation in Corsica: on the west side of the island from l'Ile-Rousse to

Propriano there is no lack of reasonable hotels and restaurants. However, on the other coasts (apart from the key resorts), and even more so in the mountainous interior, acommodation is in shorter supply. For this part of the route, note that there are good 2-star Logis (with restaurants) at Sartène, Porto-Vecchio and Zonza. Other satisfactory, reasonably priced hotels and restaurants can also be found at Corte, Bastia, St. Florent and on the Cap Corse peninsula at Porticciolo and Centuri-Port.

Island tour

1 week/750km/from Ajaccio

AJACCIO (pop: 55,000), beautifully located on a magnificent bay, is one of Corsica's two main towns, and makes a big fuss of Napoleon Bonaparte, who was born here (see his house, and the Napoleon Museum in the Hôtel de Ville). SI: in Hôtel de Ville.

Head south from here on the winding coastal road D55 (marvellous views). Stop at **Filitosa** (off the road) to see an exceptional prehistoric site. Soon after, having encircled the Bay of Valinco, the road reaches a small coastal resort **PROPRIANO** (marvellous coastal drives from here on minor roads on the south side of bay).

Take N189 inland to **SARTÈNE**, mountain town of awesome medieval aspect, with fine views, intricate old backstreets, archways, unfaced stone houses. The road continues back towards the coast — faster driving along here as it is not quite so mountainous — into **BONIFACIO**, at Corsica's southern tip. This small town attracts many visitors, who are as likely to arrive by boat as by car, and the crowds can detract from the atmosphere of this haunting location. The old part of town (*Haute Ville*), is a marvellous walled labyrinth of narrow lanes perched on a lofty outcrop of rock. The harbour clings to a narrow ledge at the foot of the cliff.

Corsica's east coast, apart from having better beaches, is also considerably flatter than any other part of the island, and the main road up this side, N198, allows easy, fast, but characterless, driving. Take it just as far as **PORTO-VECCHIO** one of the most popular beach resorts on the island. All around the town are forests of cork-oak. Turn inland on D368, climbing steeply into spectacular mountain landscapes, part of the Regional Nature Park which embraces most of Corsica's high central region. In these wooded uplands you may very likely encounter a squealing group or two of the island's half-wild pigs, which seem to have strangely little timidity about human beings. The route twists and turns, giving good views — but it would be better not to try to admire them while manoeuvring the narrow, lofty roadways. Instead, stop at one of the fairly frequent viewpoints.

D368 reaches **ZONZA**, cool and pleasant mountain town with fine views. Nearby, the island's most remarkable mountain formation, a cluster of extraordinary jagged peaks called the **Aiguilles de Bavella**

(Bavella Needles) rises up a few km north of Zonza on D268; but our route goes west on D420, through **QUENZA**, from which point the Aiguilles can clearly be seen in the distance.

At **AULLÈNE** turn right onto the dramatic mountain road D69. Tiny **ZICAVO** has become the focus of the mountain region's minor 'tourist industry' (mainly walking and cross-country skiing). D69 becomes ever narrower and more convoluted, passing through simple villages. After **GHISONI**, which instead of standing proudly on the heights (as most Corsican villages do) nestles in a deep valley, D69 meets N193, on the main road-and-rail axis which crosses the island diagonally from Ajaccio to Bastia. Turn right at this junction and head into the handsome and cultivated little university town which past and present Corsican separatists elect as the island's capital, **CORTE**.

(Immediately southwest the gorges of river Restonica make a rewarding tour from Corte into wild, beautiful country. For another fascinating excursion, travel to the rustic hill villages, Sermano, Zuani, etc., in the countryside to the northeast.) Continue north on busier N193, which sweeps round towards the east coast and makes its way — pursued by the railway line which crosses the island — to **BASTIA** (pop: 45,000), Corsica's other big town, and perhaps with rather more commercial and political importance than Ajaccio. It has a pleasant sunny atmosphere, but also, of course, plenty of tourists. See pl St. Nicholas, the large and congenial waterside main square; the old port; the walled Genoese citadel. SI: 35 bd Paoli.

Bastia stands at the southern end of that finger of Corsican territory which points north into the Mediterranean towards the French mainland. This is an exceptionally picturesque region: the journey to **Cap Corse**, at the extreme end of this peninsula, and back along the west coast, is a visual delight. The hills, formerly farmed, are now covered with wild *maquis*, with ruined villages and castles balanced on pinnacles of rock; there are wonderful walks to be made into the interior, too, and everywhere along the west side, magnificent views. The peninsula rejoins the body of the island at **ST. FLORENT**, a little resort looking out over a lovely bay (see also: 12C cathedral in Pisan style). D81 cuts across bare rocky terrain from here to popular **L'ILE ROUSSE** (good beach), and N197 carries on down the coast to **CALVI**, picturesque and popular old waterfront town (see: Genoese citadel).

Further south the coast road (D81) becomes gradually more spectacular, and after **PORTO** (famous for beautiful sunsets) reaches its most wonderful phase, clinging to strange sea-facing cliffs called **les Calanche**. Cutting inland at **PIANA**, it returns to the sea at magnificently situated **CARGÈSE** (many families of Greek descent: note Greek Orthodox church). D81 continues south back to Ajaccio.

*

Olive oil is the usual cooking medium, wild herbs are generously used, and many dishes come with pebronata sauce (green peppers, garlic, tomatoes, olive oil). The pigs which roam freely are used to make several types of sausage, charcuterie and ham. Sea fish and every variety of shellfish also feature often on Corsican menus. Farm-made sheep's and goats' cheeses are much used, especially brocciu (several alternative spellings!) which can appear in every course of the meal. Bleu de Corse is an excellent cheese which is sent 'white' to the caves of Roquefort (see p. 115), where it acquires its delicious creaminess and blue veins, before being returned to the island. Chestnuts, too, prove highly versatile, being used in soups, appetisers and desserts, even being made into flour for cakes (French-style pâtisserie is not much seen). The Italian connection is much in evidence, and pasta is popular. Island specialities include fish stew (ziminu), savoury vegetable soup (suppa), suckling pig, and brocciu omelette. Corsican wines are remarkably good: mainly red, substantial, robust and highly drinkable.

BIBLIOGRAPHY

Note: some are out of print and obtainable only from libraries.

Travels Through France and Italy, *Tobias Smollett* (OUP, London & New York) Collection of long and erudite letters to friends in England from the impossibly irascible and xenophobic invalid in 1763–5. The Italy he refers to is Nice and its region.

Travels in France, *Arthur Young* (1792) (out of print) Fascinating account of journeys made in French provinces before and during the Revolution.

A Little Tour in France, *Henry James* (Oxford Paperbacks, Houghton Mifflin) Superbly written whimsical but observant account of a jaunt in 1884 by the luxury-loving American novelist.

Easy Living in France, *John Harris* (Arrow) Funny, perceptive little volume on life in France written by English contributor to *Le Monde* who now lives in Languedoc.

France, *John Harris* (Papermac) Useful general guide for the independent traveller.

France in the 1980s, *John Ardagh* (Penguin) Prize-winning, readable study of modern French politics, art and intellectual life.

A Sentimental Journey, *Lawrence Sterne* (1768) (OUP, Penguin, Dent, Dutton) A delightful fantasy of bar-room friendships and amorous adventures while travelling in France, based in principle on Sterne's own journeys.

The Michelin Green Guides: invaluable set of some 16 detailed regional sightseeing guides (only 6 in English) with emphasis on history and architecture.

French Architecture, *Pierre Lavedan* (Pelican) Useful not only as a survey of French architecture but also for its thumbnail biographies of the great French builders, architects, fortifiers and restorers, such as Vauban, Viollet-le-Duc and the Hardouin-Mansart family.

Blue Guide France (A. & C. Black) Weighty tome detailing everything of historical or architectural importance.

North

The War Poems, *Siegfried Sassoon* (Faber) His World War I poems written at Somme front line and in hospital.

The Collected Poems of Wilfred Owen (Chatto & Windus) World War I poet killed in Somme trenches 1918.

Goodbye to All That, *Robert Graves* (Cassell, Doubleday) Written 1929, recounts his youth and early manhood, including World War I in the Somme trenches.

Before Endeavours Fade, a guide to the battlefields of the First World War,

Rose B. Coombs (1976) (Battle of Britain Prints International Ltd, London) Straightforward, factual and thorough, with interesting maps and photos.

Champagne; the Wine, the Land, and the People, *Patrick Forbes* (Gollancz)

An Inland Voyage, *Robert Louis Stevenson* (Dent) RLS' first book, very slim volume, about travelling on the waterways of N. France in mid-19C; the region has changed beyond recognition, though landmarks remain.

Normandy

The Longest Day, *Cornelius Ryan* (Ulverscroft).

The Second World War, *Winston Churchill* (Cassell, Houghton Mifflin).

Madame Bovary, *Gustave Flaubert* (Hamlyn, Penguin, Random House) Masterful 19C novel set in Normandy.

Companion Guide to Normandy, *Nesta Roberts* (Collins) Substantial guidebook to the province.

Brittany

Quatre-vingts-treize, *Victor Hugo* (1873) (Dargaud, Gallimard, Garnier and others) Little-known novel about the Royalist uprisings in Brittany after the Revolution.

Brittany and the Bretons, *Keith Spence* (Gollancz).

Early Brittany, *Nora Chadwick* (University of Wales Press).

Loire

Eleanor of Aquitaine and the Four Kings, *Amy Kelly* (Harvard University Press).

The Loire Valley, *Henry Myhill* (Faber).

The Loire, *James Bentley* (George Philip) A personal look at the region, with beautiful photographs.

La Mare au Diable, La Petite Fadette, François le Champi, all by George Sand, her novels set in the countryside of 19C Berry (Indre département).

Several novels by **Balzac** and **Rabelais** are set in the Loire region.

Massif Central

West of the Rhône, *Freda White* (Faber) Effusive, idiosyncratic, personal and occasionally inaccurate!

Travels with a Donkey in the Cevennes, *Robert Louis Stevenson* (Dent) Beautifully, amusingly written account of 12-day trek in 1878; see also **The Cevennes Journal**, his diary kept on the walk, published 1978 (Mainstream).

La Vie Quotidienne dans le Massif Central au 19ième Siècle, *J. Anglade* (Hachette).

Dordogne

Three Rivers of France, *Freda White* (Faber) In her usual enthusiastic and totally subjective style.

The Lascaux Cave Paintings, *F. Windels* (Faber).

The Dordogne, *Stephen Brook* (George Philip) Personal travelogue of the region with superb photographs.

Atlantic

Le Roman d'un Enfant, *Pierre Loti* (out of print).

Ways of Aquitaine, *Freda White* (out of print).

Cognac, *Cyril Ray* (Harrap).

W. Pyrenees and Languedoc

Montaillou, *Emmanuel Le Roy Ladurie* (English translation published by Penguin and Random House) Extraordinary, thought-provoking academic work on life and beliefs of peasants in 14C mountain village, based on actual confessions made to the Inquisition.

La Vie Quotidienne des Cathares du Languedoc au XIIIe Siècle, *Réné Nelli* (Hachette) Readable academic work on daily life of 13C Languedoc peasants.

The Pyrenees, *Hilaire Belloc* (1909) (out of print).

Languedoc, *James Bentley* (George Philip) Lavishly illustrated coffee table guide.

Provence

Travels in the South of France, *Stendhal* (Calder & Boyars) Detailed if clinical observations of towns in 1820s.

5 books by *Lawrence Durrell;* **Monsieur, Livia, Constance, Sebastian, Quinx** — together called The **Quincunx** or **Avignon Quintet** (Faber, Penguin, Viking) Mostly set in and around Avignon during Nazi occupation, evocative of the city's seediness and decaying grandeur, and the sun-baked timeless atmosphere of the surrounding countryside.

Provence, *John Flower* (George Philip) Weighty touring guide with marvellous photographs.

Aspects of Provence, *James Pope-Hennessy* (Longman) A personal look at the region by a cultured traveller in 1950s.

Corsica

Granite Island — A Portrait of Corsica, *Dorothy Carrington* (Penguin Travel Library).

Food and Drink

A Pocket Guide to French Food and Wine, *Tessa Youell and George Kimball* (Xanadu) A thorough, competent little handbook which covers the huge subject of French eating very completely in few words.

Language

Just Enough French/Traveller's French, *D.L. Ellis and F. Clark* (Passport Books/Pan Books). An essential phrasebook for getting by in French.

Just Listen 'n Learn French and **Just Listen 'n Learn French PLUS/Breakthrough** and **Breakthrough Further French**, *Stephanie Rybak* (Passport Books/Pan Books). Complete cassette and coursebook programs for learning French.

INDEX

Note: In the usual French way, placenames prefixed by Le or La are listed alphabetically according to the next word (e.g. for Le Puy, see P); and placenames beginning with Saint come before those beginning with Sainte (e.g. St. Quentin comes before Ste. Énimie)